Knowledge and Reflexivity

New Frontiers in the Sociology of Knowledge

edited by
Steve Woolgar

SAGE Publications
London • Newbury Park • Beverly Hills • New Delhi

Editorial matter and Chapter 2 © Steve Woolgar 1988
Chapter 1 © Steve Woolgar and Malcolm Ashmore 1988
Chapter 3 © Jonathan Potter 1988
Chapter 4 © Teri Walker 1988
Chapter 6 © Anna Wynne 1988
Chapter 7 © Malcolm Ashmore 1988
Chapter 8 © Bruno Latour 1988
Chapter 9 © Trevor Pinch 1988

First published 1988
First paperback edition 1991

Chapter 5 is reprinted by kind permission from Michael Mulkay, *The Word and the World* (London: George Allen and Unwin, 1985), Chapter 4.

SAGE Publications Ltd
6 Bonhill Street
London EC2A 4PU

SAGE Publications Inc
2455 Teller Road
Newbury Park, California 91320

SAGE Publications India Pvt Ltd
32, M-Block Market
Greater Kailash – I
New Delhi 110 048

British Library Cataloguing in Publication Data

Knowledge and reflexivity: new frontiers
    in the sociology of knowledge.
    1. Self-knowledge, Theory of
    I. Woolgar, Steve
    160   BD161

ISBN 0–8039–8120–1
ISBN 0–8039–8121 X Pbk

Library of Congress catalog card number 87–051528

Typeset by System 4 Associates, Farnham Common, Buckinghamshire
Printed in Great Britain by J. W. Arrowsmith Ltd, Bristol

KNOWLEDGE AND REFLEXIVITY

CANONS INVOKE
CATEGORIES THAT
CHANGE PERCEPTION

Contents

Preface and Acknowledgements

With one exception, the chapters in this volume originated as papers presented at a series of meetings known (rather misleadingly) as 'Discourse Analysis' workshops. The meetings comprised intensive small-group discussion of pre-circulated papers, subsequent revisions of which were peer refereed as submissions for this volume. My thanks to all the contributing authors for their patience and co-operation in the face of the demands of their Editor. Necessarily, only a small proportion of all the workshop papers appear in this volume. Hence, further thanks go to all the workshop participants whose work does not appear here, but whose participation none the less contributed to the project: in particular, the volume has benefited from the advice and efforts of Greg Myers, Kay Oehler and Steve Yearley. Special additional thanks to Teri Walker for her assistance with the final preparations for publication.

I wish to acknowledge the support of grants from the Economic and Social Reseach Council and from The Nuffield Foundation and to thank the various institutions which hosted the meetings: University of York (15–16 April 1983 and 7–8 April 1986); Oxford Polytechnic (7–8 September 1983); Brunel University (31 March–1 April 1984); University of Surrey (13–14 September 1984); University of St Andrews (20–22 September 1985); University of Bradford (22–3 April 1987).

All the chapters are previously unpublished, except Chapter 5 'Don Quixote's Double: a Self-exemplifying Text', which is reprinted (replicated?) here by permission of George Allen and Unwin from Chapter 4 of Michael Mulkay's *The Word and the World: Explorations in the Form of Sociological Analysis* (London: George Allen and Unwin, 1985). In Figure 1 of Chapter 2, the front cover of *The History of Anthropology*, volume 1, *Observers Observed: Essays on Ethnographic Fieldwork*, George W. Stocking, Jr (ed.) (Madison, WI: University of Wisconsin Press, 1983) (re)appears by permission of the University of Wisconsin Press; the photograph of Malinowski which (re)appears as part of that front cover (re)appears here by permission of the London School of Economics. Douglas R. Hofstadter and Daniel C. Dennett's *The Mind's I: Fantasies and Reflections on Self and Soul* (Harmondsworth, Middx: Penguin Books, 1982) provided the idea for the Reflexion which follows each contribution. This enables the Editorial Voice to reappear throughout the text, in the manner of a Greek Chorus. It is also a way of trying to ensure that the Editor has the last word.

SWW
Wolvercote

The Contributors

Malcolm Ashmore is Lecturer in Sociology at Loughborough University. His main interests are reflexive analysis and the sociology of knowledge. He is author of *The Reflexive Thesis: Wrighting Sociology of Scientific Knowledge* (Chicago: University of Chicago Press, 1989).

Bruno Latour is Professor of Sociology at the Centre de Sociologie de l'Innovation, Ecole Nationale Supérieure des Mines, Paris. He has written widely on the social history and sociology of science. His publications include *Laboratory Life: The Construction of Scientific Facts* (with Steve Woolgar; Princeton, NJ: Princeton University Press, 1986); *Science in Action* (Milton Keynes: Open University Press, 1987) and *The Pasteurization of France* (Cambridge, MA: Harvard University Press, 1988).

Michael Mulkay is Professor of Sociology at the University of York. He has published extensively in the sociology of science, his recent contributions including *The Word and the World: Explorations in the Form of Sociological Analysis* (London: George Allen and Unwin, 1985) and *Sociology of Science: A Sociological Pilgrimage* (Milton Keynes: Open University Press, 1991).

Trevor Pinch is Associate Professor at Cornell University. His interests include the sociology of science, the social analysis of technological systems and everyday economic reasoning. He is author of *Confronting Nature* (Dordrecht: Reidel, 1986) and co-editor of *The Social Construction of Technological Systems* (with Wiebe Bijker and Tom Hughes; Cambridge, MA: MIT Press, 1987).

Jonathan Potter is Reader in Discourse Analysis at Loughborough University. He has published extensively in the area of discourse analysis and is author of *Discourse and Social Psychology: Beyond Attitudes and Behaviour* (with Margaret Wetherell; London: Sage, 1987). His current interests include racism and the construction of facts.

Teri Walker has been Research Fellow in the Centre for Research in Innovation, Culture and Technology (CRICT) at Brunel, The University of West London. She is author of 'The Re-Enactment of Social Order' (PhD thesis, Brunel University, 1986).

Steve Woolgar is Reader in Sociology and Project Director in the Centre for Research in Innovation, Culture and Technology (CRICT) at Brunel, The University of West London. He is author of *Laboratory Life: The Construction of Scientific Facts* (with Bruno Latour; Princeton, NJ: Princeton University Press, 1986) and *Science: The Very Idea* (London: Routledge, 1988) and co-editor of *Representation in Scientific Practice* (with Michael Lynch; Cambridge MA: MIT Press, 1990) and *The Cognitive Turn* (with Steve Fuller and Marc de Mey; Dordrecht: Kluwer, 1989).

Anna Wynne is author of 'Re-Reading Data: On the Interpretability of Transcripts of Talk about Multiple Sclerosis' (PhD thesis, Brunel University, 1989) and has recently completed an MA in Modern European Philosophy at the University of Sussex. Her interests are in questioning the epistemological foundations of sociological research.

1

The Next Step:
an Introduction to the Reflexive Project

Steve Woolgar and Malcolm Ashmore

Although of considerable importance to the sociology of knowledge, the question of reflexivity has been largely neglected during the last decade or so. During this time, the range of knowledge activities amenable to social analysis has expanded, most notably to include detailed analyses of the production of scientific and mathematical knowledge. However, the growing confidence with which scholars have argued that *natural* scientific knowledge is a social construct, is now accompanied by growing interest in the consequences of applying this same argument to knowledge generated by the *social* sciences. Gruenberg's (1978: 322) statement of the self-referential quality of the social sciences is typical: 'Any statement which holds that humans necessarily act or believe in particular ways under particular circumstances refers as much to the social scientist as anyone else.' Increasingly, scholars are asking what significance should be granted to the fact that production of social scientific knowledge about the world is itself a social activity.

This volume addresses the phenomenon of reflexivity through the collective presentation of work developing out of the social studies of science. This tradition has been concerned, in very general terms, to specify the social and existential bases for the generation of scientific and technical knowledge. In a recent manifestation – the sociology of scientific knowledge (SSK) – this tradition has deployed a form of relativism to make the point that scientific and technical knowledge is not the rational/ logical extrapolation from existing knowledge, but the contingent product of various social, cultural and historical processes (for example, Knorr-Cetina and Mulkay, 1983). The general issue of reflexivity emerges in the specific area of the social studies of science, once it is recognized that the same point can be made about the knowledge produced by SSK. Its determinations, results, insights and so on are themselves the contingent product of various social processes.

Reactions to the issue of reflexivity are varied, ranging from the construal of reflexivity as a 'problem' to the notion that reflexivity may provide an occasion for exploring new ways of addressing longstanding questions of knowledge and epistemology. The contributors to this volume go beyond relativism and discourse analysis in an effort to explore the ways in which reflexivity has been variously ignored, evaded, diminished, pursued and celebrated.

To date, the recognition and exploration of the significance of reflexivity has been hindered because most prevous discussions have portrayed reflexivity as a 'problem' for social science. With almost no systematic examination of the topic, past discussions have simply assumed that reflexivity is a source of 'difficulties'. The exploration of reflexivity has also been hindered because most discussions have been pitched at too theoretical and abstract a level. Consequently, many social scientists have tended to disregard arguments which appear to have little relevance to their empirical research (Ashmore, 1985).

This volume addresses these sources of antipathy to the exploration of reflexivity in two ways. First, most of the contributors belong to a social study of science tradition committed to the exploration of important theoretical ideas through detailed empirical research. It is widely recognized that many of the major recent advances in sociology (in particular) have emerged from this tradition. Secondly, some of the contributors pursue the line that the apprehension of reflexivity as a *problem* for social science is an unnecessary and overly restrictive interpretation. By exploring new forms of textual expression and analysis, this volume demonstrates some fruitful lines of exploration which are opened up by a fresh attitude towards reflexivity. At the same time, other contributors recognize and comment upon some of the difficulties associated with this development...

EXCUSE ME, CAN I ASK SOMETHING HERE?

Oh, not you again. What is it?

WHAT DO YOU MEAN 'again'? THAT'S PRETTY ARROGANT, ISN'T IT, TO PRESUME READERS' FAMILIARITY WITH 'THE SECOND VOICE DEVICE'. YOU ASSUME THEY ARE ALREADY FAMILIAR WITH WYNNE (1983), ASHMORE (1985), MULKAY (1985), NOT TO MENTION NOVELISTS LIKE BARTH (1972), CALVINO (1982), FOWLES (1977, 1982) AND SORRENTINO (1979) AND LITERARY THEORISTS LIKE CAUTE (1971), DERRIDA (1977) AND SHARRATT (1982). QUITE APART FROM THAT, THIS IS ONLY MY FIRST INTERRUPTION IN THIS TEXT – WELL, AT LEAST, THE FIRST *OBVIOUS* INTERRUPTION.

Okay okay okay...readers will begin to think that I'm interrupting you! What's your point?

I'LL IGNORE THAT. I JUST WANTED TO POINT OUT THAT YOUR TONE WAS EXTRA-ORDINARILY EMPIRICIST IN YOUR OPENING PARAGRAPHS. YOU'RE NOT GOING TO TRY AND BLIND US WITH FACTS ARE YOU?

As usual, you jump in far too early with all the obvious quibbles. Why don't you just wait and see? Actually, that strikes me as a feeble excuse for a Second Voice intervention. You wouldn't have expected this text's authors to be quite so stupid as to introduce a definitive list of aims and arguments in the volume without there being some clever reflexive point to it all.

WELL I *COULD* HAVE BEEN FOOLED BY THAT, I ADMIT. DOES THAT MEAN MY INTERVENTION IS JUST A WAY OF DEMONSTRATING YOUR AWARENESS OF THE SECOND VOICE DEVICE...?

No.

...REITERATING THE TIRED OLD PLATITUDE THAT ALL TEXTS ARE MULTIVOCAL...?

Certainly not.

...TRYING TO FIND A NEW WAY OF SUPPLYING REFERENCES THAT HAVE USED OR DISCUSSED THE SECOND VOICE DEVICE...?

Look, it's *your* intervention. I don't see why you're asking me... And while you're thinking about that you might explain why you appear in UPPER CASE this time?

WHAT DO YOU MEAN?

Well you could have appeared in italics, or some other different script, or a different colour, or...the use of UPPER CASE makes it seem like you're shouting!

I'M AFRAID IT'S THE LIMITATIONS OF THE AVAILABLE TECHNOLOGY. BUT THEN AGAIN I DON'T SEE WHY YOU SHOULD HAVE THE MONOPOLY ON lower case TEXT. YOUR MONOPOLY OF THE CONVENTIONAL IDIOGRAPH MAKES *ME* SEEM LIKE THE ODDBALL. BESIDES I THOUGHT WE BOTH AGREED THAT THERE WAS NO REAL DIFFERENCE BETWEEN US: THAT WHEN ALL IS SAID AND DONE WE ARE NOT TWO VOICES BUT TWO SETS OF INTERCHANGEABLE SCRIPTED REMARKS; THAT OUR ORIGINS SHOULD NOT BE HELD AGAINST US AS SOURCES OF SANCTIONABLE CONSISTENCY, AS LABELS TO WHICH OUR REMARKS ARE HELD ACCOUNTABLE, AS...

You're going too fast again. Why don't you just say that actors' voices can emanate from quite different and interchangeable identities, and that this can be done without any evident contradiction on the part of the actors themselves?

YOU THINK THAT'S LESS OBSCURE?

Not very.

BUT THE BASIC POINT IS THAT WE COULD SWITCH ROLES WITHOUT ANYONE NOTICING?

Yes.

AND THAT WE COULD DROP THIS UPPER CASE/lower case DISTINCTION IN ORDER DELIBERATELY TO CONFUSE OUR SUPPOSEDLY SEPARATE IDENTITIES?

Right.

SO THAT NOBODY KNOWS WHO IS INTERRUPTING WHOM?

That's it.

Okay.

Right.

Yes.

Good.

Actually, we don't seem to be getting anywhere in terms of introducing our readers to our writers. Assuming, of course, that we wish to pursue the conventional function of an introduction. Why, for instance, should we concentrate on the so-called 'second-voice' device when only two of the chapters in this collection (or three, including this one) make use of it (Chapter 6 by Wynne and Chapter 9 by Pinch and Pinch)? Surely that is only one example of attempts to deal with the more important general issue: the way in which the conventions of realism constrain our exploration of knowledge practices and inhibit the development of reflexive practice. I think we have to start again.

GROAN.

Well, perhaps we *could* retain the first five 'conventional' paragraphs, just as long as it's clear that they necessarily precede their own deconstruction. Thus:

'Although of considerable importance . . . some of the difficulties associated with this development . . .'

How does that sound so far?

Frankly, it's very disappointing. I mean this is supposed to be a volume which explores new ways of broaching reflexivity. But in order to introduce these to the reader, here we are deploying the familiar conventions of realism. How unreflexive can you get?

In a sense you are right. The aim is not simply to talk *about* reflexivity, but to examine the extent to which we can profitably engage *in* it. So I agree that one would expect at least some effort to move beyond the usual forms of argument. I suppose you are going to suggest the use of dialogue?

Well, it does have the advantage of demonstrating (rather than just pointing out) the multivocal character of the text. The explicit presence of more than one voice reminds the reader (and the writer) that interpretation goes on all the time, that the idea of one reading – a singular correspondence between text and meaning – is illusory. In particular, the dialogue is one way of introducing some instability into the presumed relationship between text and reader. I am reminded of the rather nice phrase by Woolgar (1982: 489): 'We need to explore forms of literary expression whereby the monster [reflexivity] can be simultaneously kept at bay and allowed a position at the heart of our enterprise.'

I have at least three problems with this. First, and most obviously, we need to avoid giving the impression that adoption of a particular textual form will 'solve the problem' and guarantee that we achieve instability. Such a solution would also give rise to a version of the current position in the sociology of scientific knowledge. We criticize some SSK researchers for adopting a formulaic approach to the social study of scientific knowledge – a formula which enables them to be relativist about scientists' knowledge practices but realist in the production of their own research – and now we ourselves advocate a formula, as if it represents a 'solution' to 'difficulties' engendered by the realist mode! But more than that, there is the second problem that, as soon as we start using dialogue, we simply engender readers' irritations with this style. Too arch, frivolous, clever, smart-arse, trendy, fancy stuff etcetera. The same old stuff again, they will say. One or two uses of dialogic form and the effect is exhausted. Subsequent uses become 'just more of the same'.

The same old stuff, indeed! One or two uses of this criticism of dialogic form (Wynne, 1986; Pinch and Pinch, this volume) and the effect of the criticism is exhausted. Subsequent uses become 'just more of the same'. (For a similar general argument on the 'hyperageing' of new forms, see Ashmore, 1985: 428.) However, there is nothing inherent in the dialogic style which makes it more subject to that criticism than any other (conventional) form of writing. Instead of exploring the character of different forms, critics simply assume that dialogic writing is peripheral to the important stuff, that it is just playful.

I agree with that. But it's also clear that your perfectly reasonable and symmetrical counter-argument is still insufficient to offset the criticisms. It reminds me of Lewis Carroll's (1939) Achilles appealing to the force of logic in his argument with the Tortoise: you are saying that if I don't accept the in principle virtue of dialogic form, logic will jump up and seize me by the throat! Whatever the logic of your argument, readers can continue to view the use of dialogue as the easy way out, playful stuff, that serious work requires the use of conventional forms (which in virtue of their being conventional, are more persuasive).

I'm not at all sure that using dialogue is easier. For a start it's much more difficult to keep it on track, to keep it saying what you want it to say. You very easily get distracted by things that start happening.

Yes, that's self-evident. But my third problem with the idea of dialogue is the tendency to hear it as a debate between two positions: one voice has one set of views and the other voice another. (A tendency to this hearing is exacerbated by texts which are co-authored. But see Pinch and Pinch, this volume. But see Woolgar and Ashmore, this volume.) Far from introducing instability in the text, this notion of dialogue implies a debate between two identifiable and consistent positions. But some writers suggest a contrary view. For example, the important feature of Mulkay's (1984) 'The Scientist Talks Back' is that the characters in the play gradually shift position and – with no apparent contradiction – start arguing exactly the reverse of their initial standpoints.

I agree we should avoid the use of characters with clearly consistent identities and points of view.

Good.

Right.

Well.

Okay.

Okay then.

The next step then.

Beyond Dialogue

Then there's the question of whether or not we (should) have a dialogue at all. Or, indeed, of what counts as a dialogue. Presumably, the fact that the text follows a left-justified (or left-indented) format doesn't by itself make it dialogue? No, I would guess that you also need to include some notion that the sentences represent different turns by separate speakers. This is what would distinguish it from ordinary connected prose. But then again, you might argue that it is quite possible to arrange what is actually dialogue in the form of connected prose: that is, although it appears like prose, it is actually dialogue. Or vice versa. So you could say that this is dialogue. Or even that it is not!

I remember when we were talking about writing an introduction, you mentioned Cohen and Taylor's (1976) three-stage model of self-consciousness. First, you unreflectively and routinely brush your teeth twice a day. Then you realize that it is a mere habit and proceed *not* to brush your teeth at all. Finally, you realize that reacting to habit in this way is counter-productive so teeth-cleaning starts again – this time not as habit but as self-conscious *choice*. The interesting point is that there is no obvious way for an onlooker to distinguish between the first and third option. I think we have the same problem with dialogue. What is the difference between text which looks like dialogue and which is dialogue, and text which looks like dialogue but which is not? Or between straight text which is just straight text, and text which *appears* straight but is actually concealing its dialogic intentions?

More importantly, of course, the same point applies to reflexivity in general. The interesting problem is to distinguish contributions which are patently not reflexive from those which are reflexive, but which deliberately conceal any ostensive signs of reflexivity. Apparently unreflexive texts may in fact be reflexive and vice versa (see, for example, any of the contributions to this volume).

Well, that should provide a salutory reminder of the pointlessness of debates about whether or not X is actually being reflexive. ('I'm more reflexive than thou.') In a sense, Chapter 2, by Woolgar, attempts to take up Geertz's (1973) well-known suggestion on this: the only way to hope to distinguish reflexivity from non-reflexivity is through thick description of the community within which notions like 'reflexivity' have currency. Of course, that begs the question about what counts as adequately thick description. Of course, that begs the question of what counts as begging the question.

In any event, the question of whether or not our introduction should engage in one of the forms it introduces is entirely (un)resolved. Clearly it is important to provide (no) clues as to whether or not this is a dialogue. Except, of course, to state categorically that we have decided (not) to have

a dialogue. This is certainly not a dialogue (Magritte).
Magritte? This is certainly not the point. Shall we start again?
Again? Alright, but I think we need to inject some sense of progress in
the next step.

The Next Step

The exploration of reflexivity is the next natural development of the
relativist–constructivist perspective in the social study of science. It moves
beyond the familiar general position that relativism can be 'applied' to
scientific knowledge, and thus supersedes such variants as the strong programme in the sociology of scientific knowledge (Bloor, 1976), the
empirical programme of relativism (Collins, 1981c), and discourse analysis
(Mulkay et al, 1983). As is made clear in Table 1, a characteristic of each
phase of the evolution of these perspectives is the 'exposition and criticism'
(Naess, 1972) of the earlier phase. The main thrust of second-phase
criticism, especially pronounced in its more programmatic moments, is
that realist preconceptions about science (in the first phase) unnecessarily
restrict and shape the social study of science. In the emerging third phase,
we can now see, by direct analogy with these earlier criticisms, the way
in which realist preconceptions about social science have hindered the
further development of the art.

Table 1   *Evolution of Perspectives in the Social Study of Science*

Epistemological preconception	Character of study
1 Science: realist Social study: realist	Soc of *science* = soc of *scientists* Content of science is ignored Analysis is partial and asymmetric Social factors most apparent in cases of erroneous science Mertonianism
2 Science: relativized Social study: realist	Soc of scientific knowledge Analysis of 'content' Strong programme (impartiality and symmetry); Empirical programme of relativism; Discourse analysis First generation ethnography of scientific practice: what actually goes on in science (the exoticism of the other) Scientists as managers of the epistemological horrors
3 Science: relativized Social study: relativized	Reflexivity: new literary forms Second generation ethnography: uncertainty (the constitution of the other) Writers as managers of the epistemological horrors

Pre-Kuhnian (phase 1) social study of science was predominantly realist both in its preconceptions about science and its methodological commitments to the form of social science. This led to a concentration on the social relationships between scientists at the expense of attention to the nature of their cultural product. The sociology of scientists tended to ignore the content of scientific knowledge, and to concentrate on the elucidation of 'social factors' in cases of apparently 'erroneous' science, or where the impact and effects of scandal and intrigue were most evident.

Relativist–constructivist (phase 2) social study of science has relativized the topic of investigation – science – while retaining a realist methodological strategy. Work in this corpus disprivileges scientific knowledge by utilizing various strategies of deconstruction. The way in which these strategies work to construct a new *meta*scientific reality – that scientific knowledge is built in such and such a way and has such and such a character – is not a topic of examination for second-phase work. The nature of the reflexive similarity between findings and methods is not itself a live issue; reflexivity is either treated as an inherent but uninteresting characteristic of such work (for example, Barnes, 1974; Bloor, 1976) or, by contrast, is actively opposed (Collins, 1981a; Pinch, 1983). However, the move towards the analysis of scientists' discourse (Gilbert and Mulkay, 1984a; Potter and Wetherell, 1987) created the means whereby reflexive issues could take on a greater salience. This is largely because the methods of discourse analysis may be applied as effectively to the discourse strategies of metascientists as they can to those of scientists.

The impetus for the reflexive (phase 3) social study of science stems from several sources. One is the recognition that the lack of consistency between the relativized and realist poles of phase 2 work makes it inherently vulnerable to tu quoque ('you too') arguments from philosophers (such as Laudan, 1981, 1982). Since the repair of consistency recommended from such quarters is invariably the abandonment of the relativized pole, such arguments tend rightly to be treated with scant respect by sociologists of scientific knowledge. However, the principle of consistency can be upheld, and the threat of the tu quoque removed, by abandoning the commitment to realist methods (Ashmore, 1985). This volume is a forum for preliminary discussions about the problems and possibilities of pursuing this most important, yet very difficult, objective.

One source of antipathy to the reflexive project is the assumption that such work is incompatible with good (serious) research practice because of its self-regarding quality or because it leads to a regress of metastudies (Latour, this volume). Such assumptions have led researchers interested in reflexivity to develop a practice in which the interrogation of the methods proceeds simultaneously with, and as an integral part of, the investigation of the object (Woolgar, 1982).

A general influence on the development of phase 3 work is the increasing emphasis on the substantive effects of form and its self-conscious manipulation in many areas of cultural practice, ranging from philosophy (Rorty, 1978), through such neighbouring social sciences as anthropology (Woolgar, this volume; Watson, 1987), economics (McCloskey, 1985) and psychology (Stringer, 1985) to various literary–critical practices too numerous to cite here. Yet another factor is the current revival of interest in modes of self-reference as evidenced by the vast popularity of the works of Hofstadter (1980, 1985).

In short, the reflexive project in the social study of science, to which the papers in this volume are an essential contribution, is the inevitable next step in – indeed the culmination of – some of the most exciting intellectual work currently being undertaken anywhere.

I think that just about wraps it up. Except that we really ought to say something about the actual contributions themselves. And probably the best way of doing that is by pointing out how none of them fits our ironic portrayal of this progressivist three-phase model.

The Real Contents

For example, Potter in Chapter 3 rejects both this particular story of SSK and the use of 'degrees of reflexivity' as an arbiter of progress. For him, discourse analysis already involves the use of a 'new literary form' which entails a degree of reflexivity. Latour in Chapter 8, while advocating that we 'just tell' stories ('infra-reflexivity'), is highly critical of what he calls 'meta-reflexivity', as supposedly represented here in Chapter 7 by Ashmore and Chapter 2 by Woolgar (and this introduction). However, Ashmore's attempt to replicate the work of the classic phase 2 writer, H. M. Collins, clearly makes it difficult to classify Ashmore's chapter as work which in any sense goes 'beyond Collins'. Similarly, Woolgar's piece is more an attempt to delineate varieties of reflexivity than an exploration of them. Pinch and Pinch in Chapter 9 do use dialogic form, but this is done in order to make the point that stylistic experimentation is not essentially wedded to explorations of reflexivity.

Walker's contribution in Chapter 4 is impossible to classify in terms of form or method; her concern is with the way in which esoteric Discourses (bodies of knowledge) find their way into everyday discourses (speech), and vice versa. She would argue that hers was an attempt to 'bring the reflexive character of knowledge to observation', rather than an attempt to employ reflexivity as a method. Mulkay's contribution to this collection (Chapter 5) appears to embody reflexivity of the 'post hoc' rather than 'immediate' variety (Woolgar, this volume). Although Chapter 6, by Wynne, is perhaps the most successful example in this collection of work which attempts the seamless integration of its object (the diagnosis of disease) with its method (the diagnosis of diagnosis), Wynne's more recent work (1986) appears to reject this approach (see Pinch and Pinch, this volume). Finally, the 'introduction' by Woolgar and Ashmore is largely a conventional empiricist monologue occasionally enlivened with dialogic discussion – a form which the authors emphatically repudiate. Moreover, it includes several passages which attempt to propagandize the reflexive project as the most important intellectual development since SSK! Obviously, such hyperbole has little place in an enterprise which justifies itself in terms of the abandonment of realism. The authors' claim that all such passages are, in fact, ironic, is clearly a belated and transparent attempt to get themselves off the hook, and should not, therefore, be taken seriously.

Do you think that will do the trick?
Probably not. I am concerned that readers will miss the irony of our progressivist account. They may suspect that (deep down) we actually like the possibility that reflexivity is an advance on previous approaches. After all, we merely assert that the three-phase model is ironic; we do not attempt its deconstruction. Thus, we miss the opportunity of revealing that Table 1 is actually our third effort to devise a table which portrays reflexivity in a good light; we fail to present a further table (Table 2) which sets out the relative advantages of different ways of presenting tables, and so on. More generally, do you think we could *ever* have an adequate introduction to a project which attempts to engage in the kind of reflexivity it endorses? On the one hand it seems quite appropriate, indeed admirably consistent, that an introduction to this kind of work should both display and comment upon the work of introducing. On the other hand, you could say that this tactic is just self-indulgent and will succeed only in putting people off. Even a discussion of whether or not it would put people off is bound to put them off.
We clearly need to avoid that kind of discussion.
So we can conclude that our effort is bound to fail: either we restrict ourselves to a straight introduction (or at least one which – *pace* Latour – *appears* straight) which fails to exemplify/explore the forms it introduces; or we put people off.
Perhaps we find ourselves in this position because we haven't thought clearly enough about our potential audience. A lot of readers may find the issues rather obscure, and that our text demands familiarity with some very specific arguments. The point about successful instances of reflexive practice is that they are closely tied to the specific occasion of their occurrence; they are essentially local accomplishments. For example, Mulkay's (1986) Bernal Prize acceptance speech worked well precisely because the audience recognized, and was part of, the situation which the

speech parodied. Our problem is that we would very much like to produce a standard form of book, a text for anyone, which doesn't make particular expectations of its readers and which can be read in many different ways; but we would still like it to be read in a very specific way. If readers are unsure what's going on they might feel that we are making jokes at their expense. And, as before, even our reasonable attempt to make explicit our (genuine) concern about this effect might be interpreted as a further joke.

But there aren't any jokes in this text. Or at least there weren't until I said there weren't.

There still aren't!

But there are now – that was definitely a joke, of sorts.

I hope it won't put off our readers...

What readers? I'm sorry; no jokes, right? Though I think at this stage...

After all...

In the end...

...we have to trust the Reader to make of it what s/he will.

Malcolm. This is what we have so far. I'm afraid things are still very obscure. And I'm not at all sure about this ending. Do we need to start again?

Steve. This is what we have so far. I'm afraid things are just as obscure as they were, though I have tried to improve the ending. I have done this, as you will realize, by inverting your final question. Rather than re-start, I have re-ended. Do we need to end again?

Reflexion on Woolgar and Ashmore

Woolgar and Ashmore seem to be juggling with several balls at once. They raise questions about ways of exploring reflexivity, their discussion throws up more questions, questions about the questions and so on. The trouble is that, in the end, the balls remain in the air. In terms of the conventional requirements of an introduction, the piece clearly fails: the reader has no firm footing from which to begin what looks to be a potentially hazardous journey through the text.

Possibly, Woolgar and Ashmore suppose that resolution might be attempted in this Reflexion. They might anticipate that Editorial comment on their so-called 'introduction' would dwell on the way their piece seems (not) to progress, on its lack of a proper ending, and so on, perhaps culminating in a discussion of how best to end a Reflexion. But this rather tiresome move will be resisted. In any case, I strongly suspect the authors would claim that their chapter actually contains its own Reflexions, and that further Reflexion is superfluous. (It will be interesting to see how far this is also the case for the other contributions.)

Reflexions permit the reappearance of the Editorial Voice throughout the text. It is, of course, possible to discern the presence of an editor's *v*oice, for example, in the shape and direction of the arguments, their organization and juxtaposition, and so on. The use of a scripted *V*oice is intended merely to underscore this presence. This rationale poses an interesting problem. A meta-Voice (the Editor) is established in order to reassert the multivocality of the text. But, as Woolgar and Ashmore make clear, the assignation of discrete/distinct identities to voices/characters is to be discouraged, because it tends to play down the interpretive work necessary to concretize positions and views, to crystallize them as the production/possession of separate selves. Thus, the meta-Voice either undermines its own assertion or it becomes indistinguishable from the characters/voices about which it wishes to make an observation. We might also note that the meta-Voice appears to invite regression: the Editor's Voice is clearly someone else's creation. As is this. (And so on.)

Hopefully, the significance of these observations about the Editor's Voice will become clearer during the course of this volume. For now, the obvious question is whether or not there will be reflexions on these Reflexions. Leaving aside the extent to which Reflexions constitute their own commentary. My answer is no (cf. Garfinkel, 1967: 79ff).

Woolgar and Ashmore seem concerned about 'putting people off' even though they (almost) conclude that the Reader has to be allowed to make up his or her own mind. But it is axiomatic to most social science that actors are not free agents. In other words, Readers are not free to choose as they will: they are prisoners of conventions and of their own expectations. This means, of course, that many Readers will hate the Next Step despite them-Selves. Sociologically speaking, they have no option but to react in this way! Woolgar and Ashmore go completely off the sociological track on this point. By assuming the autonomy of the subject (Reader) they transgress a basic axiom of sociology. On the other hand, we should note the interpretive flexibility involved in specifying (constructing) the nature of 'constraints on choice'. In principle, a large number of alternative accounts of 'constraints' is possible. This suggests we remain sceptical about the existence of such 'constraints'. It suggests that conventions and expectations do not constrain action so much as provide a discursive register which is drawn upon in the evaluation and rationalization of action. Woolgar and Ashmore are perhaps saying that innovation requires a break with the view that conventions and expectations constrain action. But you can't please everyone all of the time. Which is why we now turn from a (possibly) reflexive non-introduction to a (possibly) non-reflexive introduction.

2

Reflexivity is the Ethnographer of the Text

Steve Woolgar

The front cover of a recent collection of essays on ethnographic fieldwork (Stocking, 1983a) bears a black and white photograph (Figure 1). A figure sits at his desk under the awning of a tent canopy. The photograph is taken from within the tent, so that the seated figure is silhouetted against the brightness of a tropical scene, from which a dozen tribal faces peer in on him as he writes.

On a straightforward interpretation, the photograph shows 'Malinowski at work'.[1] But in the mood of interpretivist scepticism which pervades much current scholarship, instances of 'straightforward' interpretation are rare. For even to speak of (or draw attention to) interpretation, far less scrutinize the nature of the interpretive act, is to begin to question the congruence of the image with its underlying reality. Once the relationship between them comes into question, a series of increasingly complex questions is set in train.

The reader arrives at the straightforward interpretation, at least in part, by using the photograph to infer the presence of 'an actual scene', a pre-existing reality which gave rise to the photographic image. The photograph both provides the 'fact' of Malinowski's observational activity and is a symbolic manifestation of his author-ity to speak of an actual place and time, to claim to have actually been there. But if we accept that this really is Malinowski and that he really was in Omarakana, there remains the puzzle of what the devil Malinowski thought he was up to.[2] To what extent does the photograph capture the nature of ethnographic work, the experience of being 'in the field'? What manner of 'work' is Malinowski engaged in? Is he perhaps more concerned with his writing than with his subjects? Indeed, is he really writing at all?

While these questions highlight the possibility of alternative interpretations of ethnographic record, they do scant justice to the essential and irremediable ambiguity about 'what the photograph shows'. A more profound set of questions arises when we notice that Malinowski shares the cover of the book with its title – *Observers Observed*. The juxtaposition of photographic image and caption unleashes queries about observation

HISTORY OF ANTHROPOLOGY · VOLUME 1

OBSERVERS OBSERVED

Essays on Ethnographic Fieldwork

Edited by George W. Stocking, Jr.

Figure 1 *Frontispiece*

which go beyond the issue of adequacy in ethnographic record. Who is doing the observing and who is being observed? The reader observes the observer (Malinowski) at work, but the photograph seems to show that Malinowski is himself the focus of attention of some of the Trobrianders. The observer is the subject of observation from within. In addition, closer inspection of the photograph suggests that some of the natives are looking directly at the camera. Thus the very observation of the observer-at-work is itself being observed. Further, we only realize this as a result of our *own* careful scrutiny of the photograph. In other words, it is through our own observation that we see the observation of the observation of the observer . . . [4]

Attention to the juxtaposition of image and caption not only alerts us to the multiple senses of 'observation' involved, but also raises important questions about their inter-relationship. In our apprehension of the photograph (and its caption) we may begin to question the nature of the 'observational' work carried out by the ethnographer. But in what sense, and to what extent, does a critical focus upon the ethnographer depend upon the adequacy of our own observations? How much can we rely upon our own observations as the basis for questioning his methods? And what are the implications of the observational work being done by the natives for our own efforts at observation? Given the multiple and interconnected levels of observation here, on what basis can we leave unchallenged the simplistic analytic distinction between the Trobrianders ('the natives') and their ethnographer ('the observer')? Our suspicions about the camera-happy ethnographer lead us to question the very basis for distinguishing between ethnographer and native, observer and observed, insider and outsider.

The Malinowski photograph provides a metaphor for exploring fundamental problems associated with the rich and complex interplay of image (observation, representation, record, text), caption (content, antecedent circumstances) and reality (object/subject, the observed). In less sceptical times, these problems did not arise. The frontispieces to the great classics in anthropological fieldwork are a motif for the self-confidence of a bygone age; matter-of-fact photographic records of the world on which they report. The observer (author, ethnographer, photographer) is notably absent from these photographs; silent, passive, behind the scene. The modern predicament about the adequacy of representation arises because the observer, the agent of representation, has once again become part of the picture. Critical accounts of the nature of observation now include photographs of the observer.

If 'reflexivity' refers, in simple terms, to the willingness to probe beyond the level of 'straightforward' interpretation, the response of social sciences to the issue of reflexivity is divided along the lines of those dismayed and those delighted by the potential complexity of the Malinowski photograph; between those who construe reflexivity as a tool for improving observational accuracy and those who view it as the impetus for exploring different ways of asking questions about knowledge practices. Once we go beyond the idea of 'straightforward interpretation', we confront a potential vortex of questions about interpretation. The interesting question is where, how and on what basis does one stop asking further questions; at what point, to use Blum's (1971: 301; Blum and McHugh, 1984) phrase, do we differentially decide to stop doubting? (And – just in case we think this provides a line of enquiry which enables us to escape from the vortex – what counts as an adequate answer to this last question?)

Most social scientists tend to steer well clear of any sustained examination of the significance of reflexivity, despite frequently acknowledging its relevance in general terms. As a result, there is much loose talk about 'reflexivity' and the term is used in a variety of often confusing ways. This chapter aims to provide an initial delineation of species of reflexivity with reference to the social studies of science and to some discussions of ethnographic fieldwork. The argument begins with a consideration of the connection between relativism and reflexivity. This is the basis for an examination of the various ways in which researchers construe the relationship between image and reality, and their conception of the role of the agent of representation (the observer). In order to show how different conceptions of reflexivity index (correspond to) deeply held preconceptions about the nature of research and fundamental ideas about the character of representation, these different stances on reflexivity are juxtaposed against one especially virulent strain: constitutive reflexivity – a slogan for which provides the title of this chapter.

The Rise of Cultural Relativism

In the 1960s, the long-standing debate about the nature of understanding and explanation in the social sciences gained new impetus by focusing on the problem of understanding the beliefs and actions of members of other cultures. Taking their cue from Winch (1958), sociologists, anthropologists and philosophers debated the problem of rationality: whether or not it was possible to translate the meanings and reason of one culture into the language of another (for example, Wilson, 1970). More recent developments in the philosophy of science, especially the post-Kuhnian revision of epistemological preconceptions about the 'special' character of scientific enquiry, gave rise to a replay of these debates in terms which more explicitly addressed the phenomenon of science. Thus, in introducing a collection intended as an update on debates about rationality, Hollis and Lukes (1982: 1) note that:

recent upheavals in the philosophy of science have turned the historian or sociologist of science into something of an anthropologist, an explorer of alien cultures. It is as if scientific paradigms and theoretical frameworks were strung out in time like islands across an archipelago.

The espousal of a relativism traditionally associated with cultural anthropology enabled the social study of science to treat the achievements, beliefs, knowledge claims and artefacts of subjects as socially/culturally contingent. The significant point is that scientific knowledge no longer needed to be considered a special case, exempt from consideration as a cultural artefact (for example, Bloor, 1976; Mulkay, 1979; Collins, 1985). In its 'ethnographic mood', the social study of scientific knowledge makes explicit its use of 'anthropological distance' as an analytic tool. The ethnographic study of science thus portrays the production of scientific facts as a local, contingent accomplishment specific to the culture of the laboratory setting (Latour and Woolgar, 1979; Knorr-Cetina, 1981; Lynch, 1985; Traweek, forthcoming; for reviews see Latour, 1982; Woolgar, 1982; Knorr-Cetina, 1983).

Does Relativism Lead to Reflexivity?

To what extent, and in what sense, does this espousal of relativism by the social study of science entail reflexivity? Although it is a philosophical commonplace that relativism 'leads to' reflexivity (for example, Lawson, 1985), the connection between relativism and reflexivity remains confused. For example, when discussing 'the mistake' of assuming the relativism can adopt an uncommittal, neutral standpoint, Nickles (1984: 307) asks: 'Is it reflexivity or lack of reflexivity with avoids [this] mistake?'

Let us take a close look at one formulation of the view that relativism leads to reflexivity. Woolgar and Ashmore (this volume, page 1) suggest that Gruenberg's (1978: 322) is typical: 'Any statement which holds that humans necessarily act or believe in particular ways under particular circumstances refers as much to the social scientist as anyone else.' According to this formulation, the relativism in the claim that 'humans necessarily act or believe in particular ways under particular circumstances' also applies to those making this claim. The general aim of the social studies of science is to produce knowledge about scientific activity, in other words, to make statements about human acts which involve the production of scientific knowledge. Since making statements is itself a human act, it follows that the social study of science is self-referring.

This argument for self-reference lays the basis for the further argument about the deleterious consequences of reflexivity. Reflexivity becomes problematic when the relativist stance is taken as both self-referential and critical. If the relativistic argument implies that human actions or beliefs are *less reliable* (valid, true) because they are specific to particular circumstances, then the self-referential argument also makes the claims of the relativists less reliable. By questioning (or merely by refusing to take for granted) the *adequacy* of observation, we simultaneously highlight the possibility of questioning the adequacy of our own observations. More generally, one potential consequence of applying relativism to the results of others' research is that we raise critical questions about our own research practice. This, of course, is the well-known view that relativism is self-defeating.

The conclusion that relativism is self-defeating (in virtue of the reflexivity it entails) depends crucially on our interpretation of the various terms and clauses which constitute the argument. For example, Gruenberg's formulation: 'Any statement refers as much to the social scientist as anyone else', draws heavily on a particular sense of what we understand by making statements, acting as a human, and being a social scientist. In particular, the claim for self-reference depends upon our seeing an equivalence between these items of behaviour which might, in other circumstances, be understood as different. Thus, we read reflexivity in this formulation by equating the class of actions of 'human' with those of 'social scientist', although in another setting we might recognize the need to emphasize a distinction between humans (subject) and social scientist (analyst). Or again, with particular reference to the social study of science, the argument for reflexivity depends on our understanding 'making statements' as the same kind of 'human act' as those 'human acts' involved in the production of scientific knowledge.

The interpretive flexibility of the component parts of the argument suggests that 'relativism leads to reflexivity' is far from the necessary connection or entailment suggested by some philosophical accounts. The 'necessity' of the connection derives from an epistemological standard imposed upon the practices of social scientists. In other words, we find the necessity of the connection between relativism and reflexivity in virtue of our conforming to a particular set of interpretations and equivalences. Clearly, most relativizing social scientists exhibit blatant disdain for the compulsion of logical entailment: they continue to practise relativism without regard for its allegedly self-defeating consequences.

The interpretive flexibility involved in the philosopher's connection between relativism and reflexivity has three important consequences. First, it makes it possible to deny that relativism leads to reflexivity.[5] This is done by assuming that the human acts of the social scientist–analyst are of a *different order* to those human acts involved in the production of scientific knowledge. The idea that relativism leads to reflexivity is thus resisted by claiming that the analyst operates at a *different level* from those being studied. Rhetorically, the 'threat' is managed by the assumption of difference between observer and observed. This difference is *assumed* rather than argued for. As we shall see, the assumption of difference is embedded in practices of argument which maintain the distance and exoticism of the target of study. Secondly, the interpretive flexibility makes it possible to admit that the social study of science is 'reflexive' in a limited sense and yet deny the significance of this for research practice. Thirdly, social scientists find it possible to practise relativism and yet subscribe to a variety of kinds of reflexivity.

Fundamentals of Reflexivity

All this suggests that whether or not relativism leads to reflexivity depends on how you construe the relation between one's own research practices and those of the subjects. The following simple schema enables us to identify the importance for different views of reflexivity of the perceived relationship between our system of representation and the properties of represented object. The adequacy of representation can be said to depend on:

1   the *distinction* (or *distance*) between representation (image) and research object (reality); and
2   the *similarity* of these separate entities.

'Method' is a knowledge community's sanctioned procedure for accomplishing adequate connections between representation and object; a guide (or set of guidelines) for generating an image which is faithful to the represented reality. But it is readily apparent that prescriptions of method fail to resolve the central tension between the postulates of distinctiveness and similarity. The image should be similar to the represented reality. But the critique of replication developed in the social study of science (Ashmore, this volume; Collins, 1985; Mulkay, this volume) tells us that a condition of faithful representation is that the image should not be so familiar to the object as to be indistinguishable from it. Hence, a faithful representation must be both similar and distinct. It is a re-presentation: the *same* thing reappearing (as image) *at a distance from* the object (cf. Latour, 1986, and in this volume). At the same time, claims for distinctiveness may attenuate claims to similarity. Given certain considerations of distinctiveness/distance of a produced representation (for example, what we know about Malinowski, his background and preoccupations), we become more sceptical about its similarity value (the correspondence of the photographic record to reality).

In every case, what counts as similar and what aspects of a 'reality' are most important are the upshot of social negotiation. And the situation becomes further complicated when we target abstract concepts for representation. For example, if I wish to make a film about boredom, does the similarity postulate suggest I should try to make a boring film? If fidelity between representative medium and subject matter is the desired aim, would the production of a boring film be a sign of successful representation?[6] More interesting is the reverse question: to what extent is it possible to *avoid* mimesis? If I try to make a film about boredom, to what extent can I *avoid* making a boring film?

These questions become especially interesting when science is our target for representation. The relationship between our object (science) and its representation (our portrayal of science) will depend on the method we deploy. But if we accept method as a means of regulating the connection between our object and its representations, we then draw upon a concept which is part of the object we wish to represent. In this way, our efforts to study science assume some of the very features of scientific enquiry we set out to reveal. The character of our object (science) shapes the character of our investigation (our method) and hence the nature of our representation (portrayal of science).

Is this necessarily a bad situation to find ourselves in? The dilemma here stems from the tension between the postulates of distinctiveness and similarity. If method and object were truly distinct, the enquirer would have no way of knowing the characteristics of the latter in advance of studying it. Consequently, in the case of science, the adequacy of our account of scientific method might hinge upon our use of some highly *un*scientific method. If, on the other hand, the means of study and the object of study are not distinct, their interdependence suggests that our research process assumes (at least part of) the answer it sets out to find.

The difficulty in managing this double-bind accounts for the awkwardness of disclaimers, made in the face of accusations that relativism is self-defeating, that the social study of science is simply trying to do no more than science itself (Bloor, 1976). For example, to justify the use of causal explanations because 'this is how science itself proceeds' apparently assumes the answer (the nature of the object, that is, 'how science proceeds') which the research sets out to reveal. The justificatory appeal to 'how science proceeds' obviously derives from some ideal conception of Science, even though this justification is usually part of an argument for the need to demystify idealized conceptions of scientific procedure.

Varieties of Reflexivity

Our discussion of representation in terms of the twin postulates of distinctiveness and similarity enables us to classify varieties of reflexivity along a continuum ranging from radical constitutive reflexivity to benign introspection.

The *constitutive reflexivity* of foundational ethnomethodology arises from Garfinkel's (1967) discussion of the documentary method. Garfinkel suggests that, in any act of representation, there is an intimate interdependence between the surface appearance (document) and the associated underlying reality (object). The sense of the former is elaborated by drawing on 'knowledge of' the latter; at the same time, the sense of the latter is elaborated by what is known about the former.[7] The establishment of a connection between document and underlying reality (in the present case, between representation and object of study) is a back-and-forth process. 'Members' accounts...are constituent features of the settings they make observable' (Garfinkel, 1967: 8). We see that constitutive reflexivity amounts to a denial of distinction and a strong affirmation of similarity; representation and object are not distinct, they are intimately interconnected.

By contrast, traditional conceptions of the natural sciences depend on the affirmation of distinction and the denial of similarity; this position emphasizes the distinction between representation and studied object and maintains that these are essentially different kinds of entity. As a result, apparent concessions to reflexivity, both in the natural sciences and in other disciplines which aspire to the Scientific ethos, usually involve an entirely different form of reflexivity, which we can call *benign introspection*. This kind of reflexivity – perhaps more accurately designated 'reflection' – entails loose injunctions to 'think about what we are doing'. It is encouraged as a means of generating addenda to research reports, sometimes in the form of 'fieldwork confessions', which provide the 'inside story' on how the research was done. Although introspection and constitutive reflexivity may be related – for example, it may be through introspection that we come to recognize constitutive reflexivity in our work – it is important to recognize their difference. An exercise in introspection is usually concerned with improving the adequacy of the connection between analysts' statements and the objects of those statements. Perforce, this maintains the postulate of distinction between representation and object. Far from raising any fundamental problem, this kind of reflexivity sustains and enhances the Scientific axiom of the research effort.

The social sciences fall awkwardly between constitutive reflexivity and benign introspection in virtue of their admission of some similarity relations and their pretensions to ideals of Scientific method. In other words, the social sciences espouse distinction and admit similarity. This is one source of tension. While constitutive reflexivity is viewed as problematic for an enterprise with Scientific pretensions because it challenges the distinction between research methods and research object, benign introspection is encouraged as an aid to science. From a literary point of view, however, the situation is almost exactly reversed. Much literary criticism explicitly encourages constitutive reflexivity; the fact that the author constitutes and forms part of the 'reality' she creates is axiomatic to the analytic style. A second source of tension thus arises because social science is attracted by the constructivist undertones of constitutive reflexivity in its literary mood, but repelled by the implications for its own pretensions to produce a 'scientific' social study.

Natural science has no 'problem' with reflexivity because its discourse banishes similarity relations of the kind admitted in the social science. The rhetoric of scientific analysis asserts a difference in level between its operations and the world of the phenomena it investigates. Problems of reflexivity would occur in the natural sciences only if it was granted that electrons (like physicists) had belief systems, their own theories of inter-action and so on (cf. Ashmore, 1985: 198–201). (The 'absurdity' of the proposition is testimony to the effectiveness of Scientific discourse.) The alleged difference in level is accomplished and sustained in the rhetoric of research practices which differentially grant and deny attributes to the objects of investigation.

The tension which confronts social science results in various ways of managing similarity relations. This variation is particularly evident in the different social science traditions concerned with the study of science. Practitioners in the *sociology of knowledge* have traditionally avoided the study of scientific knowledge, partly in anticipation of 'problems' of reflexivity. This stance effectively finesses the question of similarity; whether or not these sociologists are 'scientific' in their own work is immaterial since science is not their object. *Mertonian sociology of science* also finessed the question of similarity. Although 'science' was the avowed object, this was conceived in terms such as the social relationships between knowledge practitioners, the impact of science, its institutional growth, and the political dynamics of funding decisions. This tradition thus presumed a low level of similarity between its representations and its research objects. In short, this tradition can be understood as an attenuation of the similarity postulate. The social study of sci*ence* was effectively an unreflexive social study of sci*entists*.

The *sociology of scientific knowledge* explicitly claims scientific know-ledge as the target for sociological analysis. In other words, the researcher is required to participate, *in the course of her research*, in activities which are also the object of that research. She produces knowledge claims about the production of knowledge claims; she aims to explain how explanation is done, to understand how understanding is produced, and so on. We would thus expect that self-reference in the sociology of scientific knowledge would be of an *immediate* kind, occurring in the course of the research itself. Clearly, this is quite different from the reflexivity which might be claimed for, say, a socio-historic study of slavery. I might admit I would act like the slave of my research account if hypothetically placed in that slave's role and time, but I do not conduct my research as a slave! In this case, the self-referential move is post hoc; the application of the results of the research to the researcher is a task *disengaged* from the research process itself.

In fact, however, proponents of the sociology of scientific knowledge also declare their enterprise to involve no more than post hoc or *disengaged* reflexivity: similarity between representation and object is admitted as a matter of principle, but the implications of this are deferred or disengaged from the practice of sociological enquiry. Bloor, for example, says that the strong programme in the sociology of scientific knowledge embraces the idea of reflexivity: 'In principle [the strong programme's] patterns of explanations would have to be applicable to sociology itself' (Bloor, 1976: 5). However, while admitting similarity between methods of research and research object, adherents to the strong programme effectively recommend that the sociologists put aside the reflexivity tenet in the course of explanatory practice (Woolgar, 1982: 492). The distinctiveness postulate is thus underscored by setting the practices of sociologist and of scientist apart in time. This disengaged version of reflexivity thus leaves the actual conduct of research undisturbed. The recommended reflexivity is to be carried on separately from sociological research practice.[8]

Reflexivity in Ethnography

We have seen that a variety of positions on reflexivity arise from the adoption by social science of a cultural relativism traditionally associated with anthropology. It is therefore appropriate to return to anthropology to consider the place of reflexivity in ethnography.[9] This is particularly appropriate, both because – as mentioned before – some analysts of science style themselves as ethnographers of science, and because of the recent emergence of a critique of ethnographic method.

Concern about the ways in which anthropological scholarship achieves its effect as 'knowledge of others' is manifest as an explicit epistemological concern for the ways in which interpretations are constructed and represented as objective discourse about subjects on (or among) whom research is conducted (Marcus, 1980; Marcus and Cushman, 1982; Clifford and Marcus, 1986). 'The activity of cross-cultural representation is now more than usually in question' (Clifford, 1983b: 118). This trend is both informed by and symptomatic of a more general critique of representation (deconstruction) in literary theory. The growing concern of cultural anthropologists at the dependence of anthropological knowledge upon cross-cultural representation emerges as a form of critical assessment of ethnographic method (Stocking, 1983a; Clifford and Marcus, 1986). For our purposes, the interest is in how ethnography deals with the postulates of distinctiveness and similarity, and what kind of reflexivity ensues.

Stocking (1983b) has examined Malinowski's attempts to convince his readers of the objectivity of his ethnographic method. While his explicit models were from Science, Malinowski also drew heavily on various literary devices, especially those of Frazerian prose. His problem, 'was not so much to tell his readers how to accomplish the ultimate divinatory task, as to convince them that it could be done, and that he had done it' (1983b: 106). Stocking argues that Malinowski's use of literary devices (the ambiguous situation of reported events in time, the categories of actors in his reports and so on) works to build a euhemerist validating myth: the anthropologist as hero. Malinowski himself noted that the function of magic was to bridge 'over gaps and inadequacies in highly important activities not yet completely mastered by man'. Malinowski's own brand of magic, says Stocking, consists precisely in bridging the gaps between specific methodological prescriptions of fieldwork and the vaguely defined goals of ethnographic knowledge. Stocking suggests that this 'ethnographer's magic' has been powerful enough to shape the work of generations of ethnographers. (Not to mention its power in fostering a determined disregard among these ethnographers for the radical implications of constitutive reflexivity.)

Stocking thus produces a deconstruction of the ethnographer's text. But Stocking shows no inclination to confront his own use of textual magic – the use of literary devices to reinforce the myth of the *historian* as the provider of authoritative accounts (of the way ethnography was done). He proceeds as if writing as an historian affords a level of epistemological security not available to those writing as ethnographers. Stocking thus evades the challenge of constitutive reflexivity by claiming, in effect, that the production of historical and ethnographic texts operate at fundamentally different levels.

Clifford's (1983a) assessment of Griaule's ethnography of the Dogon starts from the difficulty of reconstructing 'what really happened' in ethnographic encounters given our dependence on the secondary accounts furbished by the ethnographer. But Clifford eschews approaches which portray ethnographic reports as partial or distorted, in favour of their treatment as 'specific inventions'. 'The historian asks *what kind of truth* Griaule and the Dogon he worked with produced, in what dialogical conditions, within what political limits, in what historical climate' (Clifford, 1983a: 125). Only recently, says Clifford, in the context of a gradual dissolution of the myth of fieldwork objectivity, can we more deeply appreciate the ironic structure of ethnographic thought and practice, 'its reliance on improvised, historically contingent fictions' (1983a: 143). Clifford advocates the dispersal of ethnographic authority in the sense that both researchers and natives be recognized as active creators (authors) of cultural representations (Clifford, 1983a: 147; cf. Clifford, 1981, 1983b). This is not just to recommend an ethnography of Dogon ethnography, a definitive portrayal of how the Dogon portray their own culture. Instead it suggests that ethnographers' and Dogon's versions of custom are 'dialogically implicated one in the other' (Clifford, 1983a: 149), and that there is no extant cultural object beyond the interconnected construction of ethnographer and native.[10] Clifford thus advocates the eradication of the distinction between ethnographer and native (cf. Sharrock and Anderson, 1982): the 'natives' are as much observers as the 'observers' themselves.

Like Stocking, Clifford deconstructs the ethnographer's text. But Clifford's position on the implications of his deconstruction is less straight-forward. Clifford wishes to avoid criticizing the ethnographer's text as incorrect or distorted, even though, in a way exactly paralleled by claims to impartiality in the social study of scientific knowledge, it is doubtful whether such declarations of intent make the project any less critical in effect (cf. Woolgar, 1983). Clifford's proclaimed impartiality with respect to ethnographic truths is compromised by his argument that all forms of textual expression necessarily embody claims to truth: his own argument is, after all, another form of textual expression. So, although Clifford advocates the dispersal of authority between ethnographers and natives, it seems that commentators and meta-analysts (historians, literary critics etcetera) still possess greater authority than either ethnographer or native. Clifford (1983a: 153) remarks that fieldworkers are currently struggling 'to improvise new modes of authority', but it is not clear that Clifford would wish to regard himself as a fieldworker of the text.

Both Stocking and Clifford ironicize the ethnographer's claim to corres-pondence between representation (ethnographic record, report) and object (the native, his views and beliefs etcetera). Yet they accomplish this irony by advancing a correspondence between their own representation (comment, meta-analysis) and object (the ethnographer's claims). In relativizing the ethnographer's practice but not their own, they lay claim to a dissimilarity between their own representation and object.

How is this move accomplished? Let us look again at the use of photo-graphs in critical accounts of ethnography. Given that photographs are a formidable source of textual authority in the ethnographic genre, it is perhaps not surprising that they are used frequently throughout these discussions.[11] The photographs are used to make the point that interpreta-tions of ethnographic records are fraught with an uncertainty which belies the objectivist claims of an earlier, more self-confident, generation of anthropologists. Ethnography is not all it is (sometimes) cracked up to be. For example, Cole (1983: 41), when discussing a photograph originally captioned by Boas (1888) – 'Eskimo awaiting return of seal to blowhole' – states (in *his* caption) that the plate is in fact based on a studio photograph of Boas in his caribou suit. Cole thus claims the camera's deceitful representation of 'the actual situation': this is not a *real* eskimo, says Cole, merely Boas posing as one. Stocking (1983b) similarly used the Malinowski photograph (with which we began) to suggest that Malinowski's method was not all it was cracked up to be: the photograph shows us what actually happened in practice! In the same article (Stocking, 1983b: 82), the caption accompanying another photograph – 'Seligman at work, Hula' – appears alongside Malinowski's (1926: 147) pronouncement that 'the anthroplogist must relinquish his comfortable position on the verandah where he has been accustomed to collect statements from informants and go out into the village'. But in the photograph, Seligman can be seen seated at a table on the verandah, ostensibly collecting statements from informants.

Undoubtedly, this kind of ironic comment on ethnographic method usefully serves the purpose of dissuading readers from taking ethnographic reports at face value. The by-now familiar point is that ethnographic texts can no longer be regarded as the authoritative and docile records which they might once have been. By casting doubt on the claims of ethnography, by drawing attention to the constructed character of ethnographic fictions, the way is opened up for a critical assessment of ethnographic method, its claims to authority, the circumstances of its rise to prominence and so on (Clifford and Marcus, 1986). But the central critical moment of this project depends crucially upon the critic's own claim to authority. In these examples, photographs are to be read as revealing the 'actual' conditions of *another* text's production. The indeterminacy of interpretation is used to contrast the claims of another text with what (after all) it was actually like. (These efforts directly parallel attempts to relativize aspects of scientific culture and replace them with alternative – sometimes 'demystified' – accounts of what science is 'really' like.) Scepticism of the ethnographer's claim depends upon our accepting the *critic*'s claim. In the Seligman example, the ironic effect is achieved in virtue of accepting an interpretation of the photograph offered by the last sentence of the preceding paragraph.

Exoticism and Uncertainty

The tendency which militates against the view that representation and represented object are essentially similar (the similarity postulate), finds expression in anthropology in the conception of the cultural other as a distinct analytic object. The tribesmen are assumed to be fundamentally different from us, and their actions are to be explained in terms of an alien and exotic culture. The distinctiveness of the cultural object is axiomatic to the ethnographer's work and her report must testify to the strangeness of the other. In virtue of the strangeness achieved in her report, the ethnographer appears to operate at a higher epistemological level than the native. Her report appears as a merely neutral representation of an actual difference between observer and observed. The exoticism of the report is tied to its certitude because analytic distance privileges and sets apart the method of the observer. Not only is the tribesman different, the implication is that this difference entails the subject's inferior access to reliable procedures for observation and report. In an almost paradoxical way, the more exotic the native, the more we can depend on the accuracy of the ethnographer's report. It is this, we can speculate, which accounts for the rhetorical importance of the notion of 'primitive'.[12] By denying the similarity postulate, exoticism acts as a buttress against reflexivity.

Conversely, the more familiar the subject (or, the more difficult it is to specify what makes the subject different from us), the less distinctively privileged is the ethnographer's method. Uncertainty presents itself for as long as we grant the possibility that the activities of our subjects/objects are essentially no different from our own, that the explanation of activities in terms of culture applies as much to our methods as theirs.

As writers like Clifford recognize, exoticism and the minimization of uncertainty are essentially textual accomplishments. It is in and through textual representation that the character of the other is achieved and that the observer simultaneously makes her author-itative claims to certitude. But what is perhaps insufficiently stressed is the generality of this argument. Exoticism and the minimization of uncertainty are crucial to a wide range of representational practices. They are as much the basis for the relationship constructed between 'ethnographer' and 'tribesman' as between any other observer and her subject/object: Malinowski and the Trobrianders; historians of anthropology and anthropologists; the physicist and her electrons; the engineer and the bridge; and so on.

The conventions of the realist genre encourage the unproblematic and unhesitant singular interpretation of text, the unreflexive perception of a reported reality (subject/object) and the essentially uninteresting character of the agency involved in the report's generation. In the realist genre, the text is a neutral medium for conveying pre-existing facts about the world. The epistemological commitment here is that subjects of study appear exotic in virtue of their inherent qualities rather than as a result of their construction in the text. An important corollary of this position is that the text's neutrality exempts it from consideration as a species of social/cultural activity. The text is thought to operate at a different level from the world 'about which' it reports. Relativism can not lead to reflexivity, in this view, because the text itself is not permitted a susceptibility to relativism.

What, then, are the prospects for a radical constitutive reflexivity of the immediate (rather than post hoc) variety? In developing a critique of representation and of the relationship we assume with our subjects/objects, a clear priority is to play down the exoticism of the other. The familiarity of our subjects/objects should be highlighted, at least as a heuristic, thereby making our own methods seem less distinctively privileged. We should recognize that there are no grounds for assuming the activities our subjects/objects to be essentially different from our own; such differences are accomplished through unreflexive observation and research. We should try to recover and sustain the uncertainty which exists in the early stages of ethnographic enquiry, before our construction of text solidifies the concepts and categories we employ. It is insufficient to reveal the actual circumstances behind the production of ethnographic texts, as if this revelation was itself a neutral, passive process. In short, we need continually to interrogate and find strange the process of representation as we engage in it. This kind of reflexivity is the ethnographer of the text.

Frames and Captions

The analyst must resist the temptation to accept at face value the conventions which structure the text and the illusion of a world beyond the text which these conventions suggest. These conventions impose order upon a fluid (pre-textual) realm of actants and entities; they produce an ordered structure of categories, objects and subjects; they define distances and relationships between these entities; the moral order of rights and obligations – which of these entities can say and do what about whom. The ethnographer of the text must not simply make these conventions his (exotic) object; they are at once his own equipment and his topic. The key principle of ethnography as applied to the text is that of uncertainty rather than exoticism.

The ethnographer must be especially wary of being seduced by the idea that different elements within the text independently converge upon the same external reality. The myth of triangulation supposes that different textual elements are equivalent to separate items of evidence. For example, the image and its frame conspire to reinforce the notion of a constructed reality beyond the text. The frame is thus the classic device of synecdoche: our picture is a mere extract from a much wider pre-existing reality; the world continues either side of the boundaries of the text (photograph); a shift in frame would reveal to us another part of the same objective world.

Similarly, the ethnographer should be wary of the conspiracy between image and caption. Just as the frame, in purporting to select from reality, further enhances the existence of that reality, so the caption enhances the idea of an objective world from which we choose items for consideration. The caption purports merely to direct our attention to a pre-existing feature of the complex reality revealed by the frame. It achieves this by posing as a neutral entity, disengaged from the world upon which it is commenting. The caption thus claims distance from the image. It is to be understood as a different kind of statement to the image itself.

The ethnographer of the text, in highlighting the curiosity of these claims for the independence of textual elements, has to insist that captions are deeply implicated in, rather than an adjunct to, the reality to which they point. The caption is reflexively tied to the image such that the meaning of the latter draws upon the sense of the former, and the meaning of the caption draws upon what is 'evident from' the image.

Possible Impossibles

The strength and obduracy of textual organization becomes clear when one considers what must be done to discourage the merely instrumental reading of texts. What would it take to disrupt the apprehension of texts as 'objective' accounts? It follows from our discussion that we should attempt to inject some instability into textual organization, to undermine the way in which different textual elements conspire to deny the similarity postulate and to project an 'objective reality' beyond the text.

The possibility for the injection of instability is suggested by one untypical example of discussion of the use of photographs by ethnographers. Clifford (1983a: 127) presents a photograph which, according to the caption, shows 'Marcel Griaule developing photographic plates'. This formulation of the image immediately rebounds upon us. We see that the photograph of Griaule is also the result of a developing process. And we are led to ask who developed and inspected *this* photograph (of Griaule), and how was *it* selected for inclusion? This unusual and interesting effect arises precisely because the standard relationship between caption and image is broken. The caption points, not (just) away from itself (to a reality beyond and distinct from its own discourse), but (also) back towards itself, reminding readers of the process whereby a 'reality beyond' is constituted in the first place. The particular relationship between caption and image in this example provides a much more striking reminder of the pervasiveness of textuality than a straightforward deconstruction of Griaule's text.

One development of this effect is achieved by juxtaposing textual elements such that no single (comfortable) interpretation is readily available. In this scheme, different elements manifest a self-referring or even contradictory relation with one another. Consequently, the interpretation of any one element is never allowed to remain at rest with itself.[13] (I take this to be the essential quality common to 'textual experiments' as diverse as Magritte's surrealism – 'ceci n'est pas une pipe', Escher's drawings and Garfinkel's breaching experiments.) Something of this effect is apparent when a photograph and its caption are devised so that possible interpretations are disrupted by noticing their dialogical inter-penetration. In Figure 2, for example, the image is organized so that its referent appears to disappear within itself.[14] The juxtaposition of antagonistic textual elements highlights (at least momentarily) the indeterminancy and ambivalence of the interpretive process. The sense of order normally associated with the triangulation of caption and image is replaced by instability; the text is both possible and impossible.[16]

Conclusion

Starting from a straightforward interpretation of the Malinowski photograph, we have drawn attention to the ways in which perspectives on reflexivity, the significance granted to its apprehension and management, mirror basic assumptions about the nature of representation. We have seen that whereas many social scientists agree that much is to be gained by

Figure 2 *The author devising a caption for this photograph*

shaking off the idea of observation as a docile record of pre-existing reality, they differ markedly as to the appropriate form of reflexive examination which ensues. Cultural relativism thus 'leads to' any of a variety of kinds of reflexivity depending on the social scientist's conception of representation. More specifically, as is well demonstrated in the case of the social study of science, the positioning on a continuum between the extremes of constitutive reflexivity and benign introspection depends crucially on the management of the postulates of distinctiveness and similarity.

The variation in reactions to reflexivity is also indicative of tensions at the heart of social science over the relationship between observation (image), observer and observed (subject/object). The pretensions of social science to Scientific ideals makes reflexivity seem, at best, a self-indulgent luxury; introspection – the disengaged reflection upon the use of observational methods – is tolerated as a way of improving research. On the other hand, the pretensions of social science to literary ideals generate the insistence that authors and readers constitute and form part of the scenes which they describe. This suggests the interrogation of the nature of textual representation in the course of research: the ethnography of the text.

Marcus and Cushman (1982) note that attempts at experimental ethnography have thus far produced no more than a few isolated techniques for pursuing reflexivity at the level of the text. Although examples like the 'self-enveloping photograph' remind us of the importance of textual organization in reinforcing our tendency towards realist readings, there remains the concern that we have thus far 'failed to overcome the impression that [the use of these techniques] is merely a self-conscious and clever device rather than an integrated narrative organization' (Marcus and Cushman, 1982: 41). This remark implies that a next task is to seek forms of narrative organization which convey more than an impression of self-conscious cleverness. But it also raises the thorny question of what counts as an adequate demonstration of constitutive reflexivity. The idea that this might come about as the result of some specific combination of techniques drawn from a set of standardized 'reflexive devices' is unlikely to prove satisfactory because it pays little attention to the concept of the reader. It follows that our ethnography of the text must develop an understanding of text as just one element in a reader–text community. Otherwise there is little hope that readers will recognize the more subtle features of textual organization; that the juxtaposition of textual elements works systematically throughout a text rather than just at odd 'reflexive moments'; or that this entire text constitutes yet one more caption (frame) for the photograph with which we began.[17]

Notes

An earlier version of this paper, entitled 'A Kind Of Reflexivity', was presented at the Discourse and Reflexivity Workshop, Surrey University, 13–14 September 1984. My thanks to participants, and especially to Malcolm Ashmore and Henrika Kuklick, for helpful comments.

1. The photograph on the cover is also reproduced in the text (Stocking, 1983b: 101), where it is captioned 'Malinowski at work, Omarakana'.

2. The trick of anthropological understanding is 'to figure out what the devil [the informants] think they are up to' (Geertz, 1975: 48).

3. Clifford (1986: 1) refers to this photograph as 'carefully posed'.

4. The dots imply, of course, that this series of iterations is, in principle, endless. This last sentence, of course, constitutes an observation about the chain of observation. And so on.

5. The philosophical objection that relativism leads to reflexivity is rarely addressed head on by sociologists (but see Collins and Cox, 1976; cf. Fuller, 1986). Indeed, it would be difficult to claim that my discussions of the interpretive flexibility in the philosophers' objection constitutes a strong refutation of their argument. Rather, the point is that logical entailment is just one possible reading. The idea that relativism leads to reflexivity remains a potential threat, but one which is unlikely to paralyse social scientific practice.

6. The problem familiar to film critics is that of using the 'character' of the film to determine 'what it is really about'. Does the fact that a film is boring necessarily mean that the film-maker intended his film to be about boredom?

7. Despite Garfinkel's discussion of reflexivity, few practising 'ethnomethodologists' have explored the application of this kind of reflexivity to their own research practice. This is consistent with the scientistic aspirations of traditions like conversation analysis. Some exceptions are members of the so-called 'idealist wing' of ethnomethodology (for example, Blum, 1971; McHugh et al., 1974; Sandywell et al., 1975).

8. The stance of those practitioners of the sociology of scientific knowledge who advocate an 'empirical programme of empiricism' (Collins, 1981b; Collins and Pinch, 1982) appears to reject any kind of reflexivity (Ashmore, this volume). They achieve 'disengagement' simply by refusing to discuss reflexivity (but see Pinch and Pinch, this volume).

9. Both social studies of science and cultural anthropology have adopted what can be broadly termed a relativizing stance towards their objects of study. As a result, both pose questions quite different from those informed by the normative concerns of earlier philosophical debates. Whereas many philosophers sought a normative warrant for explanation and understanding (with questions like: *can* cultures, other languages, other scientific frameworks be discussed only in their own terms?), anthropologists and others experienced no profound difficulty in producing descriptions of other cultures; empirical social science felt no obligation to wait upon philosophical deliberation. But while cultural relativism has long been the stock in trade of much anthropology, its application in the social study of science is both recent and has engendered fierce territorial battles with objectivist philosophy (Bloor, 1976, 1981; Laudan, 1981). On this count, perhaps, we might expect cultural anthropology to exhibit a greater general interest in reflexivity. Thus, just when some practitioners in the social study of scientific knowledge are seeking to develop a self-confident and largely unreflexive empirical research tradition, a small but growing body of anthropologists see the need for increased attention to the grounds for their practice. On the other hand, the ethnographic study of scientific knowledge entails a much closer relationship between its methods and objects of study than does cultural anthropology in general. The ethnographer of science relativizes the knowledge practices of her scientist subjects, but is responsible to the scientific pretensions of her own discipline. By contrast, the cultural anthropologist need not specifically focus on the knowledge and beliefs of her subjects, so that the relation between their knowledge practices and her own is less obvious. On this count, we might expect cultural anthropology to be less concerned about reflexivity than the social study of scientific knowledge.

10. 'The very shape (of ethnography) is a textual expression of the performed fiction of community that has enabled the research. Thus, and with varying degrees of explicitness, ethnographies are fictions both of another cultural reality and of their own mode of production (Clifford, 1983b: 144).

11. For example, the opening passage in Clifford (1981) discusses the photograph used by Malinowski (1961) as the frontispiece to *Argonauts of the Western Pacific*; Clifford (1983a) begins a discussion of ethnographic authority by referring to the use of frontispiece photographs by Lafitau and Malinowski; the opening passage of the introduction to the volume by Clifford and Marcus (1986) refers both to Malinowski's use of photographs and to a photograph (also used as frontispiece to, and cover for, the same volume) which 'shows Stephen Tyler . . . at work in India in 1963' (Clifford, 1986: 1). All but two contributions to the Stocking (1983a) volume include at least one photograph.

12. It is this which raises intriguing questions about recent attempts to generate 'primitives'' ethnographies of modern western industrial societies.

13. There are some similarities here with the notion of 'interruption' used by Brian Torode. In denouncing his own use of the 'documentary method', Torode explores ways in which the usual relation between appearance and reality can be disrupted such that we are discouraged from determining which is one and which is the other. See Silverman and Torode (1980).

14. The trick here, of course, is to supply the reader with an extra textual element (for example, this last sentence) which directs the reader to see what is actually happening in her attempt at interpretation. See note 15.

15. The trick here, of course, is to supply the reader with an extra textual element (for example, this note) which directs the reader to see what is actually happening in her attempt

at interpretation. See note 14.

16. Stability (possibility) can be restored by providing a further (objective?) account (caption) which purports to explain the genesis of the text: The photograph in Figure 2 was produced by the Time Relay Inversion Camera (Klystron) currently being developed at MIT's vision research unit. The system relay projects the received image back into the field of vision, simultaneously with its delayed conventional photographic recording (Chaudry et al., 1986). See also note 15.

17. John Barth's (1972) advice is clear: 'I would advise in addition the eschewal of overt and self-conscious discussion of the narrative process' (cited in Ashmore, 1985).

Reflexion on Woolgar

It would be too self-indulgent to let the Editorial Voice report that one referee described this last chapter as a 'clear-headed' discussion of varieties of reflexivity. But at least we now have a sensible introduction to the topic, free from all those distracting experiments with form. For example, one can now appreciate the important distinction between the 'quality control' kind of reflexivity (cf. Hammersley and Atkinson, 1983: ch. 1) which reinforces the ideology of representation (cf. Woolgar, forthcoming), and constitutive reflexivity which portrays itself as a radical challenge to this ideology. And this, in turn, suggests why these Editorial Voice commentaries are 'reflexions' rather than just 'reflections'.

On the other hand (on reflection), can we be sure that Woolgar's text fails to engage in constitutive reflexivity? If the metaphor of photograph as text is taken seriously, it is clear that Woolgar views his own text as a photograph which contains its own caption. This is obviously the intention behind the use of the self-encompassing photograph (the Figure 2). It is not just an example of what is involved in disrupting the singular, instrumental reading of texts as reporting upon objects, but also a clue for reading Woolgar's own text. Obviously, he could not point this out himself because it would spoil the effect; there is even a footnote which says as much. None the less, it is clear from other features of the text – for example, some of the opening sentences – 'the essential and irremediable ambiguity of what the photograph (text) suggests that some of the natives (objects/subjects) are looking directly at the camera', and so on – that Woolgar is insisting that the text be read on a number of different levels.

Would the point have been clearer if Woolgar had included a further Figure 3? I am not sure. But it begins to become clear why the authors of the first chapter were so exercised about the problem of what counts as reflexivity. Perhaps we should wait for Latour (this volume) on this: he'll be able to say whether Woolgar's chapter counts as infra- or meta-reflexivity. On the other hand, that's a long way off, and we are left with the impression that, despite Woolgar's efforts at a cool analysis, just about anything could count as reflexive. In order to pursue this a bit further, we now turn to an example of an argument that an apparently unreflexive style of analysis is actually more reflexive than it seems.

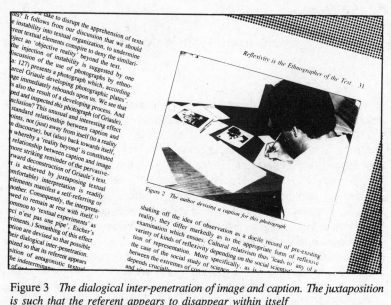

Figure 3   *The dialogical inter-penetration of image and caption. The juxtaposition is such that the referent appears to disappear within itself*

3

What is Reflexive about
Discourse Analysis?
The Case of Reading Readings

Jonathan Potter

In this chapter I am going to be concerned with the nature of the sociology of scientific knowledge (SSK) perspective known as Discourse Analysis (henceforth DA – see Gilbert and Mulkay, 1984a; Mulkay et al., 1983; Potter and Wetherell, 1987 for summaries). My central concern will be with the following question: in what sense, if any, is DA reflexive? Answering this question will involve an examination of the relationship of DA to, on the one hand, current post-Mertonian theory in science studies – the Empirical Relativist Programme (Collins, 1981a, 1983a, 1985), the Strong Programme (Barnes, 1974, 1982; Bloor, 1976) and the Constructivist Programme (Knorr-Cetina, 1981; Latour, 1980, 1983) – and, on the other hand, to recent overtly reflexive developments emphasizing the use of New Literary Forms (Ashmore, 1985; Mulkay, 1985; Stringer, 1985; Woolgar, 1983; Wynne, this volume). The answer to the question will also necessitate a consideration of the central and contentious issue of the way DA construes its subject matter, discourse itself. In fact, consideration of these issues will involve some reformulation of the way DA has been understood by both proponents and critics. To clarify what is at stake my discussion will be organized around a specific analytic example.

Stories of SSK

To start with, let us consider two alternative narratives which formulate the recent development of SSK.

Narrative One
    Stage A. After the dark ages of normative sociology of science (Merton, 1973) came an enlightened period in which it was realized that the contents of science need not be considered inviolate, and analysis must be conducted which remains impartial with respect to the beliefs that scientists treated as true or false. That is, it maintains a stance of methodological relativism

with respect to scientific beliefs. This work showed the way interpersonal (Knorr-Cetina, 1979), social (Collins, 1981d) or even political (Barnes and Shapin, 1979) factors penetrated the very stuff of scientific theory and lubricated certain paths of scientific development.

Stage B. Just as this work was blossoming into a progressive and well-replicated research programme, however, the new perspective of DA started asking unwelcome questions about the way these researchers were understanding the scientists' discourse which was their main data base. Scientists were *saying* that they were acting in certain ways – but were they really? Discourse analysts unearthed a huge variation in the versions of the world scientists offered on different occasions. They argued that Empirical Relativists, Strong Programmers and Constructivists – the post-Mertonian theorists – adhered to the tenets of symmetry and impartiality with respect to scientists' beliefs only as far as it suited, being quite happy to arbitrate as to the truth or falsity of scientists' pronouncements about the *social* world.

Discourse analysts adopted a rather different research strategy involving an impartial stance to *all* scientific discourse. Of necessity, their research questions were rather different. Instead of trying to assess the role of 'social factors' in closing down a controversy, say, they focused their efforts on the explication of the organization of scientific accounts, the nature of the linguistic and argumentative resources which scientists deploy, and the consequences of particular accounting techniques.

Stage C. Those more concerned with the issue of reflexivity, however, suggested that Discourse Analysts, in turn, were failing to confront the textually constructed and constructive nature of their own discursive practices. That is, Discourse Analysts' own discourse can be seen as yet another instantiation of the realist discourse found in post-Mertonian studies (Ashmore, 1985). These researchers suggested abandoning the empiricist logic of the standard research report and instead adopting a variety of New Literary Forms which display, and indeed celebrate, their own active, constructed nature. In this narrative, reflexivity is very much the arbiter of progress in SSK – the more the better (Fuhrman and Oehler, 1986).

Narrative Two
An alternative narrative popular among post-Mertonian theorists concurs over the significance of Stage A, but gives a very different picture of Stages B and C.

Stage B. In this narrative DA has simply renounced all the interesting questions in SSK. In particular it no longer asks *why* scientists choose a particular theory or how a specific controversy is negotiated to a close. In their place it has offered a kind of pallid neo-positivism (Barnes, 1982: 97) dependent on the mistaken presupposition that discourse is a realm of pure data (Collins, 1983a). Far from offering a critique, then,

DA merely offers groundless stipulation as to what questions can or cannot be asked and what should count as acceptable evidence.

Stage C. The importance of reflexivity is accepted in principle. That is, it is accepted that the post-Mertonian perspective could in principle be explained sociologically, but this is seen as having no practical consequences for research (Collins, 1981a). Indeed, reflexivity is a minor irritant which should not lead the SSK researcher to deviate from a basically realist research practice; it is certainly not something to focus on or celebrate.

In this chapter I shall argue that both of these narratives are crucially flawed in their construal of DA. Specifically, I shall suggest that one of the virtues of DA is exactly its incorporation of a certain type of reflexive practice which offers up detailed interpretations of scientists' texts for scrutiny. Moreover, this practice is displayed in a way which is itself a New Literary Form designed to facilitate certain interpretative procedures on the part of the reader. Rather than make this argument in the abstract I shall concentrate on a particular piece of analysis which makes problematic the whole issue of readings and exemplifies some of the procedures at the heart of DA.

Reading Readings

The Incident

The extract below is taken from the transcript of a workshop attended by a group of leading figures involved in Personal Construct Psychology. Most participants conducted research in either universities or hospitals, and between them have published many books and articles, although some participants were primarily clinicians rather than researchers. Personal Construct Psychology is a somewhat marginal field of psychology, but probably no more so than, for example, gravity wave research in physics.

The participants are discussing an incident which occurred during the previous session where a particular group dynamics exercise was suggested.

1

Dennis: 1 The group has a kind of understanding that you are going to have to *kill* the experiment if you opt out. 2 Because even if you opt out somehow you have done something that is part of the experiment, you know. 3 That is you have said something about yourself. 4 You know, it is kind of like the question of freedoms and constrictions. 5 [*Pause*]

Ian: 6 When you say the group has an understanding, I am not sure that, he was saying that the reason he didn't want to do it was for purely personal reasons, he didn't want to tighten; in other words a personal construct theory analysis of why you didn't do it. 7 I would say that we have to say more than that. 8 We have to look at the whole role structure of the group, the way it is beginning to develop and the fact that that was a piece of process that went on which was bidding for leadership of the group and saying 'I am going to structure the next half hour'.

Carol: 9 But I don't like being rejected like that. 10 And I have a personal/ [*Dennis cuts Carol off*]

Dennis: 11 We don't like...

Mike: 12 [*laughs*] And I don't like role theory. [*some laughter*]

Ian: 13 Yes, well I don't want to use the word role but that was the one/ [*Ian is cut off*]

14 [*several people talk at once, laughter*]

(Tape CC1: 226)

Discourse Analysts have approached scientists' utterances and texts in a variety of different ways, often being more concerned with the pattern of accounts offered on different occasions than with the significance of any individual account (Potter and Wetherell, 1987). However, for our purposes we shall concentrate exactly on making sense of a single utterance which is, anyway, a necessary prerequisite to broader analytic objectives (this is not to say that these tasks are separable in principle). In particular, as discourse analysts, how are we going to understand Carol's utterance: 'But I don't like being rejected like that'? (1.9 = Extract 1, sentence nine) I shall explore this question, first by providing some of my own (analyst's) readings, and then examining some readings done by participants.

We can start by looking for the 'rejection' referred to in 1.9. For example, the interaction *might* have taken the following form:

A

Ian: I think Carol's contributions to this meeting have been worthless.
Carol: But I don't like being rejected like that.

If it had, we could have produced an adequate (though preliminary) reading. Carol's contribution is described as worthless; such a description would be felt as a 'rejection' by Carol (of her ideas and therefore herself), and she is clearly not going to like it. We could have made what was said intelligible, although at the same time raising many new questions about why the speaker felt the contribution to be worthless, and so on.

However, when we come to look at the two turns of talk preceding Carol's we do not find any explicit, formulated criticism. Indeed, Carol's name is not mentioned at all. Nevertheless, in the face of the lack of an obvious, explicit (to us) criticism of Carol, we can take another interpretative option. Perhaps the rejection is not 'in' the turns of talk by Ian or Dennis but in something they are talking *about*. Again we can make up an example to clarify this.

B

Ian: Smith was being very critical of your work.
Carol: But I don't like being rejected like that.

If the interaction had happened like this we would have no difficulty in reading Carol's response as a straightforward and coherent response to the prior turn of talk. Carol is *describing* her feelings about an *earlier* point rather than *expressing* her feelings about a *current* point.

Unfortunately, we have no transcript of the interaction being referred to to help us with the mystery. However, there is anyway a basic problem with this approach. For we seem to be in danger of trying to find a *definitive version* (Mulkay, 1981) of the meaning of this interaction – a sin much identified in the work of post-Mertonian theorists by discourse analysts. If we consider 'the meaning of social action, not as a unitary characteristic of acts which can be observed as they occur, but as a diverse potentiality of acts which can be realized in different ways through participants' production of interpretations in different social contexts' (Gilbert and Mulkay, 1984a: 9 – a reference which alludes back to the work of Garfinkel and Schutz), then we must be wary of searching for *the* section of discourse which constituted/embodied the act of rejection. Indeed, we have to see Carol's statement about rejection as itself potentially constitutive. Even conversation analysts, who are bolder than most in their identifications of acts in talk (but see Levinson, 1983: ch. 5), and who routinely treat second turns as *displaying* understandings of first turns (Atkinson and Heritage, 1985), note that 'speakers may respond to earlier talk in ways which may blur, conceal or otherwise avoid displaying their true appreciation of [the first turn's] import' (Heritage, 1984: 260).

From Resource to Topic

One response to this problem would be to look at participants' own, explicitly formulated, interpretations of this piece of transcript. This would allow us to make the reassuring move from resource to topic (Zimmerman and Pollner, 1971). That is, instead of trying to interpret the extract *ourselves* (drawing upon a variety of unexplicated resources) we can look (as topic) at the interpretations of the members. That is, we can look at their readings of this discourse. I shall argue later that, at least in this simplistic formulation, this approach does not solve the problem; for the moment, however, let us see how far the move from resource to topic takes us.

To generate readings of this kind, I was able to capitalize on a fortuitous turn of events which led to a follow-up workshop to the one from which Extract 1 is taken. Not all the participants were the same but there was considerable overlap. Each person going to this second workshop received in advance a fourteen-page section of transcript from the first and it was suggested that it would provide a good topic for discussion. At the second workshop itself this transcript was discussed and the discussion recorded and transcribed. Part of the discussion concentrated on the section I have picked out as Extract 1, hingeing particularly on Carol's utterance about rejection.

The participants themselves pose the question of the meaning of Carol's utterance and stress its importance. Carol was not present at the second workshop. The first part of this discussion went as follows.

2

Neil: 1 Why did Carol say 'but I don't like being rejected like that'?
Ian: 2 I don't know. 3 It's a very important bit, isn't it. 4 I can't remember.
Dennis: 5 Again I think that there is a/ [*Mike cuts Dennis off*]
Mike: 6 It effectively shuts Carol up for about a page and a half. [*Laughs*]
Shirley: 7 Well Carol's remarkably quiet through the whole thing when you look,
   really. 8 She comes in occasionally here and there, doesn't she.
Frank: 9 Isn't it this reference about leadership that refers to there? 10 I would
   infer that, not knowing what went on, just from the text, that in fact Carol
   is reacting to Ian's previous statement that he [*Mike:* Right] simply wants to
   describe, wants to describe what's going on as a bid for leadership of the
   group. 11 And she responds by saying 'oh, that hurt', 'I don't like being
   rejected like that'. 12 And other people join in by saying 'we don't like it,
   either'. 13 And, er, you say 'I don't like role theory'. 14 That's what it *looks*
   like. 15 It may not be that.

(Tape CC2: 28)

In the first sentences of this extract (1–8) three participants who were at the original conference stress the importance of Carol's utterance – yet they do not provide any account or gloss of its nature. This is provided only when we get to sentences 9 onwards, by Frank, who did not attend the original workshop.

Frank's interpretation is quite complex. He sees Ian's initial statement (1.6–8) as offering a *description* of the earlier group process as a bid for leadership (2.10) and he sees Carol's problematic utterance (1.9) as *reacting against* this. That is, Frank is reading Carol as responding to Ian's reading of what went on. But why is this description a rejection? (Why for Frank is it a rejection, of course, not why *really* – having made the move from resource to topic its definitive nature is not now our business.) Frank formulates the consequence of the rejection further as 'hurt' (2.11), but he does not fill in why a description of events as a bid for leadership is hurtful to Carol.

To try to clarify this, I shall invent another interchange guided by Frank's gloss, and then look at it in Gricean terms (Grice, 1975).

C

Ian: What has been going on has been a bid for leadership.
Carol: But I don't like being rejected like that.

Grice suggests that for coherent and rational conversation to take place speakers must work with the basic principle that conversation is a co-operative endeavour. This means they use a small number of basic maxims both to generate and to interpret coherent conversation. For instance, one turn of talk should be relevant to the last, it should be believed to be true, no longer than necessary and so on. Crucially, if two utterances have no obvious or surface relation, conversationalists do not abandon the co-operative principle: rather, they look for more subtle ways in which the turns follow the maxims, or, in the extreme, look for ways in which maxims are flouted to (co-operatively) convey information.

We can resolve the co-operativeness in the example above by making one or two additional speculations. First, that bids for leadership are things that can be done implicitly and then exposed. Second, that bids for leadership are not (always) popular. Third, that Ian's statement implicates Carol as the person bidding for leadership. We have now reached the nitty gritty. If we accept these speculations, Frank's answer to our question goes something like this: Ian has described what has been going on in the group as Carol bidding for leadership. Carol, hurt by the negative connotations of this, treats it as an accusation and personal attack. Carol's reaction thus displays the 'natural' response to the pejorative overtones of Ian's account. So for the first time we have an answer – that is, a participant's answer – to our initial question about what is going on in Carol's utterance.

That would be fine. We have got an answer. But no sooner do we read on in the transcript than we get another, and then another! The social world once again starts to fragment into versions. We will examine some of these versions before going on to assess the significance of this analytic exercise.

More Readings of Readings (the Versions Multiply)
Extract 3 continues where Extract 2 left off and contains the rest of the discussion of Extract 1.

3
Mike: 1 But I, I think in effect Carol *loses* at that point. 2 I mean, a *bit* anyway, whatever the decision was, it took the direction of the next page and a half rather than the direction which she wanted it to go.
Ian: 3 Can you say all that again Frank. 4 I wasn't at the right place.
Frank: 5 Um, I think that there was a general reaction against the way of describing group processes which you offered in the previous piece, in which you tend to describe it as a bid for leadership. 6 And it looks like a reaction against that. 7 And it is not just Carol, it is a collective.
Ian: 8 And where's the bid for leadership? Three A? [*a reference to a page of transcript*]
Frank: 9 Er, four A.
Shirley: 10 Just at the last few lines of Ian.
Mike: 11 Towards your, towards the end of your . . .
Ian: 12 I got it, yes.
Mike: 13 You see, but I think also that whilst everybody is saying 'no' there, the actual understanding is a recognition that probably that was going on: let's

not acknowledge it, let's acknowledge it but not *say* it. 14 So there is a sort of 'let's ease it over that bump'. 15 I mean the fact that it is so universal is, wasn't a rejection of it, it was an acknowledgement of it with [laughs] 'let's not play that, play that through again'.

Jonathan: 16 I, I mean, what's the 'like that' referring to, then, in Carol's speech? 17 What is the specific 'this' for rejection?

Richard: 18 I had assumed it was being talked about in role terms, rather than the person. 19 I mean, having one's discussion reduced to role play.

Mike: 20 But I think that also hides the fact that there was an agenda negotiation going on there. 21 And that she's lost the agenda negotiation, as well as having it lost in terms of having it discussed in role terms. 22 I mean it is/ [*Neil interrupts*]

Neil: 23 I mean, she does bring up the agenda.

Mike: 24 She brings it up later, [*Neil:* Yes] yes. 25 But my feeling was that there was a negotiation about which direction the thing was going to go. 26 And I can't put my finger on it, but Carol is trying to make it go in one direction [*Neil:* Ahh] and that whilst this thing about role is put in those terms she in fact loses the agenda argument, or discussion.

(Tape CC2: 28–30)

To start with we shall concentrate on some features of Mike's contributions (3.1–2; 3.13–15; 3.20–2; 3.24–6). Mike reformulates Frank's version as the appearance to which he himself provides the contrasting reality (see Potter, forthcoming, for a detailed discussion of this reading practice).

In sentences 1 and 2, Mike interprets the transcribed interaction under discussion as Carol 'losing'. What he sees her as losing is the negotiation of the agenda (3.20–2). He describes the consequence of this loss as Carol being unable to influence the direction of the discussion in the next page and a half of text (3.2). However, in sentence 13 Mike extends the concept of loss even further, to cover Carol losing the bid for leadership.

Frank, in his readings (2.9–15; 3.5–7), had gone on to suggest that not only does Carol react to Ian's suggestion that a bid for leadership has taken place, but a *general* feeling of discontent arises among the workshop participants. However, Frank does not indicate whether he sees this discontent as stemming from a disagreement with the *accuracy* of the interpretation or disquiet about such matters being made *explicit*. However, Mike interprets Frank's gloss as definitely taking people to *disagree* with the factual status of Ian's account; he claims that 'everybody is saying' that Carol did *not* make an attempt to gain leadership of the group.

Additional implicit speech is 'reported' which explains *why* there should be this conflict between what is said and what is being done (3.14–15). Mike suggests that there will be interactional difficulties raised by making this contingent, personally motivated (Gilbert and Mulkay, 1984a: ch. 4) version of events explicit. So, to avoid these problems, there is only implicit acknowledgement of the contingent personal reality. Put another way, what everybody is rejecting, according to Mike, is not the *reality*, which *is* contingent or personal, but the problems and distractions that *acknowledging* it would create. Overall, then, Mike contrasts a contingent personal version of events which is *really* going on with an alternative version, *apparent* in the participants' talk, which contradicts this. Moreover, the very unanimity of the spoken version is used as grounds for warranting the correctness of the unspoken version.

It might seem that here is a prime instance where the special knowledge held by participants at the original conference is used successfully to give an interpretation which 'goes beyond' the restricted verbal record of events provided by the transcript. In other words, we have not really uncovered *competing* versions at all, but merely a mistaken version and a right one: that is, Mike knows and Frank doesn't. For a moment the embarrassment of versions recedes. We breathe a sigh of relief as we had been getting deeper and deeper entangled in a web of analytic complexities.

Unfortunately, there are certain indications which belie the idea that Mike is simply providing the correct version which Frank, with his lack of first-hand experience, is unable to do. These indications become apparent if we closely examine a point made by Richard (who also participated in the earlier conference). In sentence 18 Richard proposes a rather different account from Mike's (and, indeed, Frank's – the versions are breeding again) of Carol's statement about rejection. In this account 'rejection' comes not from an implicit accusation that Carol is attempting to gain leadership over the group, but from the theoretical categories used to characterize the interaction. Characterizing it specifically in terms of role theory is described by Richard as undermining the personal aspects of the interaction.

What is interesting about this for the present discussion is the way Mike, instead of disagreeing with Richard, attempts to introduce features of Richard's account into his own. Accordingly in sentence 20, directly following Richard's contribution, Mike depicts the issue of the role characterization as 'hiding' the agenda negotiation *and* the fact that Carol lost it. Yet Mike then notes that being discussed in role terms also constitutes losing the agenda argument (21).

He tries to assimilate Richard's explanation to his own while retaining the central features of each. Significantly, at this point he starts to downgrade the facticity of his own account (Latour and Woolgar, 1979). The interpretation of an agenda negotiation, which has previously been confidently asserted is now hedged as a 'feeling' (25). Moreover, although he reiterates the claim that the role characterization in some way leads to the loss of the argument (26), he this time claims that he cannot give an exact interpretation of this: 'I can't put my finger on it' (26). Mike therefore moves from the internally consistent and confident 'factual' version of sentences 13–15, to the vaguer, hedged around, 'intuitive' version of sentences 25–6.

We must, however, be careful with this line of argument. I am not trying to suggest that this kind of shift in versions is straightforward evidence of falsehood on Mike's part. For us the interest is that we end up with yet another version (one in which agenda discussions are hidden by discussions of role) leaving us with two versions to choose between offered by Mike, plus one from Richard and one from Frank. And it is not as if we can simply accept the versions which come from those people who had first-hand experience (who have, as it were, accredited memories that fill in the interpretative spaces in the transcript), as both Mike and Richard fit this bill – and besides, Mike ends up giving us the two alternatives. Moreover, memory itself is a far from neutral resource (Coulter, 1979, 1983, 1985). So our search for the sense of Carol's utterance in the reading of members has thrown us back into the very problem we started with, of how to provide warranted analysts' interpretations of discourse as the basis for DA research reports.

And Back to Reading... (Some Home Truths?)

Beyond Resource to Topic
Near the start of this chapter, I suggested that a different approach might be adopted to discourse where, instead of trying to recover its meaning, we examine the readings of the members. Yet, appealing as this sounds, there are two crippling problems with this which are amply illustrated in the foregoing analysis.

The first is the proliferations of versions. Unlike the situation in conversation analysis, where the second turn is (normally) taken to provide the members' meaning of the first turn, our participants' readings provide a number of different versions of what is read. Such variability comes as no surprise, of course, as even 'professional' readers like literary critics ceaselessly produce varied interpretations of texts (Belsey, 1980; Culler, 1981; Crosman, 1980 – although see Hirsch, 1976, for an argument in favour of the search for definitive versions). Examining variations in reading is an extremely useful way of addressing the specific problem of scientists' readings, as it allows the analyst to lay bare the ways different readings are constructed and naturalized (Potter et al., 1984; Stringer, 1985). However, the proliferation of versions thrown up in this analysis suggests that soliciting participants' readings is not going to be a magical solution to the analyst's problem of making sense of sections of scientists' discourse.

The second problem is, if anything, even tougher than the first. The crucial point is that there is no principled difference between our readings of the original extract and our readings of *participants'* readings of the extract. In other words, there is no basic distinction between scientists' texts and texts-which-are-readings-of-those-texts (Potter et al., 1984). The latter species of texts are not somehow transparent and straightforward in a way other texts are not. For instance, I have concentrated on Carol's utterance as a piece of discourse whose meaning is cloudy or mysterious, and treated the meaning of the *readings* of Carol's utterance given by Mike, Richard and Frank as more open to analytic scrutiny. Yet as analysts our readings of readings are interpretative in the same way as our readings of discourse are. And, as we have seen, analysts' readings reveal variation in readings just as much as they reveal variation in discourse.

This analysis therefore encourages us to question the topic resource move I drew upon early in the paper, at least in its most simple version. The idea is that when social researchers are constructing analytic stories about a chunk of social reality they draw upon unexplicated resources. The (now conventional) response asks us to 'step back' and take these resources as the topic itself, and thereby avoid introducing unnoticed participants' assumptions and proto-sociologies into research conclusions. Yet this just pushes the issue further back; for what resources are we going to draw upon to explicate the resources which are now the topic (see Ashmore, 1985)?

All this is not to say the topic resource problem is unimportant – rather it questions our construal of the traditional move and that move's complete-ness. I suggest that if relativism is to be taken seriously we do not need *a* move at all, but to be in a continual state of motion. That is, we need continually to shift the analytic searchlight on to new analytic resources and turn them into topics. For example, in the above analysis I have taken the scientific credentials of the workshop participants as unproblematic – yet another analysis might have been conducted on the way these researchers were made out to be 'proper scientists' or 'acting scientifically'. On the other hand, I have focused on the issues of reading as an analytic topic, but I am not suggesting that discourse analysts will not, following this study, be able to use reading as a resource.

DA as a Reflexive Practice

So where does all this leave discourse analysts? First of all, I hope it makes very clear that the kinds of characterizations of DA as a form of neo-positivism made by Barnes (1982) and Collins (1983a) are wide of the mark. Just like the participants, the analyst is constructing readings: categorizing discourse into different types and proposing acts which it is performing. The difference between analysts' readings of Extract 1 and those of the workshop participants is not one of principle (for a deconstruction of the principle/practice opposition see Ashmore, 1985: ch. 5). Looked at another way, discourse analysts would be unwise to draw on the general rhetoric of 'objectivity' when contrasting the claims of discourse analysts with those of workers in other perspectives. If the difference between analysts' and participants' readings is not a principled one, what is it? How do discourse analysts provide readings of discourse?

In one sense, the response to this question is relatively straightforward. Discourse is read in the ways displayed in the various studies of scientific discourse. This suggestion is not as empty as it appears; for one of the features of these studies is that they attempt to make the process of interpretation as explicit as possible. Typically this has involved presenting as much of the transcript as is manageable to the reader, and where selection does take place to make it as representative as possible of the variation in the materials studied. This is combined with a fine-grain approach which links interpretation to specific parts or features of the discourse. These procedures contrast markedly with the textual practice common in other approaches. They allow other analysts some opportunity of assessing the value of particular interpretations and contesting them if they wish (Potter and Mulkay, 1985; Potter and Wetherell, forthcoming).

There is another, more subtle aspect to this question. In their analytic practice, discourse analysts strive to offer close readings of passages of discourse. It is an inescapable fact that the production of such readings is a craft skill which requires considerable practice to acquire. Just like the scientist readers in the above example, our initial tendency is to attempt a neat analytic story which fits together various accounts in a seamless coherent narrative. Academic training teaches people to read for gist – which is precisely the wrong spirit for discourse analysis. If you read an article or book the usual goal is to produce a simple, unitary summary, and to ignore the nuance, contradictions and areas of vagueness. Like the scientist readers, again, we have a variety of reading techniques to assist us in this aim. For example, we can make contrasts between what people *seem* to be saying and what they are *really* saying (Potter, forthcoming), or we can selectively ironicize and reify different statements (see Woolgar, 1983; Potter and Wetherell, 1987: ch. 3 for a discussion of these reading practices).

Doing DA involves a constant struggle to make sense of discursive organizations while avoiding reading practices of this kind. That is, the concern is with the discourse *itself* rather than with the assumptions, expectations and ideas we might smuggle into it. The process of analysis is, much of the time, one of actively purging our readings of these things. In this sense, then, DA is a reflexive practice – it is a debate with our own taken-for-granted reading practices. Moreover, viewed in this light DA is not an attempt to sweep problems of reading under the positivist rug. In many ways it is a celebration of these problems. Part of the process of analysis inevitably involves a critical interrogation of our own presuppositions and unexamined techniques for sense-making. The analyst constantly has to ask: why am I reading this passage in this way? And what features of the discourse allow me to produce this reading? The studies draw attention to the detail of their readings of transcript. To this extent they are drawing upon a reflexive analytic strategy.

This reflexive aspect to the work is not something hidden in the phenomenology of analysis; it is displayed in the analytic write-up. The report of such research is much more than a presentation of findings from the researcher's prior readings, it constitutes a reading in itself. The form of the write-up, illustrated in the analytic sections above, involves passages of scientists' discourse which are explicitly linked to specific interpretations. In this way the researcher's entire reasoning process from discursive materials to conclusions is documented in detail. The discourse analytic report is thus itself a New Literary Form; that is, a specific textual organization designed explicitly to draw attention to the constructed nature of the analyst's readings. As such the reader is given the opportunity, indeed challenged, to offer alternative readings or better constructions.

DA and Post-Mertonian Theory

This stress that DA is fundamentally an interpretative analytic strategy, and that discourse is not transparent or brute data, does not imply that it is a misguided development and that workers should return to the post-Mertonian fold. For the important arguments discourse analysts have made against studies produced within these perspectives do not rest on the idea that these approaches make inferences 'beyond' the discourse. If discourse analysts were simply formulating an a priori critique, these theorists would justifiably berate them for groundless methodological purism akin to positivism. But this is not the crucial argument.

The criticism that post-Mertonian theorists are constructing definitive versions has two facets. On the one hand, it is based on an appreciation of the variability in discourse, which is a consequence of the many constructive uses to which participants put their language. This throws doubt on the use of scientists' statements or writings as a document of their activities or beliefs. On the other hand, it is based on detailed examinations of the way these approaches use inconsistent and unexplicated procedures for dealing with scientific discourse and thereby start to move away from the impartial, symmetrical stance which post-Mertonians themselves deem essential in the study of science (Bloor, 1976; Collins, 1981a). For example, discourse analysts have pointed out the way a number of post-Mertonian theorists from different perspectives have drawn on scientists' discourse in a highly inconsistent manner, sometimes treating it as literal and sometimes ironicizing as lies or rhetoric, without providing warrant for this variable practice (Mulkay et al., 1983; Potter, 1983: ch. 1; Yearley, 1982).

Given that discourse analysts' criticisms have been of this kind it is perhaps significant that the commentators from relativist, interest and constructivist approaches who have chosen to discuss DA have treated its claims as methodological stipulations abstracted from the analytic findings (Barnes, 1982; Collins, 1983a; MacKenzie, 1981; Shapin, 1984a).

By doing this their arguments appear most powerful because attention is directed away from the specific instances of inadequacy identified by discourse analysts. Indeed, by tarring DA with the 'positivist' label (which I hope the above discussion will have shown to be ludicrous) the research can be all too easily dismissed.

Collins (1983a) has noted that the kinds of extracts from participants' discourse used in these studies are open to alternative interpretations. And he infers from this that discourse is not grounded in objective data. However, this possibility is not denied by discourse analysts – indeed, such variation is documented in detail above. What Collins, or any other critic, needs to do is demonstrate, if they are going to respond properly to the criticisms made by discourse analysts, how an alternative interpretation can be sustained in practice and therefore how the kinds of variability and interpretative procedures identified by discourse analysts do *not* undermine the status of post-Mertonian studies. This is not, of course, a suggestion that they must start to do DA themselves; rather that they show how their positions can deal with the potentially anomalous findings that DA has thrown up. Simply to claim that DA is an interpretative exercise is no response at all; if they are to rebut criticisms they must undermine the *specific* interpretations which have been produced; they must either work up alternative readings or deconstruct those of discourse analysts; a priori legislation is not enough.

DA and Reflexivity

The tension between DA and advocates of more militantly reflexive work is a much softer one than that with post-Mertonian perspectives. This is probably because much reflexive work has originated in problems of DA and many reflexive proponents share a central interest in scientists' discourse. However, as I indicated in the introduction, some narratives of SSK view reflexivity as a progressive step away from an essentially flawed perspective of discourse analysis. This view is expressed most strongly by Fuhrman and Oehler. For example, DA 'could not succeed as its supporters originally envisioned it, because they did not deal adequately with the issue of reflexivity' (Fuhrman and Oehler, 1986: 293).

There are two basic problems with this criticism. The first is that it is directed at the version of DA which is taken to treat discursive data as an unproblematic bedrock on which to base analytic conclusions. Fuhrman and Oehler's point draws attention to the fallibility in discourse analyses and parallels this to problems which discourse analysts have pointed out in post-Mertonian research. That is, they claim to identify problems in DA which discourse analysts have found in the work of others. However, as I have argued above, the critique made by discourse analysis of post-Mertonian research can be seen in a very different way, which does not draw on the fallibility or otherwise of different kinds of data.

From this revised perspective on the nature of DA this critique, and other similar ones (Ashmore, 1985: 285; Woolgar, 1982: 488–9), cease to be damaging. Indeed, DA can itself be seen as a form of reflexive practice.

The second problem with this criticism is that it starts to equate increasing reflexivity with increasing progress, and suggests that there are reflexive problems which can be 'solved'. The danger is that 'the great scientific progress towards truth' is replaced with 'the great SSK progress towards maximum reflexivity'. Ironically, this form of criticism mimics the very critique which discourse analysts were accused of making against post-Mertonians: post Mertonian work is not acceptable because it does not look at the only proper data (discourse); DA is not acceptable because it does not use the only proper approach (reflexivity). The important questions which reflexive work pose do not need to be propped up with the rhetoric of progression (Ashmore, 1985).

Another Story of SSK

In this chapter I have explored the way DA construes the nature of discourse and its relation to post-Mertonian theory and the reflexive New Literary Forms movement. In the light of this discussion let me offer up some conclusions and suggest another narrative of the development of SSK.

The picture of DA given by critics (and some proponents) which has it claiming to discover a neutral analytic data base is a misguided one. DA is fundamentally an interpretative exercise which offers up readings of texts for scrutiny. In this way DA embodies one kind of reflexivity, which is reflected in the very form of its writings. Disagreements with post-Mertonian theory do not stem from its discovery of safe data, but from specific readings of bodies of discourse which conflict with readings implied in post-Mertonian research. Unfortunately, post-Mertonians have ignored the substance of these readings in favour of generalized attacks on discourse as proper data. Some proponents of reflexive work have made similar generalized attacks on DA for not dealing with reflexivity.

The picture of DA which I have offered suggests the potential for a different and much more fruitful relation to post-Mertonian and overtly reflexive work. By avoiding the legislative debate about the nature of acceptable data and concentrating instead on specific analytic issues there is scope for DA *complementing* post-Mertonian work rather than standing as an irreconcilable alternative. This is not to deny points of conflict, but these should no longer concern the very existence of the positions. By emphasizing the reflexive concerns inherent in DA itself, it ought to be able to continue to foster reflexive work and respond to the implications of this work – after all, much of the current interest in this area has originated from within DA (this chapter; and see, for example, the chapters by Mulkay and by Wynne in this volume). In general, then, the SSK narrative which I would like to offer avoids both the rhetoric of progressive stages and the idea of perspectives which have renounced the interesting questions. It opens up the possibility of much fresh dispute, but dispute which will be more constructive and exciting than what has gone before.

Reflexion on Potter

Potter's central argument is that Discourse Analysis (DA) is misunderstood. His strategy is to draw upon issues arising in a particular example of analysis, in order to argue that two common versions of the status of DA are 'crucially flawed', that DA does indeed constitute a kind of new literary form, and that this entails a type of reflexive practice.

Does Potter's argument constitute an attempt to advance a definitive version of (the actual character of) DA? Is a flawless version of DA possible (or even desirable)? His objections to others' characterizations of DA suggest an affirmative answer: 'DA is actually like *this*, not the way others portray it.' On the other hand, parts of his chapter imply that DA does not wish to claim privileged readings. This follows from a central axiom of DA that all discourse admits an essential variability of reading; alternative versions are always possible; and particular versions arise in the light of specific reading practices (cf. Mulkay et al., 1983). On this basis, we would not expect Potter to advance a strong claim about the 'actual character' of DA, but to portray his characterization as an alternative version, not necessarily any better than the versions produced by critics. In this formulation, Potter's version sits alongside those of the critics of DA; it increases the choices available to readers; and readers make their choice using particular reading practices.

Potter suggests that doing discourse analysis is itself a constant struggle to make sense of discursive practices while avoiding reading practices which tempt the analyst into a definitive version. On the other hand, it might be observed, there are few signs of any struggle involved in his producing this version of DA.

Of course, this Reflexion would not want to claim that it represents a definitive version of what Potter is actually saying. The version presented here is an alternative to what Potter is claiming. (Or at least, an alternative to what the Reflexion *claims* Potter is claiming.) This Reflexion thus represents one further formulation to be added to those initially set out by Potter. On the other hand, we might observe, this Reflexion exhibits few signs of any struggle involved in producing this version of Potter's argument.

Perhaps Potter feels that manifestations of the analyst's struggle would only 'put people off' in the way that seemed to concern Woolgar and Ashmore, and that's why he plumps for something midway between reflection and constitutive reflexivity. But is this the only reasonable response to the twin demands of challenging empiricism and not putting people off?

In the next chapter we see an alternative view: reflexivity can be conceived not as a stance to be adopted with respect to empiricism and anti-empiricism, but as an unavoidable feature of knowledge.

4

Whose Discourse?

Teri Walker

There are many souls one will never
discover unless one invents them first.
.(Nietzsche, 1909: 69)

Recent Discourse Analysis includes attempts to look at what comprises
expert and non-expert knowledge. These studies show how the distinction
between expert and non-expert is managed, in interactional communication (Ashmore, this volume; Wynne, this volume; Mulkay, 1984.) This
chapter takes as a starting point the central finding of those studies: that
the distinction between expert and non-expert is inconcludeable or
indiscernible or both. The main aim of this chapter is to discern the
constitutive bases of both expert and non-expert knowledges within
discursive practices.

I shall argue that these discursive practices or discourses emerge, merge
and re-emerge in and through a particular kind of communicative action:
the cultural dissemination of knowledge (for a different kind of exposition,
see Habermas, 1984). This dissemination, I suggest, is a discursively
circular form of Discourse within discourse.[1]

Discourse within discourse refers to the discourses of disciplines or
bodies of knowledge (Foucault, 1972) recognizable as such within
discourse (interactional communication) at the point of its articulation:
speech. I shall refer to these two formulations of the term as Immanent
and Transcendent discourse respectively. Although at first glance this
distinction might seem perverse or merely a semantic error, it is neither.
It is, as I shall attempt to show, a possible consequence of the cultural
dissemination of knowledge. Put another way, the cultural dissemination
of knowledge provides the conditions of possibility for the transformations
of expert and non-expert knowledge. The effects of this are twofold. First,
on the knowledge itself; and secondly, on its status *qua* knowledge. In
order to demonstrate this argument, I begin with a particular text of talk
and trace its genealogy to a specific body of knowledge. The text of talk
is an excerpt from a transcription of a recorded therapy session; and the
genealogically traceable body of knowledge is the psychoanalytic tradition.
The juxtaposition of this talk with a different kind of text of talk – excerpts

from a film script – serves to demonstrate the cultural dissemination of knowledge. In other words, the transformation of Immanent and Transcendent discourse.

To talk of a genealogy rather than a history of an event, object or activity pre-empts any claims for a uni-directional course or process. This is not to suggest that there is a multi-directional course, for this would still imply an historical account.[2] To trace the genealogy of an event, object or activity is to seek the conditions of possibility for its emergence in discourse; not in one or other of the formulations of discourse posed above but in both. It is not that we have a general or common-sense knowledge about an event, object or activity because there is a discipline or body of expert knowledge available. Nor is there an expert body of knowledge because there is a general or common-sense knowledge waiting to be reified.[3] The two knowledges, or discourses, inform and constitute each other and provide what Foucault (1972) calls 'the surface of emergence' of the object. In this case the object is counselling. The object is the formation of discursive practices and discursive practices allow for the formation of objects – always in tension. A tension that is itself, I suggest, the condition of possibility for the cultural dissemination of knowledge and, therefore, the transformations of discourse. But I go too far too soon. The notions of Immanent and Transcendent discourse did not arrive fully fledged in thought needing only to be spoken or written for them to be considered a cultural possibility. Bearing in mind the Husserlian dictum of 'to the things themselves' (Husserl, 1931), before proceeding with the argument I should perhaps begin at the beginning. Not with the text of transcribed talk as might normally be expected but at an earlier stage: the initial recording of the talk.

This beginning is necessarily somewhat arbitrary and anecdotal but, to paraphrase Schegloff, discursive oaks may from discursive acorns grow (Schegloff, 1968). At the same time as (audio) tape-recording therapy sessions, I watched the interaction on closed-circuit television. While watching and listening to this particular session I found myself thinking something like: so Freud was right, it (life and its vicissitudes) is all about sexuality in childhood. Almost simultaneously it seemed, I was aware of what I was doing and began to question it.[4] Because the session was being recorded live I could not immediately pursue these questions and all I could think of doing was to make a note of the time and the last words uttered, and concentrate on what came next. To my surprise what came next was all the evidence one would reasonably need to substantiate that earlier thought. The counsellee (L) provided information like pieces of a jigsaw just waiting to be put together. Indeed the jigsaw seemed to me to be so complete I began to wonder if the exams she talked of taking, or her course of study, included psychology. Uncharitable? Cynical? Maybe. Yet the account she gave of her life experiences would not have been out of place as one of Freud's case histories. Or so it seemed. The question this raises is, how did this seem to be so? The attempt to answer this 'how' question by tracing its genealogy provided the conditions of possibility for the emergence of the apparently counter-intuitive notions of Immanent and Transcendent discourses.

A basic tenet of Freud's philosophy is that conflict is basic to the human condition (Freud, 1930). This conflict has its roots in the irremedial antagonism between the demands of instinct (id) and the restrictions of civlization (super-ego). It is the demands of instincts that are initially pertinent to the how question raised above. These demands of instincts, otherwise libido, otherwise sex drive[5] are, according to Freudian dictates, polymorphously innate in us all; along with the civilizing inheritance of the incest taboo (Freud, 1912). The antagonism between these instincts and civilization is the site of the oedipus conflict (Freud, 1905). Put simply, if somewhat crudely, the oedipus conflict is the sexual desire of the child for its opposite sex parent versus the incest taboo. The child's sexual desire is manifest in real or imagined sexual activity between parent and child (Freud, 1905, 1909; but see Masson, 1984). The transcript[6] illustrates the pertinence of this for the arguments proposed earlier.

The counsellees (M and L) have a relationship problem. L's response to the counsellor's (H) opening remark: 'Right, how have things been over the last week?' lays the groundwork for what is to follow: L replies to the effect that she is 'finding it difficult to deal with any sort of pressure' and feels 'pushed into a corner with nowhere to turn'. She gets 'really frustrated and very annoyed with herself' because she seems 'unable to forgive and forget' and finds herself 'festering over arguments'.

Such expressions are interpretable as classical symptoms of neurosis (Crowcroft, 1967) which, aetiologically speaking, originate in the unsuccessful resolution of the oedipal conflict.[7] This conflict is apparent in the L that 'loves my father *so* much' and appears distraught because she 'can't *touch* my father now'. This raises two questions: in what way is the resolution seen as unsuccessful; and of what would a successful resolution consist? To respond to this requires the introduction of two definitive psychoanalytic terms: sublimation and repression (Freud, 1898). The unsuccessful resolution of the basic condition of conflict stems from desires or instincts which have been merely or overly repressed and are, therefore, ready to re-emerge at some later time; while successful resolution consists in the sublimation of appropriately repressed desires or instincts.[8] The re-emergence of repressed desires or instincts takes the form of a re-enactment of that earliest, oedipal, conflict in a transposed form.[9]

From the text of talk it is possible to identify both the presence of the oedipal process and its re-enactment when the conflict between desire and civilization re-emerges in this couple's relationship. Of her relationship with her father L said:

> I used to sleep *between* my parents right up to the age of ten. They did not
> have sexual intercourse. I used to sleep between them, so I know.

At this point in her life L and her mother were unavoidably separated
from L's father for six months. When the family were reunited, the sleeping
arrangements changed: L now slept in the same room as her parents, but
not in the same bed. L describes her feelings about this change in the
following way:

> I kept my parents apart because I loved my father *so* much and that relation-
> ship between my father and me *broke* when we were separated for six months.
> After that, he was never the *same* towards me. Then, sleeping in the same
> room and seeing them *together* like that, maybe I felt that he's really *gone*
> from me now and maybe that's why I started crying at night.

Her current feelings toward her lover (M) were expressed in a somewhat
ambivalent fashion:

> He brought something out in me and I became free sexually. I became more
> secure and was able to make the first move. But at the same time I feel used
> I think. Making the first move sexually makes me feel loose. It makes me feel
> as though by doing that he will lose his respect for me. It's crazy but that's
> how I feel.

To some extent L is aware that she is inhibited sexually and emotionally
and that this is somehow connected to her early relationship with her father:

> I'm very inhibited. I can't seem to let myself *go* and relax and enjoy myself.
> I *feel* very used very easily, and I feel very loose. I was very close to my father.
> I was very very close to my father and I think that has a lot to do with it. Perhaps
> I think it would be terrible to enjoy myself.

However, apart from what L says, what grounds would there be for
claiming an unsuccessful resolution of the oedipal conflict? That is, for
mere repression rather than the cultural or super-ego preference for
sublimated repression. Once again, the counsellee (L) provides the clues.
When the counsellor (H) interprets L's comment that 'it would be terrible
to enjoy myself' as L really referring to her relationship with her father,
L responds by displacing, in psychoanalytic terms, her desire for her father
on to her brother. She is not sure about H's interpretation and offers another
example of familial relationships:

> also I realized that at the time I stopped sleeping in my parents room, my brother
> came on the scene. I mean he came in and he and me got very very close.
> When he left to get *married* I became very very upset about that and very jealous
> about that so maybe I looked upon *him* in a way to try out my sexual attrac-
> tiveness and things like that.

The explanation for L's account would be something like: the deep-rooted
fearfulness of the oedipus conflict cannot be directly faced by the patient.

She can admit the facts of her involvement with her father and demonstrate to the discerning listener her reluctance to relinquish that involvement, but attempts to neutralize it. The counsellor hears all this and, repeating L's interpretation, suggests that:

> I hear that as 'to enjoy myself with my father would be terrible' because yes, that would be terrible. That it is *still* thought with regard to other men, is the problem. I'm trying to say that there's some connection there.

L's response to this was to shift the conversation away from how terrible it would be to enjoy herself sexually with her father, towards her brother. This would appear to be a clear case of resistance in that it seemed easier for L to admit to the sexual nature of her relationship with her brother than her father. This resistance was helped to some extent by some confirmatory remarks made by a second counsellor (B) about the sexual nature of the siblings' relationship. It might be interesting to consider whether B's remarks are a collusion with L's resistance; or a confirmation of the a priori status of sex; or something else altogether. However, this is not an attempt to interpret what is really going on, but an attempt at genuine description (Husserl, 1931).That this is a re-enactment of primal lust, is the point H is concerned to make when she says, 'This is noticeable in your relationship with M'; and, 'how similar do you think that your relationship and those sorts of feelings with M and your father are? Is what happened with your father also happening now in this relationship? How much does M resemble your father?' H concluded her questions and interpretation with the following:

> You see, the problem you are faced with is, what are you going to do with your sexuality? and that may be how you still relate to men when sex comes into a relationship. You call that loose and say they won't respect you, and so forth, but I wonder if that is really what it's about. Or if it is some confusion about whether you could actually be a sexually responsive woman in a relationship with a man. Or whether that is too destructive or very frightening. You know, feeling that something awful is going to happen if you allow yourself to be sexually free and responsive.

It is really all quite obvious.

It is in these obvious terms that it seemed to be an ideal case history for Freud. Perhaps too ideal; even, in Weberian terms, ideal typical (Weber, 1947). This might account for my initial sceptical reaction but can hardly be grounds for dismissing the account as given. It would be more fruitful, perhaps, to consider the accounting practice itself; and to accept the account as the counsellee's true version of her experiences (Coulter, 1984).[10] By this I do not suggest that we go in search of the action (Gilbert and Mulkay, 1983) in order to derive true statements or claims about actual actions and behaviour on the basis of an account of actions and behaviour (cf. Woolgar, 1986). Nor do I suggest there would be any grounds for knowing or assuming that the account is really true. Rather, what I am suggesting is that it is possible to view the accounting practice itself as a true version without making any claims about truth or validity as such.

My own accounting practice (knowing that the counsellee's talk was about childhood sexuality and so forth) will emphasize and clarify the distinction I am making between a true version and a truth claim when referring to the accounting practice itself. My account of this event is that subsequent to my recognizing the problem, L provided all the information one could ask for to substantiate both my claim to have realized what the talk was about, and the claim of psychoanalysis that the aetiology of neuroses (that is, normal behaviour in aggravated or extreme form) is to be found in the unsuccessful repression of the innate polymorphous sex drive or instinct. I have tried to demonstrate the reasonableness of this account by referring to what was said in the therapeutic setting. Namely: L's problem is her inability to accept and enjoy her sexuality; and that this inability is apparently due to the constraints of socialization as she experienced it. However, from the perspectives of the two experts (the client-centred B and the psychoanalytically oriented H) this inability is rather more to do with what might be called 'faulty learning'. This is illustrated by B in his account of how a 'young lady learns (through familial interactions) to be an attractive woman'; or, as H is concerned to demonstrate, by the repetitive nature of L's relationship going back to the 'entangling and confusing relationship between father and daughter'. So far, so good. Despite, or in spite of, their professional differences, both B and H locate the site of the problem in the incestuous nature of the father/daughter relationship.

There is then, nothing remarkable in someone (myself) who had been sensitized by watching some hundred and ninety hours of therapy, recognizing a real problem when she saw one. Given the event as a whole account, that is, as presented in the transcript and as witnessed, there is a certain appeal in experiencing the 'ah-ha' effect – knowing what the talk is all about. Freudian theory itself is so seductively appealing with its total explanatory form (Freud, 1901).[11] However, it is the form that appeals, not the content.[12] It is the form of argument as much, if not more, than the content that makes it recognizable as belonging to the body of statements that belong to a particular discipline or body of knowledge (Foucault, 1972, 1974). On this basis it may be that there is something in the form rather than the content of the talk that provided the conditions of possibility for the 'ah-ha' effect. Perhaps it is possible to ignore the content and look instead at the form.

Taking the whole of the talk itself by itself there is nothing, as far as I can see, in the content that warrants claiming that it is about childhood sexuality. Childhood, yes; sexuality, yes; the counsellee does talk of both, but separately and as distinct experiential entities. For example, L initially talks about her actions, behaviour and responses, of now. After a directional prompting from M her talk becomes more about her childhood actions, behaviour and responses. More particularly about her (traumatic) experiences of relationships formed while at school. It is only after these separate accounts that there appears, in the talk itself, a link between then and now. At one point L says 'and it [what happened at school] happened later with other friends too'. From this point onwards the talk takes on an altogether different tone. Or does it?

Certainly there is considerably more in the content that could be seen as evidence for proving the facts of the problem: L actually talks about how her feelings now may be left over from childhood. For example, anger; suffering; sexual ambivalence; difference; and so forth. Throughout the remainder of the transcript these stated links become both more frequent and more explicit. Evolving into a slowly-emerging picture of an adult person with relationship difficulties caused by trauma when her relationship with her father was broken in early childhood.[13] What this suggests is that the condition of possibility for both my recognition of the real problem and the emergence of the true picture begins with the appearance of an apparent link between then and now: 'and it happened later with other friends too.' But does it?

To address the form of talk rather than the content, however, would not only undermine the already tenuous conclusions reached above but, as I will argue later, also provide the grounds for locating Immanent and Transcendent discourse (everyday and esoteric knowledges) within discourse (speech). The warrant for claiming the tenuousness of the conclusions reached above is grounded in taken-for-granted epistemological terms rather than on the grounds of whether it is true, or an accurate version or interpretation of events. All of which rests upon an equally tenuous assumption: that the emergence of the true picture begins with an apparent link between past and present and that this link is the counsellee's utterance 'and it happened later with other friends too'. Again, all resting on a single, simple supposition: that I had the thought when I thought I had it. Put another way, that it occurred precisely when I think it occurred. There may be grounds for claiming knowledge of the organization and operation of brains, but there are no proven claims or knowledge about how the mind is organized and operates; nor whether the mind is confined to, or predicated upon, conscious thought.

It is not the tenuousness of the conclusion (that the talk is about childhood sexuality) that necessarily occasions further analysis. Rather, it is how the conclusion is reached. In this particular instance, having located an origin (that is, a condition of possibility), it is not its flimsy character, though it is perhaps flimsy evidence, that persuades me to look further. Rather, it is something of an automatic reflex. Having looked at counselling talk in various ways on previous occasions (Walker, 1984) it seems right and proper that, having looked at the counsellee's talk, I should also look at the counsellor's talk. Predictably, it is not at all difficult or surprising to find a similar condition of possibility. In the utterance immediately prior to my recognition of the problem, H says of L's relationship with her father, 'You can notice this happening now in your relationship with M'. Given my knowledge of the psychoanalytic dictum regarding problematic relationships as re-enactments of earlier relationships, it could just as easily have been the counsellor's utterance that had the appearance of an apparent link between then and now. Thus either counsellor or counsellee's talk make L's utterances hearable as about childhood sexual experiences; but the utterances themselves are not hearable as such. The question then is not how did I know *that* to be the case; but *how* did I know that to be the case.

In addressing the form of the talk in relation to the form of argument in Freud's work the how of the matter becomes a possible hearing. There is a danger that this may sound merely tautological (in contrast to all the best arguments which are just tautological) or as another way of arriving at the same conclusions reached above and this would be a pity. To dismiss the possibility of another way of looking at discourse, that is, at form rather than content, would be to dismiss what I hope to show is both a fruitful and reflexive way of looking at talk.[14]

Earlier I suggested two things: first, that Freud's work comprises a total explanatory form; and second, that counselling talk is, perforce, genealogically traceable to the psychoanalytic discipline. Thus it is explanation as form that I suggest consists in both Freud's writing (discourse *qua* Discourse) and the text of talk (speech *qua* discourse). It would serve no useful purpose for this text to review either Freud's work or the psychoanalytic literature. Instead I propose a gloss on both. In my view the most fruitful way to approach the Freudian perspective is as a metaphor for understanding society and its constituent parts: culture and people (Fromm, 1957, 1980; Bocock, 1976). The predominant approach in the psychoanalytic and other literature has been rather more concerned, whether for or against Freud, with its power, or the lack of it, to explain societal and individual events and actions.[15] Explanation thus dominates the forms of psychoanalytic argument; hence explanation as form in Freudian discourse. Furthermore, it is within the (often blurred) distinction between understanding and explanation that the cultural dissemination of knowledge provides a warrant for categorizing discourse as either immanent or transcendent. Before proceeding with the argument it is necessary to provide (rather more than gloss)[16] the grounds for arguing that the text of talk consists in an explanatory form.

The interview begins with H's request for information: 'How have things been over the last week?' L responded with a description of how things had been with her: what she did; what she thought; what her reactions were; what she felt; and so forth. But H appears to interpret the actions that L describes as really a desire to talk: when L begins to describe her likely attitude to certain events or actions, H interjects with what appears to be a helpful and innocuous suggestion that L's attitude is one of 'liking to talk things over'. At the level of what H is saying, the words are perhaps helpful and innocuous. However, at the level of things said, a different appearance emerges. In Austin's (1962) terms, words are performative: we perform social actions when we say what we say. The action performed by the saying is not itself present in the saying of the words but in what is being said. That is, in what the words do; and what words do is categorize. What H says, then, is not so much a suggestion as an assumption based on categorization. In other words, what H is doing when she says what she says is categorizing.

I am proposing that the 'helpful and innocuous suggestion' works as a device, a Membership Categorization Device (MCD) (Sacks, 1972) for locating L within the category of persons who like to talk things over. This location, or L's membership of that category, operates at three levels. First, L can be located (with M) as a lover; that is, a member of the category interpersonal relationship. Secondly, L can be located, (with counsellors H and B) as in therapy; that is, a member of the category therapeutic relationship. Thirdly, L can be located (with all others) as a member of our society; that is, a member of the category societal or social relationship. In other words, L can be located as a person who categorically talks, or who talks categorically. These three locations or categories – dyad, group, and society – are different, but not distinct categories. They are different in that the relationships are of a different character or nature; but they nevertheless have a commonality of action: talk. By this I mean that talk in its specificity is a prerequisite for those categories *qua* categories. It is not simply that lovers talk, group participants talk and people talk. Of course they do, but they do other things as well that help differentiate one location or site of action from another. It is talk, in its specificity as precondition, that provides for a commonality. This point is illustrated in Barthes's (1977) elegant and mimetic *A Lover's Discourse*; in the fact that most forms of psychotherapy, not least psychoanalysis, rely upon talk as the major therapeutic technique; and, finally, in the notion that people's actions are peculiarly social rather than purely instinctual – a notion that is predicated on the idea that it is language that separates humans from other animal species. This idea has been the condition for theorizing as diverse as Romantic Humanism and Positivistic Scientism. This commonality is captured in the everyday or common-sense knowledge that everyone needs someone to talk to.

Thus it is that 'likes to talk over' may not be the innocuous saying of a helpful therapist, but something said about our knowledge, as members, of individual and collective, societal and cultural, requisites. Furthermore, 'liking to talk things over' categorizes L the individual as a member of the collections dyad, group and society: all perceived requisite elements of our social world. Put another way, sociableness in our relationships with others as couples (i.e. marriage); as groups (i.e. family, employment); and as social beings (i.e. community, nation, humanity); is deemed essential for our individual and collective well-being. It is from this position of essentiality that explanation as form emerges in discourses. By now it should come as no surprise that I shall address this rather sweeping statement in terms of how this explanatory form emerges, rather than from a causal type explication. To restate a point already made in various ways: I am not concerned to show that any one thing causes or has priority over any other.

I do not, therefore, suggest that 'liking to talk things over' explains anything per se. Rather, that if sociableness is essential for individual and collective well-being then that explains, or accounts for, why everybody knows that everyone needs someone to talk to. For whether we as individuals are narcissistic or altruistic; conformist or non-conformist; do we not strive for well-being in whatsoever form our preferred state of well-being consists? It may be asked, how is this an explanation and not an understanding of a self-evident truth about ourselves as individual and collective beings. For if sociableness is essential, and we as individuals or collectivities recognize this, have we not then understood a simple fundamental truth? Here we have the crux of the matter: explanatory form is not necessarily, or even, explanation as such. Which, of course, raises the question of what, exactly, explanatory form is; and in what ways it differs from explanation. One way into discussing both questions and their propriety or appropriateness is through epistemological enquiry: how do we know what we seem to know?

I suggest that our knowing, and the belief in that knowing, is grounded in knowledge-based systems of thought which are themselves constituted in bodies of knowledge. In this particular instance, the knowledge-based system of thought is that which constitutes the ethos of the psychoanalytic tradition. This is not to suggest that we are all psychoanalysts or potential analysands, though of course Freud might (Freud, 1926), but that the psychoanalytic tradition founded by Freud changed dramatically, fundamentally, irrevocably and persuasively, the way people thought, and think, about themselves and others as human and social beings. The kinds of evidence for such a claim can be located only within the bodies of knowledge, or disciplines, that constitute systems of thought. In other words, it is only by being constituted as a thinking self within a particular system of thought that I can make such claims. I could of course say 'and so I rest my case'. Now, while there may be a pleasing satisfaction to be gained from this tautological ipso facto, this is hardly grounds for convincing others. What might be convincing is an exploration or discussion of bodies of knowledge.

For this exploration I shall not have recourse to the abundant critical literary sources that have culturally located Freudian precepts and psycho-analytic concepts within art, drama, literature, music and dance; nor shall I take recourse in the academic literature that posits the same location within individual and societal actions and activities, in order to prove the point (see, for example, Fromm, 1980; Marcus, 1984; Marcuse, 1955; Ricoeur, 1970). Rather, I shall take as an occasion for exploration another, different, text of talk. More accurately, I shall take a talking text as data that both encompasses and comprises all the elements contained within that earlier sublimely grand and general statement: the psychoanalytic tradition founded by Freud changed dramatically, fundamentally, irrevocably and persuasively, the way people think about themselves and others as objects of knowledge; or as knowable objects. The talking text is a film entitled *Nineteen Nineteen* (Brody and Ignatieff, 1985) that:

> ...began with some photographs of vanished Viennese rooms (Freud's consulting-room), with some case histories (The Wolfman and The Psycho-genesis of Homosexuality in a Woman), and ended with a script about a man and a woman (Alexander and Sophie, one-time patients of Freud) in their late sixties, in search of each other, in search of the impalpable shape of human life, one afternoon in Vienna. (Brody and Ignatieff, 1985: 15)

At one level this film is about two people, some-time patients of Freud when they were young, who meet through chance: a television programme, apparently about Freud, in which they both featured. In watching the broadcast Sophie resolves to go to Vienna to meet Alexander. They spend an afternoon together when they talk about themselves, often to themselves, and remember their respective pasts. We know this because film tech-niques provide for flashbacks: Alexander and Sophie as young people with their families or friends; in their homes and in public places; in Freud's consulting-room on the analyst's couch. We see them in their young pasts and in their older presents; with others and when alone. We hear them talking to Freud, even though we never see him; to others; to themselves in their thoughts. Because we see and hear all these things we know the real story behind the case studies. We know, in short, what Freud never knew: what was really going on in their minds. And, from the case studies themselves and the mass of Freud's clinical writings we know also what Alexander and Sophie at the time never knew: what was really going on in Freud's mind. On the basis of all that we really know, we can draw our own conclusions as to whether Freud helped or hindered his patients: Sophie not only does not admit her homosexual encounter to Freud, she actually denies it, and tells Alexander that she could not have told Freud. We discover that Alexander did not have the breakthrough to the woman that his marriage to Nina signified for Freud when we learn that he never had any desire for her. Both show their anger at Freud's misunderstandings:

Alexander: He thought my problem was in my mind, in my childhood. You read what he said about me? That when I first came to him I couldn't even dress without the help of a servant? That I couldn't put on my own trousers? A complete fabrication. He just wanted to believe that I owed everything to him. A mistake...A mistake...(Brody and Ignatieff, 1985: 30)

Sophie: They all talk – my mother, my father, *you* too – as if I had some disease. I'm in love with a woman. *That's* why I'm here. (Brody and Ignatieff, 1985: 30)

their ambivalent need of him:

Sophie: He was a good listener. I hated him. He threaded every word, like pearls on a necklace. Those theories...But *you*...There isn't anything left of you, is there? [*She pauses but cannot control her despair*] He's gone. Anna's gone. And now you're gone. (Brody and Ignatieff, 1985: 53–4)

Alexander: We talked. I gave him what he wanted. But I kept saying, 'When can I marry my Nina?'...I was unsure. I needed to make up my mind...about Nina. I depended on him. (Brody and Ignatieff, 1985: 64–5)

and the non-resolution of their neuroses:

Alexander: [*talking to Sophie of Nina's suicide and their marriage*] We were married for twenty years. In the same bed. Night after night. [*Wildly*] I never had any desire for her. Do you understand that? I had to make myself. I loved her. The breakthrough to the woman [*suddenly shouting*] what woman? What breakthrough. Remember. Just remember. That's what he said! It doesn't make any difference. (Brody and Ignatieff, 1985: 73)

Sophie: [*talking to Alexander of her night with Anna; and her resistance to Freud*] That was the happiest night of my life. Why did I think you would understand? For that one night I spent years explaining myself. I thought you might at least begin to understand *why* I fought with him [Freud], why I had to. (Brody and Ignatieff, 1985: 53)

Which all goes to show that even the great Freud can get it wrong. After all this time and all that these two people had been through, including their analysis with Freud; their attempts at living normal lives; and their obvious awareness, or self-knowledge, of both the nature and the persistence of their respective neuroses, 'Nothing had changed'. If Freud can get it wrong; if self-knowledge cannot, after all, help; what then of the talking cure? Could the bedrock upon which the discursive practice of counselling is based turn out to be less than solid?

Perhaps it is time to reintroduce the authors of the text (see Mulkay, 1984). Brody and Ignatieff (1985) say: '*Nineteen Nineteen*...does not purport to represent actual relationships between Freud and any of his patients.' And yet, in the responses of the audience there is no discernible recognition of this caveat. That people do get caught up in the stories they view is evidenced in the way soap operas become newsworthy. But, as the film's director said in a seminar discussion of the film: 'It is something of a mystery why a film that began life as a minority audience production, could even be called an art film with all that that implies, ends up being seen as suitable for popular or mass audiences' (ICA, 1986a). The questions this raised for the ensuing discussion became questions about film-making institutions; the politics of funding; and the controls of distribution. The talk shifted away from 'why has this film been so popularly received; why is it seen as being powerfully relevant; and how can we understand this as a phenomenon'; towards questions that 'raise political issues and questions of class and power and oppression' by 'challenging the bourgeois preoccupation with self that is the heart of psychoanalysis', itself a perceived bourgeois or middle-class activity.

While attempting to wrestle with this shift of emphasis I experienced a sense of *déjà vu*: a sense of knowing what the film was about – even though I had yet to see it – just as I had known what the counselling talk had been about. Why this film, like the topics of my research for me, had caught the audience's imagination was blindingly obvious and really quite simple. It brought to observation what everybody already knows: that everyone needs someone to talk to:

> In our story Sophie suddenly resolves to confront her past, in which Freud now figures as a problem among problems: she must return to Vienna. But to whom can she return? There is only one possibility: another patient. (Brody and Ignatieff, 1985: 14)

and how they already know it: in and through discourse; in other words, in and through the cultural dissemination of knowledge:[17]

> *Nineteen Nineteen* speaks directly to what we know about life, composed inextricably of the most intimate movements of the heart, accident, and the remorseless movement of history...The originality of *Nineteen Nineteen* as a film is that it offers an example of how this problem (of private and public; of past and present) can be addressed and of how a story must speak to what we know in our hearts. (Berger, 1985: 93 and 96)

What is so striking about the observations made in subsequent discussions of the film (ICA, 1986a) is what is absent: any fundamental questioning of Freudian precepts or concepts. Just as in the original study that prompted and informed this writing (Walker, 1982) where concern was directed towards whether or not to engage in counselling and how best to go about it, and not to questioning the premise of counselling as a good thing; so the talk about the film seemed to be concerned with arguments about whether or not Freud got it right. Whether the how-to knowledge of psychoanalysis where Freud stopped doubting (Blum 1971) is any longer relevant; or whether the updated versions of psychoanalysis found in Kleinian or Jungian theory, for example, were more relevant to, or tell us more about, the modern human condition. In these discussions, the evidence put forward in support of both views was largely anecdotal:

> I have a friend who was a patient of a patient of Jung's and she said...

or,

> Of course, Freud was afraid that Jung's superior theories would supplant his...

and,

> Well, it is quite obvious that Jung was merely acting out the oedipal conflict. The problems between Freud and Jung were clearly problems of transference and counter-transference. It is ironic that Freud could not recognize this of course, but then his cocaine habit or his cancer might have had something to do with that.

Exactly what either might have had to do with anything was not explicated. However, there were murmurs of agreement and much wise nodding of heads among the listeners.

If it were only this lay audience that fell back ('in conversation') on anecdote to silence dissent, one might dismiss the observations as merely anecdotal. However, professional speakers in a series of lectures on *Talking Psychoanalysis* (ICA, 1986b) also resorted to anecdote in a similar fashion, and for similar reasons:

> As I said to Winnicott...

or:

> Of course, Melanie [Klein] could never entirely refute Freud's major insight. As she herself always acknowledges, she *built* on Freud.

and:

> Well you know, I have been an analyst for over thirty years now and I can honestly say that, despite all these attempts by so-called post-modernists to show that psychoanalysis is socially constructed, people are *helped*. And that's what it's all about, gaining a greater understanding of yourself and others. And of course I've been in analysis myself too [*everyone laughs*] so I should know.

It is never explicitly acknowledged that theorizers and practitioners of psychoanalysis, as much as lay people, ground their knowledge at this conversational level (as I said to Winnicott...). It might sound good 'in conversation', but would never do for the more serious task of written exposition. I am not suggesting that speech should take priority over writing. That is, that these theorizers and practitioners dress up anecdotes to look like real evidence when formally presenting their case, but that both anecdote and the evidences of serious research inform a person's knowing. Indeed, the research that grounds this writing could be said to have derived from a piece of anecdotal evidence: everybody knows everyone needs someone to talk to. However, while not wanting to deny this – wanting, perhaps, to celebrate it – I would want to claim that it is a serious piece of research, and seriously undertaken. Furthermore, that it is the undertaking of a serious piece of research that informs the hearing of anecdotal evidence *qua* evidence. The difficulty, of course, is in trying to decide which came first.

It is always possible to impose chronological order, but when and where the thoughts that made both possible come from is addressed, the order, as in the chicken and egg story, becomes an impossible imposition. And where the thoughts come from, I suggest, can only be located in the cultural dissemination of knowledge; or what Durkheim (1912) called the ideas residing in the *conscience collective*. Put another way, it is the knowledges available to us, knowledges that both constitute us as objects of knowledge and knowable objects, that constitute both our objective and subjective knowing. Genealogically, the conditions of possibility for our knowing in this context are traceable to the psychoanalytic tradition: another way of saying, system of thought. This system of thought is itself a surface emergence. That is, the knowledges or discourses of the prevailing milieu provide the conditions of possibility for the emergence, as a system of thought or body of knowledge, of psychoanalysis. The state of the art of knowledge then and since, is one of scientism; and scientific knowledge represents, or attempts to represent, then and now, reality. Science explained what and why things are. Emerging in an increasingly scientistic society, small wonder that the new knowledge of psychoanalysis should be perceived in terms of explaining the human condition.

It is within this sense of explaining reality that it is possible to locate discourse within Discourse; the anecdote within evidence; the film within reality. In other words, in order to arrive at what is reality, the further one needs to go away from it (Walker, 1986: ch. 6; Latour, this volume). No one would want to claim that the anecdote was really evidence; or that the film was of real events or relationships. Rather, it is the persuasive power of the medium that brings reality into focus. Thus, in a discussion about psychoanalytic theory and techniques, and about the founders and practitioners of both, it is the anecdotal 'what Winnicott (or Klein etcetera) said over coffee' that has an undisputed quality of reality about it. To expound on someone's ideas or theories from their writings or their lecture presentations is a scholarly and academic reality; to divulge what they actually said under conditions of mundane human activity such as coffee breaks, catches the imagination in a way that even the most erudite of discourses does not. It is precisely its everydayness that makes it real. It is one thing to expound and explicate for special occasions, it is quite another to say the same thing, or something different, in everyday life. The anecdote serves to ground the evidence of theoretical constructs.

The same can be said of the film. No one actually believed the characters were real; everyone knew they were only actors playing a part written for them.[18] The authors of *Nineteen Nineteen* make it quite clear that their writings are fiction: '*Nineteen Nineteen* is a work of fiction inspired by case histories written by Sigmund Freud' (Brody and Ignatieff, 1985), and no one would want to claim that either the characters or the plot was real or even representative. Yet it is precisely the realness of both that provides for the film's authenticity. It could be argued that, inspired as it was by Freud's writings, there is an element of reality in the storyline that gives the illusion of reality to the film. Certainly the authors acknowledge both the facts and the fictions of their story. And yet, the facts and the fictions appear from the outset to be entangled; to be unbounded: *On the Psychogenesis of Homosexuality in a Woman*, from which Sophie is created: '. . . we felt that the logic of the struggle, the real story, remained hidden. Here was a mystery, an incitement to fiction. . .' (Brody and Ignatieff, 1985: 14) and on *The Wolfman* from whom Alexander is derived: 'We set about imagining the events that Freud's account leaves out. In this way we invented a new character' (Brody and Ignatieff, 1985: 15). Though the authors may not wish to claim reality for their character, the events in their characters' lives or their characters' relationship with Freud, even without the authors' acknowledged inspiration, would we not all recognize their source? Could such characters ever be the figments of a writer's imagination?

Real or imaginary, facts or fiction, case histories or inspired stories, the film appeals; and does so to a much wider audience than anyone concerned with its production imagined it would. I suggested earlier that the reasons for this were blindingly obvious: the film brings to observation what we already know. It is, of course, the histories of its main characters; it is, of course, a history of world events; it is, of course, all our histories; and, above all, it is the story of our culture's history, or the history of our culture's story. Perhaps it is also our present: a present of predicament; of uncertainty. A present in which all our modes of knowing are being critically questioned, and possibly found wanting. A most modern predicament. A predicament that is also the story of our culture's history. A history that has been shaped by, and shapes, the knowledges that constitute it. A shaping and a culture that owes much to Freud: Freud, a presence made larger than life by his absence; the star of the film, still playing a leading role in the cultural production of our knowledge. As Ricoeur puts it: 'Psychoanalysis belongs to modern culture. By interpreting culture it modifies it; by giving it an instrument of reflection it stamps it with a lasting mark' (Ricoeur, 1970: 4).

The 'mysterious figure that brought them [Alexander and Sophie] together' is, as precursor and founding father, a starting or departing point for bringing together theorizings about the human condition. This 'lasting mark' is so not simply because Freud offers a theory of the human condition that subsequent theories agree with or dissent from, but because his theory is also an interpretation of culture in which the human condition resides; and from which it derives.[19] An interpretation that is often conceived as a demystification or unmasking of repressed drives or instincts. At best, it is an explanation for neurotic, obsessive or hysterical reactions to suppressed desire; at worst a reduction of human aspirations to illusions that ultimately ends in discontents.

It is this absent presence that has provided both explanation and modification of selves and culture that, I want to argue, gives rise to the 'ah-ha' effect of knowing what things are and what they are about. Knowing that the counsellee's (L) problem was all to do with childhood and sex; and the blindingly obvious answer that the film was the story of our culture's history and thus all our histories, could only be possible, could only make sense, within the context of a culture 'stamped with the lasting mark' of the psychoanalytic tradition. How I knew what the real problem was and what the film was really about, then, is because, as Alexander said, 'I read everything he wrote, you know.' Put another way, just as Alexander could not answer the question about cure without recourse to Discourse, so one cannot answer the epistemological how questions without recourse to discourse and Discourse. This one line of the film script has been the subject of much discussion: critics, as in film critics, discussants or audiences, use this line as proof that Freud hindered or helped (depending on their point of view) his patients: that Alexander, not getting the help he needed from Freud himself, read everything he could in order to help himself, only to discover that, despite the talking cure, there are no cures. Alternatively, only by understanding Freud, that is, getting to know his writings, could Alexander be helped. Through understanding that there were no cures, Alexander could be helped, that is, could come to terms with his predicament.

Michael Ignatieff has said[20] that the insertion of a pause by Paul Schofield (the actor playing Alexander) after saying 'I read everything he wrote, you know' created a whole new meaning for the words. Thus it is not so much the words themselves that convince hearers that Freud did get it right, or not, but the reading or hearing of the pause. Whatever it is that is being heard or recognized is hearable and recognizable in its absence. Arguably, is only hearable and recognizable in its absence. While there has been much debate within the philosophy of language and linguistic theory concerning words and their meaning, perhaps only Heidegger (1967) and Derrida (1976, 1978) have explicitly looked less to the connection between words and their meaning and more to the space between them. It is to the space between, or to what I shall term the relation between discourse and Discourse, that I shall now attend. Before doing so, however, it is necessary to make at least some connections between the texts of talk discussed thus far and their relation to the issue of explanatory form.

Quite reasonably, one might want to ask what all this has to do with the text of counselling talk with which I began.

From the position of the psychoanalytically-oriented counsellor in the counselling session (H) one might reasonably infer that explanation of the counsellee's problem in psychoanalytic terms is a prime concern. One could not quite so reasonably infer the same of the other counsellor or the counsellees. In order to address the relation between the texts of talk it is necessary to make a distinction between a form of explanation and explanatory form. A form of explanation is but one way to address a problem, whether of the human condition itself or of an individual's actions. Explanatory form is what constitutes both the actions as an explanation of the problem and the account as action to be explained. To illustrate: L's actions and attitude as she described them served as explanations of her problem in terms of her state of mind: she would like to talk things over. How this is an explanation rather than, for example, merely an expression of the 'everybody knows everyone needs someone to talk to' kind is, perhaps ironically, best addressed in terms of why. Why did the therapist think (assume, presume) that all the talk about finding it difficult to deal with any sort of pressure, feelings of frustration, anger and annoyance, and L's inability to forgive and forget and so on, could be reduced to wanting to talk things over? Why? Because it is entirely an (occasioned) expression of what everybody knows: that everyone needs someone to talk to. Whatever the problem is, it is both generally and specifically one of talking things over.

Generally, it is the everyday, taken for granted, response; specifically, talking is what comprises counselling. If L has problems and needs help with those problems, of course she would like to talk things over. What else would she be there for? As the problems of interpersonal relationships are reducible to problems of not talking, or non-communication, then of course, what she would want to do is to talk things over. Why else would she be seeking counselling? If she had in M what everybody knows she needs – someone to talk to – she would not need therapy. However, M does talk to her; L says so, often. Also, much of what is wrong seems to centre as much around what M said as what he did not say, that angered, hurt and upset L. However, it is not just any talk that is needed. Quite the contrary; most of it seems to be the problem. It is really talking that is needed. The kind of real talk that goes on in counselling. Which is rather strange when the real talk of counselling is looked at: the counsellor says very little. Real talk seems to be recognizable by its absence.

How is one to make sense of this? Not, it seems to me, from the form of explanation. That is, that everyone needs someone to talk to: L needs someone to talk to; M is someone to whom L talks, and who also talks to L, but their talking is not really talking. M does not tell L of his feelings and so forth, so L talks to the counsellor; who also does not talk to her, but this is helpful. M will not tell L what he feels and this is non-communication; the counsellors will not tell L what they feel, and this is communication? Counselling is communication, so it must be. When looked at in this way, explaining actions or attitudes as that of wanting to talk things over falls rather short of expectation. Minimally, one might expect talking things over to be more of a dialogue than a monologue. For the counsellees, of course, talking things over is meant to be a dialogue: they are supposed really to talk to each other. The whole problem of lack of communication has been characterized as people talking at or past each other, rather than to each other.

It would be temptingly easy to suggest that counsellors are not very good models in that they do not practise what they preach: that they say one thing and themselves do another. Preserving, perhaps, a privileged position of telling-how rather than showing-how; of saying rather than doing; of theorizing rather than practising. Put another way, that counselling is the ultimate in standing for: silence stands for talking. One immediate response to this might be that counsellors are precisely not there to talk but to listen. That if one were to talk of models and things that stand for other things (Walker, 1986: ch. 6) then there is in Freud not so much a model but an exemplar: he did not talk to his patients as such. Apart from the occasional observation, he listened and his patients talked. It is not that silence stands for talking; but that listening is Freud's, and therefore the counsellor's, technique, and the talking (cure) is entirely the counsellee's. Maybe, when he listened from behind the patient, from out of sight, Freud gazed absent-mindedly at those wonderful artefacts of ancient civilization he collected; or fidgeted or sprawled in his chair; or doodled on his notepad. If he did, was he therefore not listening? The detail of his case studies suggest this could not be the case unless, as Alexander intimated, Freud was not above embellishment, even fabrication. However, Alexander is not real; he is just a fictitious character in a story.

Just as we know that Alexander is not real, so we know that counsellors are not really being silent when they are not talking: they are actively listening. But what are they actively listening to? Something, I suggest, that is akin to the hearings of Alexander's pause. They are listening to what they already know: the problem, however it is presented, is one of not having someone to talk to, properly. A form of explanation then, would be that when L talks of her actions and attitudes in terms of her difficulties, anger, frustration and so forth, she is really talking of her need for someone to talk to. When counsellors are being silent in terms of not talking they are really actively listening – that is, communicating. When Freud's patients talk of what befalls them they are really talking of their thwarted desires.

Explanatory form, however, comprises both explanation – the actions stand for symptoms of repression, or the real problem of non-communication with self or others – and form: the account of the problem (or the symptoms) is the action that has to be explained as non-communication or repression. In other words, explanatory form is that which explains in terms of the thing to be explained. Put yet another way, explanatory form is another way of saying *explanans*.

One might reasonably ask why I did not say this at the outset. It is because I had no wish to reduce psychoanalytic theory to mistaken positivism. Rather, I wished to demonstrate its place within scientific discourse without wanting to make any claims, or refutations, as to its scientific status; or lack of. To locate it within our culture's scientism: those bodies of knowledge (natural sciences) that purport to represent reality and those (human sciences) that purport to interpret reality; in order to bring to observation the similarity between representation and interpretation without obscuring the differences. Taking psychoanalysis as exemplar: a scientific representation of reality in terms of culture; and a scientific interpretation in terms of individual symptomatology. In other words, both a representation and interpretation of the human condition can be found in Freud's writings (Freud, 1909, 1912). The similarity between representation and interpretation is that they each stand for something else; some really real thing; out there, somewhere; waiting to be discovered.

In the meantime, what we have so far discovered will serve as knowledge and provide the building blocks for further increased knowledge (see Walker, 1987). Representation and interpretation is the form our knowledge takes. Furthering knowledge, then, becomes a task of re-representation and re-interpretation. Within the social sciences this takes the form of re-presenting theories; and the re-interpretations of theorizers. Discovering, as it were, what X really is; or what X really said. The content of that re-discovered knowledge may vary but the form remains constant. The form of knowledge, or Discourse, will inevitably inform what we say and what we can say about our individual or social world. Therefore, what we can know is what can be said.

Concomitantly, what is said can be explicable only in terms of, or of conforming to, what is known: knowledge. It is not because there is a body of knowledge, for instance psychoanalysis, that explains actions that accounts of actions, or symptoms, become explanations; nor is it because there are accounts of actions to be explained that there is a body of knowledge to explain them. The two work in tension to create, and re-create, the explanatory form. For the body of knowledge to explain the problem, the problem must be seen in terms of needing explanation; and explanations take the form of why and what questions. Thus L, for example, says, 'I don't know why I am like I am', from which one might infer a request to the experts to explain one's self – why one is what one is;

why one acts as one does; rather than how does one understand – how one is what one is; how one acts as one does. I am not suggesting that L does not understand herself nor that she does not want to understand. Indeed, the fact that she is in therapy might indicate the opposite. I am suggesting that the form of explanation gets in the way of her being able to understand her self in terms of herself. The why and the what infer something other than what is, and thus tend to take attention away from it. In trying to change something attention is given to the why and the what on the presumed assumption that changes in what is, will follow. I would not wish to imply that this does not or could not happen. It just seems strange, even perverse, that a perspective that stresses the importance of knowing one's inner or real self should also stress the primacy of knowing other than what is, in order to explain it rather than to the knowing of self through understanding what that self is.[21]

This notion of knowing self through understanding has been much debated within philosophy and the social sciences (for example Ricoeur, 1981). Much has been made of what may be termed the nomothetic mode of knowing, the most important aspect of which is that knowledge ought to permit exact predictions; almost to the exclusion of what may be termed ideographic knowing, in which objects are not instances of universal laws, and therefore predictable, but singular events that can neither be replicated nor predicted.

The story that unfolds in L's telling of it could be said to be entirely a replication and therefore entirely predictable. It could be seen as a replication in two ways. First, her account of her early experiences, or traumas, centres round her position vis-a-vis her parents and their sexual activities, and the effect of this on her own sexual relationship with her partner. Which is exactly what Freud discovered. L's story then, is a replication of Freud's case studies. Secondly, Freud's argument is that these early experiences, or primal traumas, are the basis of our culture and therefore replicated in all of us. Thus her story is also a replication of Freud's theory. If Freud's theory and his reporting of his case studies is in any way accurate (leaving aside truth or reality for the moment) then L's story becomes entirely predictable; again, in two ways. First, Freud's theory of culture posits this replay of primal relationships in us all. Secondly, his clinical studies posit that we all, to a greater or lesser degree, in reality or phantasy, experience this primal relationship. Thus, whether her story is real or fiction, whether she is familiar with Freud's theory or not, is beside the point. Those early experiences, real or phantasized, explain her relationship with M.

Prevailing knowledge-based systems of thought thus not only consist in explanatory form but insist on it. Explanatory form elicits explanatory form. Thus, within an explanatory mode of being, that is, members of a scientist or explaining society, we are condemned not only to seek explanation, but to find it; often, I suggest, to the detriment of understanding. However, as suggested above, the two forms of discourse do not exist in isolation but each forms and informs the other, in tension. Thus what is said in Discourse becomes sayable in discourse; that is, Immanent Discourse. While saying in discourse becomes, or stands for, what has been said in Discourse; that is, Transcendent discourse. Thus our discourse is informed by Discourse; and our Discourse by discourse: Discourse within discourse, socially produced and transmitted. In the process of transmission a transformation occurs: what was once esoteric or transcendent knowledge becomes everyday or immanent knowledge; and what is everyday knowledge becomes esoteric or transcendent; the process of transformation is necessarily one of transmutation.[22] It is not a question of what Freud really said; whether his writings have been misunderstood or misappropriated. Rather, that whatever he may or may not have said; whatever he may or may not have intended or meant to say; as hearers constrained by our culture the reality of what Freud said is hearable only in terms of cultural propriety. A propriety which divides knowledge or knowing into two distinct categories: authentic knowledge, or expert/scientistic knowledge; and inauthentic knowledge, or non-expert/intuitive knowledge. Within this division of knowledge a hermeneutic-intuitive knowing is totally opposed to the culturally preferred scientistic-explanatory knowing. In this way discourse, or everyday speech, is subordinate to Discourse, or bodies of knowledge. Or is it?

Is it not the anecdote, the speech of fictitious characters, that speaks most directly to us? For our understanding, facts and fictions reside comfortably together; they merge and become indistinguishable. It is only when trying to arbitrate or legislate; that is, explain, that facts are taken from their fictive surroundings and become matters of fact. Standing alone, bereft of what makes sense of them, or makes them sensible, facts are then challenged, usually by other matters of fact. Inevitably then, facts alone are always challengeable, as indeed are fictions. However, it is facts and their challengers that take priority in our society. And how could it be otherwise? Who would want to challenge fiction, and on what grounds? Their claims to knowledge?

Fictions, however, are not knowledge in our society, only facts are. We live in a society of scientistic experts who, arguably since the Reformation, have attempted to distinguish facts from fictions and then explain them; leaving the fictions for the rest of us to grapple with, or to abandon in the pursuit of knowledge. It is in these terms that I suggest that being condemned to seek and find explanation is detrimental to understanding. This being condemned to seek and find explanation is not a wilful act; rather we are all, as non-experts and experts, culturally constrained to do so. Explanation tyrannizes modernity; our modern culture or society consists in our explanatory forms of knowledge; that is, is constituted in discourse. Part of our cultural heritage is the knowledge-based system of thought inculcated by Freud and textually transmitted through cultural artefacts. Two such artefacts have been directly addressed here: counselling, a perceived social and individual view of expressions; and film, a perceived social and individual expression of views. Culturally speaking, the listening ear and the seeing eye of our society. Counselling is where we speak of our world; film is where our world speaks of us. The powerfulness of both rests upon them having found a collective someone to talk to.

Once again, whether counselling or film expresses or is expressible in terms of truth or reality is neither here nor there. Indeed, counsellors will say that whether their particular theoretical and practical preferences are true or not is inconcludeable. The point is, the activity of counselling helps people understand themselves and others better. The questions raised concerning the reality of either Freud's real relationships with his patients or of his conclusions in treating them, is equally inconcludeable. The point is, the portrayal of both helps people to understand themselves and others better. At least, in principle, this is what could happen. Or may even be what does happen. It is just that in trying to describe what is experienced, the temptation to explain surfaces.

Often the explanation offered is in terms of the thing to be explained. Thus in describing the explanation of counselling, for example, one is constrained to describe it within the terminology of the explanatory form. To illustrate: one might say, I gained greater insight into my needs and desires. And, when pressed for more detail, one might explain within discursive theoretical terms what either insight or needs and desires are. That is, insight, within the framework of this discussion, is the recognition that one's relationships with an other is a replay of earlier relationships; and needs and desires are really needs for the mother's breast or desires for the father; and so forth. It is not a question of truth or reality as such, always assuming either exists, but of what it is possible to say discursively and Discursively.

While we, as experts or non-experts, concentrate on explaining what is in terms of something else there is a twofold danger: first, in explaining it, whatever it may be, away; and secondly, in forgetting what it is. For example, to explain away repression and its recurrent manifestation in the problematics of relationships in terms of the oedipal conflict is to forget what the oedipal conflict is: a metaphor – a fiction, or just-so story (Walker, 1986: ch. 8). And what a metaphor precisely is, I suggest, is the relation between, or what grounds, discourse and Discourse; facts and fictions; reality and non-reality. Metaphor, then, not only constitutes and comprises the relation or connection between the two kinds of discourse, it is what makes of them sensible and knowable discourses as such. How we know whose discourse a discourse is and what Discourse it is, is by the story being told and the teller of the tale.

Notes

1. The lower and upper case formulation is a practical and pragmatic distinction only. It allows us to identify or keep in mind what exactly is being referenced: discourse = speech or everyday talk; Discourse = discipline or body of knowledge.

2. Foucault (1972) identifies two major forms of historical investigation: the search for continuities, and the ultimately convergent discontinuities. His notion of genealogy neither presupposes either form nor attempts to combine them. Rather, he simply disallows both on epistemological grounds.

3. In the literature on counselling much emphasis is placed on it being a major technique for the helping professions. For example, social work, various guidance and advisory services; and equally, how it should play a major part in other practices, for example, medicine (Silverman, 1986); and the judiciary (Atkinson and Drew, 1979).

4. The experience is something of an irony. I consider that the emphasis on Freud's clinical writings in psychological studies and the psychoanalytic literature is to be regretted. His more sociological writings such as, *Totem and Taboo*; *Moses and Monotheism*; *Figure of an Illusion*; and *Civilisation and its Discontents*, have always seemed to me to be the most interesting and fruitful; while the clinical studies appear to be (less than fruitful) attempts to ground those philosophical reflections in scientific proofs. Finding myself thinking along those lines was therefore an uncomfortable surprise.

5. I prefer the interpretation of libido as drive or life force (Fromm, 1980). However, my own preference notwithstanding, the ᵕ nhasis has more usually been in terms of libido = sex drive.

6. The excerpts presented here are a tidied version taken from a full transcript (Walker, 1984: ch. 4).

7. The social construction of problems is taken for granted. I have argued elsewhere (Walker, 1984) that the occasional setting of the therapeutic interview renders the problematic (i.e. what the problem is) unproblematic.

8. Sublimation, in my reading, is the redirecting of the life drives, eros and thanatos, for the enhancement of the individual and collective 'Kultur' (civilization); repression the necessary and successful redirection of polymorphous drives towards culturally preferred activities. Erikson documents this distinction between repressed drives (1964) and sublimated desires (1958) and their preferred outcomes rather nicely.

9. While this may appear to be presented rather simplistically, even crudely, the in-principle perspective is simple. If the oedipus myth is accepted a priori with the resultant basic human condition of conflict, then resolution of the conflict becomes paramount, for not to do so is to retain the primal states of individual and society.

10. Coulter (1984) proposes, as a way of categorizing persons, that there are two true versions available: agents' (self) 'Opaquely True' version; and reporter's (of agent's action) 'Transparently True' version of an action or behaviour. He suggests that a hearer opts for the former. I have borrowed this notion but have taken it in a different direction to that proposed by Coulter. I suggest that agent and reporter are not necessarily different persons. In the example to hand, agent (L as subject) is also reporter of agent's action (L as object). Thus while in Coulter's formulation, I (as hearer) have a preference for not accepting the transparently true version, hence the scepticism, I can accept it as being the report, or account, of the agent's opaquely true version. In other words, one need not dismiss the obvious because it is obvious.

11. Denial of repression is itself proof of the theory. The pun in the sentence went unnoticed for a long time. The presence here in the use of 'seductively' could also be said to be a proof of Freud's theory (see, for example, Freud, 1901).

12. By this I mean the distinction Simmel (1950) makes between form and content. See especially ch. 1, part 1. At least, I mean what I think Simmel means by...

13. Mighty oaks from little acorns...?

14. I have to admit to some bias here. Any way of looking at social action, which is what I take talk to be, that attempts to avoid either the interpretation or privileged accounts of reality so endemic to much sociology has got to be fruitful. Equally, a reflexivity that has more in common with Garfinkel's (1967) Documentary Method and less to do with an introspective dwelling on what one does as a researcher/analyst can only further our individual and sociological understanding (see Woolgar, this volume ch. 2).

15. This approach can be heard in various schools of thought: Marcuse, 1955; Klein, 1948; Foreman, 1977; Barton, 1974, representing critical sociology, psychoanalysis, Marxist feminism, and psychotherapy respectively.

16. To go through the whole transcript utterance by utterance would be the ideal procedure. However, the amount of words needed to talk about other words is inversely proportional to the amount of words anyone could be expected to have to deal with. So, what follows in the text must necessarily be only rather more than a gloss.

17. It is this tangible cultural dissemination of knowledge, the cinema, that makes this film as data and evidence so appropriate and, to me, so appealing.

18. That said however, it should be acknowledged that what the actors bring to their character roles is precisely what makes of them real people; also, what they bring to their reading of the script can be crucial for their performance. An anecdote, rather than an analysis of acting techniques and theory, will serve to illustrate this: when Alexander is asked by the television interviewer 'were you cured?' he replies: 'I read everything of his, you know' and takes a long pause before continuing with his lines. The pause, so poignant and so telling, was inserted into the script by Paul Schofield who played the part of Alexander, and not written into it by the authors. (In conversation with Michael Ignatieff.)

19. That Freud interpreted the human condition, rightly or wrongly, is the focus and impetus for much of the theoretical work in counselling and psychotherapy: Jung, 1954; Klein, 1948; Rogers, 1942; Berne, 1961. That he interpreted the culture that gives rise to the human condition, rightly or wrongly, is the focus or impetus of much of the work in the human sciences: Fromm, 1980; Ricoeur, 1970; Marcuse 1955. That Freud's most illuminating writings: *Totem and Taboo* (1912–3); *Moses and Monotheism* (1939); *Civilisation and its Discontents* (1930); and *Future of an Illusion* (1927) are those which provide metaphoric understandings, rather than interpretations or explanations of our culture, is a premise that has been the impetus for much of my theorizing.

20. In private conversations – to which I am greatly indebted for my enhanced understanding.

21. This is something of an irony in that it was precisely through his own introspection that Freud arrived at his findings and precisely what he advised against. Perhaps Alexander got it right when he said 'He just wanted to believe I owed everything to him.'

22. Even at the simple level of the text of talk that provides the basis for this writing, transformation from speech to writing involved transmutation. The audio-recording of what was said in the therapy session has a sensibleness about it that the transcript in written, though exact, form does not: the transmission from audio-recording to text transformed speech into writing, transmuting sense into non-sense. Likewise in the creation of *Nineteen Nineteen*: 'when the script was turned into a film, other forces started to work their changes. Characters became actors, each of whom had his or her own understanding of their part in the story' (Brody and Ignatieff, 1985: 15). Thus transmuting through transformation.

Reflexion on Walker

It must be said that Walker's chapter provides some unusual problems for the Editor's Voice. For the clear message is that direct intervention in the text is inappropriate. Whose Discourse?

Walker's chapter is an attempt to bring to observation the reflexive character of knowledge (Woolgar and Ashmore, this volume: 9). So we are bound to ask whether or not this is something we already knew. Although the question seems precious, it offers an important test of the status of Walker's argument. If the answer is yes, then the argument is self-exemplifying and we have at least a sufficient condition for construing her piece as knowledge. If no, the argument is a standing refutation of its own claim to knowledge. Hence, one is tempted to ask, in what *sense* is the argument self-exemplifying? One might, for example, point out and examine those passages which contain subtle hints about the self-referring character of the argument. But one of the interesting features of the text is the lack of any explicit claim to self-reference. Or at least, taking the whole of the text by itself there is nothing, as far as I can see, in the *content* that warrants the claim that it is self-referring. For an example of a self-referring claim about self-exemplification we turn to the piece by Mulkay.

5

Don Quixote's Double:
a Self-exemplifying Text

Michael Mulkay

There can be no doubt that 'replication', in ordinary language, has something to do with the 'sameness' of or 'close similarity' between two or more events or objects. Likewise, 'experimental replication' in science seems to refer to attempts to 'copy closely' a prior set of experimental procedures and to obtain 'the same results'. Replication in science is usually taken to contribute to the process whereby experimental claims are validated. Valid claims are supposed to be 'reproducible' by other competent experimenters and it is often assumed that experimental observations come to be accepted only after thay have been successfully replicated, that is, repeated exactly, by numerous independent observers (see the discussion in Zuckerman, 1977).

Described in this way, experimental replication appears to be fairly simple and straightforward. But recent work by several sociologists has begun to show that the process is much more complex than may at first appear (see Collins, 1975; Travis, 1981; Pinch, 1981; Harvey, 1981; Pickering, 1981). The following quotation is taken from Collins's recent article on scientific replication in the *Dictionary of the History of Science*:

> Werner Heisenberg (1901–76) has written: 'We can finally agree about their [physicists'] results because we have learned that experiments carried out under precisely the same conditions do actually lead to the same results.' The view that replicability is essential in science is widespread. This view has only recently been examined in detail, the major problem being the meaning of 'the same conditions'. Since no two events are identical a set of *relevant* conditions must be specified. But ideas of relevance will rest on an understanding of the [scientific] phenomenon in question and this will be incomplete where the very existence of the phenomenon itself is in doubt. (1982c: 372)

In this passage, Collins makes problematic our initial, straightforward account of experimental replication. He does this by emphasizing the literal impossibility of *exact* experimental replication. He points out that no two experiments can ever be exactly the same. For if they were exactly the same, we could speak only of one experiment and not of two. Collins suggests, therefore, that when scientists treat two or more experiments as the same or as different, their judgements of similarity depend on criteria of relevance which do not inhere in the experiments themselves but are formulated and applied by the scientists involved.

Collins's final point in this quotation is that scientists' criteria for judging experimental sameness/difference often derive from, or at least vary with, their views about the scientific phenomena under investigation. Consequently, it seems to follow that experimental replication is not an invariant criterion for establishing the validity of new experimental results. Rather, the very meaning of 'replication', in any particular instance, is bound up with and dependent on scientists' potentially divergent scientific views about the very phenomena whose existence and character are to be established by means of experimental replication.

Making the 'Same' Experiments 'Different'

Collins's central points, then, are that the sameness/difference attributed to two or more experiments depends on interpretative work carried out by the scientists concerned; that the sameness/difference actually attributed will vary in accordance with other aspects of scientists' interpretative work, for example, in accordance with the scientific viewpoints they profess; and, consequently, that judgements of experimental replication can be highly variable (see Collins, 1981a, c, e). Let me illustrate this variability by means of a set of quotations from interviews with biochemists, in which each of the speakers is referring ostensibly to the 'same' series of experiments. These are the 'stoichiometry experiments' and they include the experiments by Spencer and Marks discussed by Mulkay (1985: ch. 1). The names given at the end of these quotations are pseudonyms of biochemists working in the same field as Marks and Spencer. The number following these names are the relevant pages of the interview transcripts. Each 'sentence' has been numbered for ease of reference. For further details, see Gilbert and Mulkay, 1984.

A 1. Then we verified that the number through the ATPase was two in intact mitochondria. 2. There is still an argument about that because one is somewhat bugged by the porter systems. 3. The ATP has got to get in and the ADP has got to get out. 4. The Pi has got to go through... 5. There's a controversy at the moment as to whether Pi can also get in by another route. 6. Because we think we have identified a calcium phosphate porter. 7. And almost without exception everyone else at the present time says it doesn't exist. 8. But none of these people who say it doesn't exist have really repeated our experiments in detail. 9. Our feeling is that if they do, they will – well I think it may turn out that it does exist. 10. So that there is a little doubt about the ATPase stoichiometry. (Spencer, 43–4)

B 1. We repeated all [Spencer's stoichiometry] experiments. 2. We can get the same answers that he did. 3. There's no question of not believing his data. 4. It's not a question of that at all. 5. We reported this and we showed that with our experiment and everything we get exactly the same answers. 6. That's all recorded in our papers. 7. But what was wrong was...(Marks, 13)

C 1. These proton stoichiometries, now there you have a series of discrepancies. 2. But if you look, no two people have done exactly the same experiment. 3. So this is part of the reason why I am somewhat cynical about the whole business. (Pope, 35)

D *Interviewer:* 1. Is there in fact any disagreement about actual observations? *Respondent:* 2. Nothing major. 3. There *are* some disagreements, but they're not very important ones by and large. 4. Not between the position that Spencer holds and the position that Marks and I have held, or are holding... 5. We can do the same experiments and get the same results. (Crane, 24)

E 1. Crane and Spencer disagree on one particular issue. 2. On others they merely disagree on their own interpretation. 3. On one they seem to disagree on fact. 4. They have not actually done the same experiment twice. 5. But they have done two different experiments that should be the same. 6. Spencer says that if you reduce the temperature, to reduce the rate of the phosphate porter to such an extent that you can see the phosphate going in and you can see the rate that it is going in and you can see that you are *not* missing protons. 7. Crane says that if you slow the phosphate porter, you can see the slowing of the phosphate porter going in, but the stoichiometry rises to three and not two. (Read, 29)

F 1. I really don't know what the battle is all about. 2. But [Spencer] seems very adamant in sticking to his numbers of two. 3. I could not care less, if I was him. 4. Whether it is two or four, it makes no difference... 5. The fact as to whether it's two or four is irrelevant. 6. Basically, it supports [Spencer]. (Peck, 30–1)

In passage A, Spencer notes that there is some controversy in relation to the stoichiometry experiments (A2, 7, 10). He mentions his basic experimental finding that two protons cross the membrane for every ATP formed and he draws particular attention to experiments in which he claims to have identified a 'porter' which carries phosphate across the membrane (A5–7). The existence of this porter is said to be denied by most other scientists in the field. But Spencer suggests that this is partly because they have not done the same experiments as he has (A8). Despite some hesitation at the end of the passage, Spencer seems to imply that if other scientists were to repeat his experiments in detail, they would reach the same scientific conclusion.

In passage B we have Marks, who is regularly described in our interviews as Spencer's main opponent on the issue of stoichiometry. Marks maintains that he has repeated all Spencer's stoichiometry experiments and has published his results (B1, 5). Furthermore, although he does not mention here any specific experiments of Spencer's, he stresses that there is no question of not believing Spencer's data (B3–4). Thus Marks seems to be saying that he has repeated many, perhaps all, of the relevant experiments, that he is able to obtain the same results as Spencer, and that if there are experiments which he has not repeated, he does not doubt that they are repeatable. However, whereas Spencer proposes in passage A that repetition of his experiments by others would help to convince them of the validity of his scientific interpretations, Marks maintains that his scientific viewpoint has been unaffected by this experimental replication. Immediately after this passage he explains why Spencer's conclusions are wrong despite their reproducibility.

In passage C, we have a speaker who forcefully denies that there has been *any* experimental replication at all in this area, thereby clearly contradicting Marks's claim to have repeated Spencer's results (C2). In passage D, however, we have another participant maintaining that at least Spencer's major experiments can be, and have been, repeated by Marks and himself (D2–5).

The speaker in passage E, Read, returns to the specific experiment on the phosphate porter mentioned by Spencer in passage A and compares it with the wider debate about stoichiometries. Read claims that most of the disagreement about stoichiometries between Crane (the speaker in passage D) and Spencer is merely a matter of divergent interpretations (E2). Given the way in which Read uses terms in this passage, this seems to imply that, in relation to the stoichiometry debate in general, Crane and Spencer have not carried out identical experiments. In relation to the phosphate porter, however, they are said to differ over a matter of fact (E3). Even here, they are not described as performing *exactly* the same experiments (E4). Nevertheless, their different experiments are treated by Read as being scientifically equivalent; so much so that their observing different numbers of protons is treated as being a simple observational discrepancy which is not to be explained as due to variations in experimental procedure (E4–5).

The treatment of experimental sameness/difference in passage E is, in one respect, more complex than in the previous passages. Unlike the previous speakers, who treat sameness/difference in these quotations simply as observable features of experiments (e.g. 'no two people have done exactly the same experiment'), Read maintains that two experiments which are undeniably different in detail may be taken to be indistinguishable for certain interpretative purposes. Thus, for Read, it is possible for two given experiments to be both different and the same. In this respect, passage E resembles passage F, where all the stoichiometry experiments, no matter what their detailed findings, are treated as much the same. The final speaker, Peck, a vocal opponent of Spencer's chemiosmotic theory, is able to treat any experiments which purport to show that protons contribute significantly to the production of ATP as scientifically equivalent. In passage F, all the fine distinctions provided by previous speakers are obliterated. In this passage, all the stoichiometry experiments are basically the same. They are equally Spencerian and equally misconceived.

These quotations illustrate how a specific set of experiments can be variably depicted by different speakers as the same, as different and as different yet the same. This supports Collins's suggestion that participants' statements about experimental sameness/difference, and therefore their statements about experimental replication, depend on complex, and potentially variable, interpretative work. Thus in order to understand scientists' claims about experimental replication, we must understand how attributions of sameness/difference are linked to other aspects of their interpretative work. This implies that we should try to understand how attributions of experimental sameness/difference operate within scientists' discourse. Accordingly, our central questions become: what do scientists accomplish interpretatively by means of such attributions? What further claims, portrayals, evaluations, and so on are made possible through specific attributions of experimental sameness/difference? The underlying assumption here is that, because the sameness/difference of any set of experiments can always in principle be depicted in varying ways depending on the kind of interpretative work which is being carried out, we can gain some insight into the nature of such attributions by examining how they contribute to the discourse in which they are embedded.

Experimental Differences as a Means of Validation

Our customary view of scientific replication leads us to expect that scientists regularly claim support for their own and others' experiments through assertions that the same experiments have been repeated by other researchers and the same results obtained. This view is epitomized in the statement by Heisenberg quoted above. In my material, however, claims of this kind occur infrequently. Much more frequent are claims that given experimental findings have been and should be validated, not by the *same* experiment, but by something experimentally different. Consider the following example.

G 1. Whether or not any scientific statement is true, I mean, is very – I mean there isn't really any great deal of argument about it as a general rule because, 2. although nobody – well people very seldom test precisely the same experiment, 3. if it is of any significance it leads to predictions which other people will use in their own experiments 4. and either it stands or falls according to the results other people get. 5. So I think the experimental thing is a test which enables all these scientists who are just like anybody else, just as bigoted and prejudiced and emotionally involved as anybody else would be, 6. I mean it actually enables people to be objective – because there is an alternative criterion. (Bamber, 23)

In this passage, the speaker is talking in general terms about the validation of scientific statements (G1–2). He suggests that, on the whole, the validation process operates without a great deal of argument (G1). However, he then rejects the view that such validation depends on scientists' performing precisely the same experiments (G2). He appears to begin to say that *nobody* ever does exact replications, but changes this in mid-sentence to the more moderate claim that testing precisely the same experiment occurs very seldom. The speaker then tells us how scientific validation normally operates. He does this by contrasting the customary account of exact replication with an alternative account which portrays scientists as exploring the validity of others' important statements by investigating how far predictions derived from those statements are confirmed by the results of 'their own experiments' (G3). Thus the speaker's alternative account depicts researchers as being able to test any specific scientific claim by carrying out new experiments which, despite their differences from the original experiment, can have clear implications for the original claim (G3–4). The speaker makes no attempt to explain, either in the quoted passage or subsequently, how these new experiments can have such unequivocal consequences for the validity of the original claim. Rather, he achieves interpretative closure by treating the scientific meaning of these new experiments as entirely unproblematic; even although his initial interpretative task was that of showing how scientific claims, *in general*, are validated.

This speaker's presentation of an apparently 'objective criterion' for assessing the validity of scientific claims is accomplished by his first identifying all scientific claims and experiments as problematic and, in principle, in need of validation; and then by his introducing a sub-set of 'new, different experiments' which can in some unexplicated way, despite their being themselves implicit members of the initial problematic set, be used to check the adequacy of the original experimental conclusions. When re-described in this way, after detailed re-examination, Bamber's account of the process of experimental replication seems weak and unconvincing. During the interview, however, it went unchallenged. The interviewers seem to have accepted it as an entirely plausible account of experimental replication. Thus the speaker in passage D furnished an interpretatively successful account of the process of scientific validation which denies the importance of exact replication or close experimental copying and stresses instead scientists' reliance on experimental variation.

It is clear that validation of scientific claims in general can be discursively accomplished by emphasizing experimental differences. The same pattern can also be found in the next two passages.

H 1. . . . many times you have an observation, interesting, that relates only indirectly to something I'm doing. 2. And I will take that observation and extend it. 3. That's what in fact is much more common [than exact replication]. 4. An extended observation into your normal area of research. 5. And does it work, here, in these particular conditions? (Shaw, 62).

I 1. If [an experiment] is really important you will end up doing something. 2. Maybe not repeating that experiment exactly. 3. But you will repeat some variant or some other thing to show the same thing. 4. Yes, I think it is important that more than one lab do the experiments, if they are important experiments, or do experiments bearing on the same point. (Fasham, 13)

The speaker in passage H begins by referring to his own practice. Much of his own work, he says, consists of taking up observations made by other scientists which appear to relate in some indirect fashion to his experimental concerns (H1–2). In sentence 3, he can be read as widening his frame of reference and as talking about biochemists in general. But this is uncertain. He may still be talking only about his own work.

At this point the speaker, Shaw, proposes that taking somebody else's observation and extending it is much more common than some form of action which he does not specify at this point, but which he takes as being obvious to his audience (H2–3). It is clear from the full interview transcript that he is speaking here of the act of doing 'exactly the same experiment' which he had referred to previously. Thus, like Bamber in passage G, Shaw also explicitly denies the importance of exact replication in scientific practice and emphasizes the role of experimental variation. Furthermore, once again like Bamber, Shaw seems to treat experimental variation as having some kind of validating effect. The point of extending somebody else's observation into your own area of research is said to be to find out whether it 'works' under these new conditions (H4–5).

The account given so far by our respondents of the process of experimental testing does not depend on different researchers being able to agree that their experiments were conducted under exactly the same conditions. Their version emphasizes that validation is achieved, rather, when another researcher's observation works under distinctly *different* conditions. Nevertheless, speakers like Shaw cannot claim to be checking somebody else's experiment, that is, finding out whether it works, without asserting *some* degree of 'sameness' for the two experiments. Thus, in passage H there is an unspecified something which is treated as common to both experiments and which is taken to be open to validation through its reappearance in the second experiment, despite the variation in experimental conditions (H5).

This combination of 'scientific sameness despite experimental differences' is repeated in passage I. Like our two previous respondents, Fasham tends to minimize the role of close experimental copying (I2) and to stress the importance of doing something different in order to check other scientists' important experiments (I3–4). But, in his words, 'you will repeat some variant or some other thing *to show the same thing*' or 'bearing on the same point'.

This formulation of the process of scientific validation seems to imply that the scientific statements which are being tested are more general than those embodied in the observations furnished by any particular experimental set-up (Mulkay and Gilbert, 1984). Only if this is assumed is it possible for speakers to maintain that there is some element of scientific knowledge which persists across varying experiments and which can be verified, validated or replicated by means of various experiments, each with different experimental conditions. This recurrent discursive form, then, avoids the participant's interpretative problem identified above by Collins, namely, that of how to decide whether or not two experiments have exactly the same experimental conditions; for differences in conditions are treated as an essential part of the validation process. Nevertheless, its users are able to sustain the claim that they are engaged in experimental replication by assuming that experiments which differ in detail can have the same scientific meaning at a higher interpretative level.

The Prevalance of Triangulation Accounts

Accounts in which scientists assert validation of given experimental results by reference to other different experiments, I shall call 'triangulation' accounts, because the need for *three* different experiments is so frequently mentioned (see Mulkay, 1985: ch. 1). I shall provide no further examples of triangulation accounts here. This pattern has been documented in detail elsewhere (Mulkay and Gilbert, 1984). The point I wish to emphasize is that triangulation accounts occur much more frequently in my interview material than that of validation by reference to exact replication or to close experimental copying. In this material, the ratio is about two to one in favour of triangulation accounts. In addition, references to validation through exact replication tend to be noticeably weaker, that is, more tentative and qualified, than references to triangulation. Compare, for example, Spencer's formulation in passage A with that of Bamber in passage D.

Spencer: But none of these people . . . have really repeated our experiments in detail. Our feeling is that if they do, they will – well I think it may turn out that it does exist.
Bamber: . . . if it is of any significance it leads to predictions which other people will use in their own experiments and either it stands or falls according to the results other people get.

Such differences in the interpretative strength of the two forms are typical. There may, of course, be many reasons for the relative strength and prevalence of triangulation accounting. However, one possibility is that such an interpretative form becomes dominant, within certain kinds of interpretative context, because it facilitates other types of important interpretative work. I suggest that one recurrent concern in scientists' discourse, and perhaps particularly in their interview talk, is that of scientific originality. Thus the specific possibility which I shall investigate is that triangulation accounting enables scientists to accomplish validation while at the same time helping them to make certain sorts of originality claim. I shall begin to pursue this idea in the next section by means of a short digression into the realm of literature.

Borges, Cervantes, Menard

In a story entitled 'Pierre Menard, Author of the *Quixote*', Jorge Luis Borges (1970) explores the problem of how to reconcile exact literary replication with literary originality. Borges's story concerns a (presumably fictional) little-known author, Pierre Menard, who writing during the period 1899–1934, is said by Borges to have included with his *oeuvre* 'the ninth and thirty-eighth chapters of the first part of *Don Quixote* and a fragment of chapter twenty-two'. Borges recognizes that 'such an affirmation seems an absurdity'. Nevertheless, he tells us, 'to justify this "absurdity" is the primordial object of this note'. By including these fragments of *Don Quixote* within the list of Menard's writings, Borges depicts himself as rectifying a previous incomplete catalogue of Menard's work from which they had been omitted. Thus Borges's text implies that the prior catalogue had, incorrectly, treated these fragments as not a genuine part of Menard's original writings. Borges's aim is to convince us that these fragments are not mere copies of parts of a prior work of genius, but original contributions to world literature.

According to Borges, Menard dedicated much of his life to the remarkable objective of writing *Don Quixote*. Menard 'did not want [merely] to compose another *Quixote* – which is easy – but *the Quixote itself*. Needless to say, he never contemplated a mechanical transcription of the original; he did not propose to copy it. His admirable intention was to produce a few pages which would coincide – word for word and line for line – with those of Miguel de Cervantes.' Thus, in so far as Menard succeeded in his task, we have two identical texts each with a separate author. Borges claims, however, that Menard's text is much more original than that of Cervantes and massively superior to it in terms of literary merit. The way in which Borges establishes Menard's literary originality, despite the textual identity, is evident in the following quotations.

> To compose the *Quixote* at the beginning of the seventeenth century was a reasonable undertaking, necessary and perhaps even unavoidable; at the beginning of the twentieth, it is almost impossible. It is not in vain that three hundred years have gone by, filled with exceedingly complex events. Among them, to mention only one, is the *Quixote* itself.
>
> In spite of these. . .obstacles, Menard's fragmentary *Quixote* is more subtle than Cervantes'. The latter, in a clumsy fashion, opposes to the fictions of chivalry the tawdry provincial reality of his country; Menard selects as his 'reality' the land of Carmen during the century of Lepanto and Lope de Vega.

What a series of *espagnolades* that selection would have suggested to Maurice Barrès or Dr Rodríguez Larreta! Menard eludes them with complete naturalness. In his work there are no gipsy flourishes or conquistadors or mystics or Philip the Seconds or *autos da fé*. He neglects or eliminates local colour. This disdain points to a new conception of the historical novel. This disdain condemns *Salammbô*, with no possibility of appeal...

Cervantes' text and Menard's are verbally identical, but the second is almost infinitely richer. (More ambiguous, his detractors will say, but ambiguity is richness.)

It is a revelation to compare Menard's *Don Quixote* with Cervantes'. The latter, for example, wrote (part one, chapter nine): '...truth, whose mother is history, rival of time, depository of deeds, witness of the past, exemplar and adviser to the present, and the future's counsellor.'

Written in the seventeenth century, written by the 'lay genius' Cervantes, this enumeration is a mere rhetorical praise of history. Menard, on the other [hand], writes: '...truth, whose mother is history, rival of time, depository of deeds, witness of the past, examplar and adviser to the present, and the future's counsellor.'

History, the *mother* of truth: the idea is astounding. Menard, a contemporary of William James...

What Borges does in such passages is to make Menard's verbally identical text *different* from Cervantes's at the level of literary meaning by linking it to its differing historical, literary and intellectual context. Whereas Cervantes's literary aims are described as reasonable and appropriate for their time, Menard's undertaking is said to have been almost impossible some three hundred years later. Borges's emphasis on the differing contexts of the two texts enables him to attribute radically different meanings to shared stylistic features and to identical verbal sequences. For instance, whereas the avoidance of 'espagnolades' can be treated as a routine feature of Cervantes's text, for Menard, aware of nineteenth-century popular writing about Spanish life, it can become a praiseworthy accomplishment of stylistic restraint. Similarly Menard's conception of history can be treated as truly remarkable for a man writing at the same time as William James.

In short, we can see that Borges creates for himself an artificial situation in which, initially, the literary originality of the supposed author appears particularly doubtful owing to the identity of his text with that of Cervantes. However, the subject's originality is established by Borges's use of various interpretative techniques which enable Borges to treat Menard's text as different from that of his predecessor and to attribute new and remarkable meanings to the content of the second text. It is clear that without a display of interpretative differences between Menard's and Cervantes's *Don Quixotes*, Menard's originality cannot be sustained. Thus Borges's story helps us to see how claims for originality depend on the recognition of differences; and also how differences can always be created at a higher level of meaning, even in situations where there is in some sense undeniable identity.

Borges's accomplishment in this story has clear implications for our understanding of scientists' routine emphasis on experimental differences in their talk about replication. Like Borges, scientists are, at least partly, referring to similarities and differences among texts. For Borges the texts are literary products; for scientists they are research reports. Like Borges's texts, scientific reports can always, as we have seen, be construed as the same, as different or as both different and the same. Some element of sameness between texts is a necessary component of any claim for experimental validation in science. Exact duplication of literary texts, in contrast, appears to be a very unusual occurrence. Borges introduces this element artificially into his narrative as a way of making the interpretative production of originality particularly difficult to achieve. He then accomplishes originality by establishing differences between the texts in question. In the next section we will examine how scientists accomplish originality in a manner analogous to that used by Borges, that is, in their case, by using the attributions of difference which are characteristic of triangulation accounts as a basis for claiming scientific originality.

Originality and Difference

It has been suggested elsewhere that, when scientists talk about their research to outsiders, each speaker typically claims and/or assumes that his view of the scientific phenomena under investigation is, at least basically, correct. It also seems likely that most speakers take for granted that they have made some kind of original experimental contribution to the understanding of these phenomena (Gilbert and Mulkay, 1984). The interpretative accomplishment of validation and originality are, in fact, closely connected in much of scientists' informal reports about their own and others' experimental activities. Scientists employ forms of talk which enable them to accomplish both self-validation and the attribution of originality. More specifically, by linking experimental validation to differences as well as to sameness, speakers create interpretative space in which to establish their own and others' originality without thereby jeopardizing their own claim to be advancing experimentally validated conclusions. In other words, the element of difference enables them to attribute originality and the element of sameness enables them to attribute validity.

Consider the following exchanges between interviewer and respondent.

J *Respondent:* 1. If something has been published, a phenomenon, and it has been explained in a certain way, and you believe the phenomenon but you don't believe the explanation; 2. then you are necessarily obliged, I think, or practically so, to repeat the phenomenon, 3. but now you'll need to take samples here and there and go and measure what *you* think is causing the effect. 4. Everybody does this, constantly. 5. It's perhaps one of the commonest ways in which progress is made, I would say . . .

Interviewer: 6. So you're seldom in a situation where you are repeating very closely and trying to reproduce exactly the work which you find in research papers.
Respondent: 7. No I wouldn't say very seldom. 8. It really can be quite frequent if one is going up a different path. 9. Do you see what I mean?
Interviewer: 10. Yes. So you're seldom interested in pursuing exactly the same path.
Respondent: 11. This, as far as it goes, may be right. 12. It's both boring, uninteresting and unpublishable, *just* to repeat it. 13. It's really only if you can add something. 14. If you can find out *why* something has happened, instead of just saying 'this happened'. (Howe, 26–7)

The speaker in passage J begins by identifying the kind of situation in which he would engage in replication. He describes this as a situation in which he believes the phenomenon reported in a research paper, but did not believe the explanation (J1). As he talks, it gradually becomes clear that he is assuming that the reported phenomenon or the experimental effect is reproducible in principle and that he will be able to repeat it (J2–3). Thus the goal of his own experimental work is not depicted as that of experimental repetition, but as that of providing a new, and scientifically more satisfactory, interpretation for this reproducible effect (J3).

The reproducibility in principle of most published findings is widely taken for granted in biochemists' talk about replication (Mulkay and Gilbert, 1984). Hence, they regularly describe themselves as making special attempts to replicate others' work specifically in situations where, like Howe, they have identified some interpretative defect in that work. Accordingly, although they portray their actions as in part a repetition of another's previous experimental work, this is always accompanied, as in passage J, by an emphasis on their own additional and different contributions (J3–5).

In passage J, the interviewer attempts to clarify how far Howe is claiming to repeat other scientists' actions very closely (J6). Howe's reply is subtle and difficult to grasp; a point which the speaker himself seems to recognize, when he asks; 'Do you see what I mean?' Whatever the exact meaning of J7, Howe seems to be proposing that he quite frequently does repeat others' experiments closely, but also that he combines such repetition with 'going up a different path'. Thus Howe maintains a careful balance between experimental sameness and experimental difference. In J10, the interviewer reformulates the issue of sameness. He is so emphatic this time about the high degree of similarity that he has in mind that Howe is led to deny that his work is ever *quite* that repetitious and to make it clear that, if his work added *nothing* different, it would necessarily be 'boring, uninteresting and unpublishable' (J12–14). In other words, the series of exchanges between interviewer and respondent leads the latter to express explicitly the interpretative difficulty of reconciling close experimental repetition with the attribution of scientific originality.

The following quotation has a very similar structure to the previous passage.

K *Interviewer:* 1. In fact, do you repeat, replicate, other people's experiments quite often?
Respondent: 2. Never for the sake of it, no. 3. I never go into the library and say: 'So and so's seen this. I will also see if I can see it.' 4. The way I would do it would be: 'So and so's seen *this*, and using *my* set of prejudices, they ought to be able therefore to show that like *that*.' 5. So I'd set their experiment up and first of all demonstrate to myself that I can repeat it, 6. and then try and show that and that as a test of my hypothesis or a test of my theory, that they're working on the wrong hypothesis. 7. This, therefore, makes all their assertions fit in with my hypothesis. 8. Something like that. 9. I do *know* people who will do experiments just to repeat them, to see if they can do other people's experiments. 10. But that strikes me as a futile way of behaving. (Crane, 46)

The speaker in this passage claims at the outset never to repeat others' experiments 'for the sake of it' (K1–2). He does not seem to mean by this that he never repeats their experiments at all. For he states clearly in K5 that he does, on occasion, set up other people's experiments and demonstrate to himself that he can, in some sense, do the same experiment. However, he seems to be suggesting that when he does repeat others' experiments it is never 'mere repetition'; that when he repeats other's work, something more is involved than simply making sure that he can observe the same phenomenon (K2–6).

Like Howe in passage J, Crane seems to assume that he will engage in replication only when he has some kind of doubt about somebody else's claim (K6), but, also like Howe, that he *will* be able to reproduce the other researcher's observations (K5–6). Thus the goal behind Crane's concern with replication is depicted as that of adding new and different observations to the initial findings in such a way that he can reinterpret that finding in accordance with his own scientific viewpoint (K6–7). Hence it follows for Crane, as it does for Howe, that 'just to repeat' others' experiments, that is, to make no original contribution, is scientifically futile (K9–10).

Both Crane and Howe portray their attempts to check the validity of others' claims as involving a necessary element of experimental sameness or experimental repetition. These speakers' assumption of sameness follows from their taking (most of) their colleagues' observational claims to be reproducible in principle. But the similarities between their and other people's experiments (texts) are treated as relatively uninteresting and scientifically unimportant. Experimental copying, like literary copying, is deemed to be trivial and both scientists deny that they ever engage in such a boring and futile activity. Both speakers also stress that the process of validation depends on their doing something different from other scientists; and both emphasize that the correct scientific meaning of others' observations can be established only through new and original experimental

contributions. In this way, by making the process of validation appear
to depend more heavily on experimental variation than on experimental
repetition, Howe and Crane are able to depict themselves as engaged in
validation, and even in replication, while simultaneously depicting themselves as making original contributions to scientific knowledge.

In the two examples examined so far in this section, speakers have treated
replication as essentially a negative procedure, that is, as a way of checking
doubtful claims. But replication can be treated in a more positive fashion.
For instance, when scientists talk about replications of their own work,
they usually maintain that other people have repeated, and thereby confirmed, their findings. Even in such cases, however, some degree of
experimental variation is routinely identified and used to display the
originality of the replicators.

L *Interviewer:* 1. Can I ask if anybody has replicated *this* paper, or done what
   you might call a replication?
   Respondent: 2. Yes. There's a lab in Amsterdam that has done some of this
   work. 3. I mean, not all the way through. 4. They've used some of the tricks
   that we've used here, yes. 5. If they'd just done *straight* replication, they
   probably wouldn't even write a paper. 6. But they've used the ideas and the
   methods for their own particular problems. 7. And also two labs in the States
   as well have also taken this thing further on. 8. Again, with different objectives.
   (Peck, 25)

In passage L, three replications of the speaker's paper are mentioned
(L2, 7). But it is stressed that these are not *straight* replications. As in
the two previous passages, the idea that competent researchers would 'just
repeat' (L5, K9, J12) somebody else's experiment is treated as most
unlikely. The speaker makes it clear that replication has occurred as other
researchers have used the content of his paper to solve their own particular
problems and to attain their different objectives (L3–8).

No indication is given in passage L, however, that the three replicating
labs were in any way involved in *re*-interpreting the original findings. In
this respect, passage L differs from the two previous quotations. Although
the speaker makes no explicit claim that these replications confirmed his
results, it seems to be presumed that the methods and ideas contained in
his paper were deemed to be adequate by these other researchers. In this
passage, then, a standard triangulation account is used to validate the
speaker's own experimental findings while attributing scientific originality
to those carrying out the replication.

Sameness and Lack of Originality

In the same way that attributions of difference can be used to display the
originality of the speaker and of other researchers, attributions of sameness
can be used to deny scientific originality. There are no examples in my
material where such denials are self-referential. In other words, all the

denials of originality in my data are applied by a given speaker to other people. As I suggested above, speakers' originality, as well as the validity of their scientific views, is routinely taken for granted and continually reproduced through their discourse.

M *Interviewer:* 1. If I could go back to that question of replication. 2. You wouldn't say that you never replicate other people's work or would you? *Respondent:* 3. You might try to on your own system, if somebody had shown something on mitochondria. 4. Surely you would go into the lab: 'I wonder if *bacteria* do that?' and try it. 5. Yes, of course you'd do that. 6. But you would hardly go in and repeat the same experiments on mitochondria. 7. I have never done that. 8. Other people have, particularly with Spencer's proton-pulse experiment. 9. They have gone and tried this experiment. 10. Potter and Travis is an example of work there. 11. And many other people have repeated these experiments and improved them or found out new things about them. 12. They've gone on to do that. 13. Not just repeated them and stopped there and said: 'That's nice, they do work, he's right you know.' (Jay, 26)

In passage M, the interviewer begins by returning to a previous statement by the respondent that he did not try 'to repeat much of other people's work'. The interviewer's question is organized in a way which encourages the respondent to say that he does sometimes replicate other scientists' experiments: 'You wouldn't say that you never replicate, would you?' Not surprisingly, this question elicits the kind of response that it appears to take for granted. The researcher replies that he may well sometimes try out other people's results on his own system (M3–5). Nevertheless, he consistently adopts the standard triangulation account of experimental replication when talking about his own actions and he strongly rejects any implication that he might ever repeat another scientist's experiment exactly (M6–7).

At this point, the respondent extends the original question and applies it to other people. He appears, quite clearly, to claim that some other scientists *have* carried out exact replications or very close experimental copies. He seems to be saying that these scientists have 'repeated the same experiments as other people on mitochondria' (M6–8). 'I have never done that', he continues, but 'other people have' (M7–8). As he proceeds, however, the conception of replication which is being applied to these other scientists seems to be revised. In M11, these third parties are credited for the first time with having improved upon the prior experiment and with having 'found out new things'. Thus, whereas the speaker had previously contrasted the mere repetition carried out by these scientists with his own strategy of experimental variation (M7–8), he now seems to be acknowledging that these scientists have also done something different and that they have thereby achieved some degree of scientific originality.

In the final sentence we find, as in previous quotations, the implicit comparison between 'just repeating' somebody else's experiment and doing something new. The speaker seems here to be unambiguously retracting what he had previously implied, namely, that these other scientists had made no original scientific contribution. By the end of the passage, therefore, the speaker has rescued these other scientists from the charge of 'mere replication', by reformulating their actions in such a way that they can now be seen to have been involved all along in experimental work which combined an element of repetition with a scientific component which was different and original. Passage M, then, appears to be an instance where the difficulty of reconciling sameness with originality is dealt with in the text by the withdrawal of the attribution of sameness and by the introduction of differentiating features which are used as the basis for attributions of originality.

The following passage has a somewhat similar structure. In this case, however, the denial of originality is the main interpretative accomplishment and the accusation of experimental sameness is not withdrawn.

N   *Interviewer:* 1. How often do you actually check out in your own laboratory the kinds of results that you are finding in other people's papers? *Respondent:* 2. We don't make *any* effort to repeat what somebody else does. 3. We have so many problems unexplored that result from our own initiative, that we would never think of going back to repeat something that Joe Blow does. 4. It's interesting, there is a laboratory that I've never visited and which shall remain nameless, but I have a colleague who has visited and he says that when you go there the Professor says, 'Well, here is Mr So-and-So, he's working on the Marks phenomenon. Here's Mr So-and-So, he's working on the Perry stuff.' 5. They actually take pride in the fact that they are checking papers that have been published by others, with the result that a great deal of confirmatory work precludes their truly innovative contribution to the literature. (Long, 15–16)

This passage begins with the interviewer asking how often the respondent checks other scientists' experiments. Long provides an emphatically negative response (N2). He then goes on to provide a justification for not repeating other people's work (N3). The justificatory effect of this sentence depends on the assumption that experimental repetition as such is less valuable scientifically than the exploration of his own original contributions. The relative triviality of repetition is not stated explicitly here, but is implied by the dismissive turns of phrase, for example, 'we don't make *any* attempt', 'we would never think of', 'something that Joe Blow does'. In this respect, Long's discourse resembles previous speakers' references to the triviality of 'just repeating' others' experiments.

The invidious comparison between repetition and original research is developed further in the rest of the passage by means of an implicit condemnation of a laboratory which is supposed to specialize in replication. In N4, the speaker decides not to reveal the name of the laboratory. The only other situation in which respondents insisted on the need for other scientists' anonymity was when they were making allegations about fraud.

Thus, in this passage, the act of simply repeating others' experiments seems to be treated as improper; more specifically, as infringing taken-for-granted norms requiring scientists to make original contributions to knowledge (N5). In addition, because the members of the nameless laboratory are depicted as pursuing goals which are, scientifically, largely irrelevant, the speaker treats their actions as puzzling. 'They actually take pride' in replication, when they should obviously be doing what Long does, namely, making truly original contributions to the research literature (N5). In short, the contrast between experimental sameness and scientific originality provides the interpretative basis in this passage for the condemnation of other scientists' actions.

Analytical Self-reference

In this chapter, I have used Borges's story, along with my own sociological data, to show that resemblances between texts (or between actions) can be, and regularly are, constructed and reconstructed by participants in diverse ways. At the start of this chapter, I illustrated how participants can variably construe the degree of similarity among a set of scientific experiments. Once we recognize the existence of this kind of interpretative variability among scientists' attributions of experimental sameness, it becomes difficult to pursue any form of sociological analysis which treats replication as a stable feature of scientists' experiments in themselves, rather than as a contingent feature of scientists' interpretative work.

In this text, therefore, I have tried to identify some of the interpretative outcomes which scientists routinely accomplish through their variable attributions of experimental sameness/difference. I have tried to show some of the things that scientists do with similarity attributions. Specifically, I have maintained that attributions of experimental difference enable scientists to display their own and others' scientific originality; and that attributions of sameness can be employed to condemn others for lack of originality. I have also suggested that respondents use a standard triangulation account, combining the attribution of sameness at one level with the attribution of differences at another level, which enables them interpretatively to accomplish scientific validation along with the allocation of originality.

Although I have emphasized above the import which Borges's story has for *participants'* interpretative work, I must accept that it has similar implications for the composition of the present text. Like Borges, and like my biochemists, I have constructed this chapter by identifying, compiling and using a series of similarities/differences. For example, I have presented various passages from different interview transcripts in which are to be found different combinations of words. Yet I have claimed that some of these passages exhibit 'the same interpretative structure'. Although these similarity claims always have some basis in the original texts, the identification of 'the same features in different texts' depends on and exists through the interpretative work I have carried out on those texts; in the same way that the sameness/difference of Cervantes's/Menard's texts is accomplished in a particular way through Borges's interpretative work. The similarities which I have identified above could, by means of different textual work, be interpretatively deconstructed.

This 'admission' may appear to imply an inadequacy in the present text. For, it may be argued, if the sameness/difference of texts is always interpretatively accomplished, there is no compelling reason to accept the analyst's attributions of sameness/difference in this text. However, this criticism, in turn, can be said to adopt 'the same position' as that proposed in this chapter; that is, although it rejects the particular readings of sameness/difference advanced above, it accomplishes this rejection by assuming that sameness/difference is interpretatively accomplished. Thus, it seems to be possible to read this criticism as both a rejection and a confirmation of this chapter's central conclusion; or, to put it in the terms used above, as a replication through difference.

Another view of the present text can be obtained by addressing my own analytical question to it: namely, what does it accomplish through its attributions of sameness/difference? (see Ashmore, 1983). One of the things it can be said to accomplish is a replication of the sociological claim about replication which is contained in the papers by Collins and others cited above. In other words, it can be taken to be one more study confirming 'the potential local interpretative flexibility of science' and further establishing the 'socially negotiated character of experimental replication' (Collins, 1981c: 4).

Although the present text has certain distinctive features, this need not affect its being treated as primarily a repetition of prior work. For example, Collins treats a paper by Travis (1981) on 'a new area of science' as, 'in the main, a replication of earlier work on replication!' (1981c: 4). Thus, the fact that the present text also contains new empirical data need not necessarily prevent it from being deemed to be the same as, a straightforward replication of, previous sociological research. At the same time, however, the present paper can be read, like that of Travis, as having a certain degree of distinctiveness and, thereby, of originality. For instance, it is the first replication study which uses data obtained from bioenergeticists; it is, possibly, the first such study to compare the attribution of scientific originality with that of literary originality; and it is, perhaps, the first replication study to emphasize the interpretative connection between replication and originality.

I can, therefore, easily link the present text to certain predecessors by means of a standard triangulation account. I can provide textual evidence to show that it reaches basically the same conclusions as these predecessors, but that it does so by an analysis which differs from previous studies in various ways. Accordingly, we might conclude that the present study serves to validate the prior conclusion; whilst making an original contribution of its own.

Possible readings of the sameness/difference of the present chapter do not stop here, however. For this text can also be read as radically different from those of Collins and as fundamentally incompatible with Collins's main conclusions. There are various ways of doing this, one of which is as follows. In this concluding section of the present chapter, I am extending conclusions which I have derived from data on natural scientists to the realm of sociological analysis. My argument, in this sense, depends on an assumption of sameness between the two realms of intellectual endeavour. Collins, however, denies this sameness in several of his texts (especially 1981a). In these texts, Collins prescribes that we should 'treat the social world as real, and as something about which we can have sound data, whereas we should treat the natural world as something problematic – a social construct rather than something real' (1981a: 217). In other words, whereas I am trying to explore the self-referential implications of my own analysis, Collins rejects this degree of analytical reflexivity because it is taken to lead to 'paralysing difficulties'.

In so far as I take my concern in this part of the chapter to be with the way in which we, as sociologists, interpretatively construe the social world, my conclusions seem to be diametrically opposed to those of Collins. Whereas Collins proposes that we should only treat the 'natural world' as interpretatively accomplished, whilst treating the attributes of the social world (such as the sameness/difference of texts and actions) as 'real', my conclusion is that both social and natural worlds are variably constructed through participants' discourse. It appears, then, that not only can the present chapter be read as the same as Collins or as the same but also different; it can just as easily be read as fundamentally incompatible with Collins's claims.

All of these readings of sameness/difference can be textually legitimated and strongly defended. I do not, therefore, wish to insist on the validity of any one. They are all viable readings. The final reading above, however, is particularly interesting for it depicts Collins as basing his claims about the social world upon a privileged form of 'realist' discourse available only to the sociologist. Scientists, in contrast, are denied access to such privileged discourse. From this analytical position, participants' discourse is to be deconstructed through the supposedly superior discourse of the analyst. This arbitrary interpretative asymmetry seems to me to be untenable, even though I have myself, like most other sociologists, taken it for granted in previous work. It is for this reason that I have tried to emphasize in this final section that the analysis presented in this chapter is self-referential and self-exemplifying. The textuality that I have tried to display in participants' discourse is an inescapable feature of my own discourse. I suggest that the self-referential character of the sociological analysis of discourse is not something to be rejected or hidden, but rather to be welcomed and celebrated as in the chapter which follows.

6

Accounting for Accounts of the Diagnosis of Multiple Sclerosis

Anna Wynne

It is a commonplace to describe this as the scientific age; that the definitive phenomenon of modern western society is 'science' – a form of knowledge that is accorded both an overwhelming legitimacy and the power both to describe and control the physical world. However, although in recent years sociologists of science have turned their attention to the practices and institutions of science and to the content of scientific knowledge (for example, Knorr-Cetina and Mulkay, 1983; Latour and Woolgar, 1979), little attention has yet been paid to whether (and if so how) lay people, non-scientists, conceive of and use a notion of science in their everyday practices. Do they, in fact, operate with a hierarchy of knowledge, with an idea of 'science' as the epitome of truth? This paper draws on a study of the chronic neurological condition Multiple Sclerosis (MS) in order to begin to address this question.

MS has been the object of scientific research for more than a hundred years since it was first described by Charcot working at the Salpétrière in Paris in the 1870s.[1] Yet according to the current expert literature, the aetiology, morphology, symptomatology and prognostic patterns, the incidence and prevalence of MS worldwide are still not unequivocally established (McAlpine et al., 1972; Matthews et al., 1985).

In the absence of a definitive diagnostic test or any universally agreed clinical criterion, the diagnosis of the disease also remains intensely difficult to establish with certainty, a problem both for sufferers and for the conduct of medical research. The category 'certain MS' is reserved on many criteria for those diagnoses made in the course of post-mortems. The advent of the NMR scanner which is able to discern the typical plaques of demyelination in the Central Nervous System of living persons has only compounded the ambiguities of the condition, for there appears to be no straightforward correlation between the site of plaques and the manifestation of symptoms (cf. for example Gilbert and Sadler, 1983; Herndon and Rudick, 1983). Thus the current 'expert knowledge' of MS states that it is a condition which continues to defy the most concentrated scientific study (Kurtzke, 1980: 170).[2]

For individual sufferers, then, the experts' admitted lack of substantive knowledge about a condition they can more or less define but do little about would seem to make knowledge problematic. MS would thus seem to provide for a sociologist a salient occasion for looking at lay conceptions and use of a notion of 'science'. Drawing a parallel with Garfinkel's famous breaching experiments, where his students breached the taken-for-granted rules of ordinary behaviour in order to bring those rules into analytic visibility, I am regarding MS as itself a 'natural' breaching experiment which, by its violation of the expectations of lay people about what science is and can do, may bring to visibility what those expectations may be (Garfinkel, 1967).

Thus for this paper a fundamental question is whether, and if so in what ways and on what occasions, people speak of distinguishable categories of experts and expert knowledge. What counts for them *as* knowledge?

How can an examination of the data upon which this study is based, transcripts of informal interviews conducted with twelve people about their MS, bear on this question?

There is an irony for an analyst such as myself, whose theoretical auspices are an epistemological scepticism, in producing an analysis still based on data collected in the real world rather than on, say, imagined conversations between fictional characters.

One could of course side-step this irony by saying that I'm not claiming these data are really true, nor that the talk is evidence of what these people actually think; this analysis does not claim any special status in virtue of the data's relationship to a 'real' world. I am, I might say, simply conforming to the usual requirement to base analysis on data collected in the field, complying with that convention merely in order to remain within the discourse of sociology. There is no harm in going along with it.

But this 'instrumental' conformity has profound epistemological consequences. For the data are very seductive; they have the feel for both researchers and readers of the stuff of life. Before you know where you are they have convinced you that they *are* reality, reality captured, preserved outside the moment of its original existence for the remembrance of others who were not there. The people whose talk this is are so immediately recognizable as members, with us, of the everyday. They are describing a world we know to be like that. *Ergo*, the data not only are the reality of talk preserved on tape, but analysis based on them is about the world outside the talk.[3]

This conclusion is deeply ironic in that it itself exemplifies how we reflexively create reality from what we take to be the documents of it – and the talk of others is one such document.

But this irony is intrinsic: it cannot be expelled from analysis since it is itself the outcome of the very theorizing which has made it visible; it is rather a matter for rejoicing – even though how to express such rejoicing is tantalizingly unclear.

The traditional form of writing sociology makes invisible the role of the writer and the reader in creating a reading of a text; it displays what is written as if disconnected from the processes which made it possible. The form of writing itself creates what can be said.[4]

The people in this study knew they had MS.[5] In seeking to understand how they came to 'know' that fact, it is possible to discern what for them counted as definitive knowledge, and how and from what that was distinguished, and in this way begin to tackle the broader question of lay beliefs in science.

This paper focuses on those sections of the interviews concerned with the process of achieving a diagnosis of MS. The point of diagnosis is taken for analytic purposes to mark the achievement of correct knowledge, the taken-as-authoritative statement of 'what is wrong'.[6] What then counts, for the people in this study, as a correct diagnosis? How, and from what, is this distinguished? And what does this have to say about their belief in science?

The interviews were designed to explore what having MS meant to individuals, and to allow them to tell their stories in their own ways rather than in terms assumed relevant beforehand by the researcher (myself). To this end I did not compose a prior list of questions to be answered or topics to be covered. The interviews were so unstructured that they might be better characterized as 'conversations'.[7]

To suppose that each interview begins from the same point of 'strangeness' – in the Schutzian sense – for the interviewer is to ignore the existence of the researcher as a continuity behind and between each interview. Although the interview may have been the first occasion on which each interviewee represented their experience of MS in this particular form, the interviewer, me the researcher, is present in each of the interviews. Consequently, the interviewer is cumulatively learning what constitutes 'talking about MS' from one interview to the next, and is feeding that knowledge back into each subsequent one as the then taken-for-granted assumptions grounding *that* talk; and thus eliciting 'MS talk' whose appropriateness is self-confirmatory.

Although the interviews were designed to be unstructured, over the period of the interviewing the interviewer works with an increasingly narrow theorizing base, rather than with the presupposition-free situation I supposed I was providing each time for each of the participants.

If an interviewer could be the passive recorder of subjects' talk about MS (the objective interviewer *par excellence*) then this would not matter: but interviews, these conversations, are *inter*actions, mutually created by both speakers. What the interviewer already knows helps constitute what is said.

And yet to point out that this researcher's learning of the MS culture and her active participation in its creation as a phenomenon through the talk matters, is to imply that this is a distortion of some other, more pure, way of researching; is to suppose that there could be a collection of data that was unmediated.

nd Gilbert (1982b) found that when scientists talk about the
or of competing scientific findings, they employ a flexible
social and psychological mediating factors. These factors
are invoked to account for what are deemed to be errors, but they are
not invoked when referring to what is considered to be correct knowledge.
This asymmetrical accounting practice, Mulkay and Gilbert argue, allows
for and continually re-creates the traditional conceptualization of science
as a body of knowledge which arises rationally and objectively simply
from the unmediated discovery of the nature of the physical world.

Can the notion of asymmetrical accounting be used to discern what the
people in this study view as differential statuses of knowledge about their
condition? If this asymmetry should be found to be present, does it work
similarly to preserve people's faith in the truth and power of scientific
medicine; a faith which, from the long history of failure both in the case
of the disease in general and their own cases in particular, would seem
to be fundamentally undermined?

For an analyst seeking to discern the accounting practices of individuals which
may work to manage the challenge to their confidence in knowledge posed
by the phenomenon of MS, it is also an occasion for reflecting upon how
analysts settle these challenges for themselves. How is it possible for me, as
analyst, to account for how people accounted for their knowledge of their
condition?

Since this analysis is interested in lay beliefs in science, it begins by
looking at how the people in the study initially accounted for their going
to the doctor rather than anywhere else; for to ask the general question
presupposes that it is from doctors as experts that the most authoritative
knowledge is sought. The analysis then focuses on those sections of the
interviews which relate the process of discovery of the diagnosis of MS.
Examination of the data shows, however, that, by contrast with Mulkay
and Gilbert's simple dichotomy between correct and incorrect, people used
several distinguishable categories of incorrect and correct diagnoses. The
analysis is organized around these categories, viz: doctors' 'incorrect'
diagnoses; patients' incorrect diagnoses; patients' 'correct' diagnoses; and
doctors' correct diagnoses. The inverted commas are used as a textual
device to distinguish between what were deemed apparent and actual
instances of correct and incorrect. The paper concludes with a consideration of how the analysis of the data relates to the broader question of lay
beliefs in science.

Going to the Doctor/Alternative Medicine

Bearing in mind Mulkay and Gilbert's notion of asymmetrical accounting,
are there differences in how the patients accounted for their recourse to

medicine and to its alternatives? First, then, what was an interactionally sufficient way of introducing 'going to the doctor' as topic? The following extracts show how, typically, the topic was introduced.[8]

Daniel: [symptoms] and I didn't know what it was and the doctors . . . first I went to an eye doctor because that's what was worst affected.

Anne: This [symptoms] lasted, went on for about two or three weeks. I thought well I'd better go and see the doctor.

Des: but [symptoms] so I went to the doctor and I saw the elder statesman of the practice and he . . .

George: [symptoms] just didn't make sense to me and I went to the doctor you know and . . .

Each account comprises a list of 'signs of something wrong', immediately followed by 'the doctor' and what the doctor said or did. The decision to go to the doctor (rather than to anyone else) was simply reported. The reason lies implicit in the sequencing – first symptoms *so then* doctor. What is taken to be the most natural requires the least explication (Sacks, 1972).

The symptoms were the documents of an underlying reality, signs of 'something wrong', of an underlying reality whose nature was not known by the patient although its signs were discerned. The patients thus had knowledge of 'the facts' but not what the facts meant. It was because 'I didn't know what it was' (Daniel), and it 'just didn't make sense to me' (George) that makes the hearable implication, with what is spoken of next – 'the doctor' – that the doctor would obviously posssess the knowledge that they lacked (Woolgar, 1980). The interactionally adequate reasonable-ness of the related course of action – symptoms followed by going to the doctor – relies also on members' intersubjective knowledge of the relation between a conceptual category 'symptoms' and the category of person 'doctors' with whom it is natural to consult.

That one will inevitably have to discard the vast majority of the data so painstakingly collected is an admonition commonly proffered to neophyte sociological researchers.[9] The tapes used for this study consist of over twenty-five hours of talk. The quotations used here constitute only a minute fraction of that mass. The practice of selective quotation is one way of coping with such overabundance; and that selection is usually passed off as a solution to a merely technical problem.

Yet what does the practice of selection assume? First and crucially that an extract, a few lines *ex*-tracted from their original site in the whole talk, can be read independently of that context; and second that they can adequately 'stand for' a set of 'similar instances' in the whole corpus of data.

At one level this is sheer delusion, as known by all aficionados of playbills which so judiciously quote from press reviews. But even granted the faith of the reader that I have not practised quotation quite so creatively, the matter remains fundamentally problematic. For the in-principle indexicality of documents (here, extracts of talk) is (only?) managed in practice through reference to context; context and extract reflexively producing meaning through their juxtaposition (Garfinkel, 1967). Extracts divorced from the contexts in which they originated and inserted into another – the context of my analysis – would seem to be particularly vulnerable to a radical distortion of their original meaning.

But to make this objection is to propose that they have *an* original meaning which is fixable – even if fleetingly and reflexively-tied-to-context; that there is, potentially, a crucial difference in meaning between the same words in their original context and in another.

Taking each quotation from its original site in each person's whole talk and re-placing it together with others in a common context – the context of analyst's topic – facilitates the interpretation that the quotations are, singly and together, about the topic: going to the doctor, for example.

But the in-principle flexibility of reinterpretation is not unlimited. For it would be difficult to select just any quotation and, by the same process of recontextualization, make it work as relevant to *any* (analyst's) topic. For example the extract:

Meg: I do respond to cortisone very well so that I suppose my own sort of peculiar psychological defence is that every time I get it I'm going to have cortisone, I'm going to get better.

would not work as a convincing account of 'going to the doctor'. Why not?

One way for an analyst to discern what may be a noticeable absence (here the absence of reasons provided for going to the doctor) is through comparison with similar yet different instances. Patients referred in other parts of their talk to alternative medical practitioners, for example acupuncturists and faith healers. Was a different kind of account provided for going to these alternative resources?

The greater complexity of the accounting practices concerning recourse to 'alternative medicine' both requires and is demonstrated by the necessity for longer quotations from the data.

George: Someone said try faith healing, I tried him and he did nothing. Mind you I had no faith in anything before I went so you know...and basically being scientifically-minded myself, I think that's the way it's [a cure] going to come...I went to an acupuncturist, not an acupuncturist, a faith healer. He moved me around and asked me you know he sort of twisted me in various directions and said what was the major problem and I told him and he said, sounds to me like MS. *Oh*, he was the one, thinking back now...yeah I think in the meantime I had decided that's what I had.

AW: So you'd seen the television programme?

George: I'd seen the television programme, *then* I went to him and he really confirmed my beliefs.

Meg: From my own point of view the *most* difficult thing about having an illness like this is that everybody has a cure for you [. . .] all of which sound fine but if you, I mean if you can picture a situation where you've come out of hospital, you're feeling fairly shattered, you you're not you definitely don't feel as strong as you used to feel and you get this *barrage* of advice and you must try my osteopath, you must try my this and and [. . .] and 'a' you find it difficult to resist it but 'b', which is much worse, is that – now now whether this is sort of conjectural or whether this is true, but I was left feeling that if you don't do it, then it's your fault that you're so ill [*laughs*]. So I went through a stage where I just thought, well, I had nothing to lose...

AW: Mm and how did that end then?

Meg: Oh well because I was talking to my neurologist about it and I said that I found this quite a pressure and he said well fine, he said, well look, he said, if you come across a faith healer or a homeopath or anybody else who can cure this *please* ask them to get in touch with me because believe me, he said, I'll go along with *any*body who can cure you. And so then when people sort of wanted to do things I just ask them if they would mind talking to my neurologist, and that sort of stopped it all.

Meg provides an elaborate account for her resort to alternative medicine – the grounds of social pressure from others combined with her initial vulnerability to such pressures. By contrast, talking to her neurologist appears the normal thing to do and requires no explanation. By appealing to 'proper' medicine, she eventually managed to resist the pressure. Even though her neurologist was clearly prepared to listen to any genuine alternative ('*any*body who can cure you') Meg implied that the people who had pestered her were too afraid that their alternatives would not stand up to scientific scrutiny to take up his eminently open-minded offer. The implication is that should alternative medicine be endorsed by 'proper medical knowledge' then Meg, like her neurologist, would have accepted it; but it was unlikely. Real medicine is the natural and final arbiter.

The data also included an account of why an individual did *not* go to alternative medicine:

Daniel: Yes the whole thing with that [the 'laying on of hands'] is you believe in it. It may well have an effect for people who believe that whatever charlatan offers them something is going to work. Maybe it will. But since I think they're charlatans I'm not going to accept that they might work, and therefore they won't work for me. Which leaves me a rationalist loser in an irrational environment.

For both Daniel and George (quoted earlier), the efficacy of alternative medicine depends on a person's belief in its power. They both invoke 'science' as the reason for their own lack of such belief. George's comment suggests that being 'scientifically minded' is just one of his personal quirks, a personal rather than a universal faith. Certain treatments are not considered either credible or effective because they are grounded in an alternative knowledge (not-science). It is not that he regards science as an absolute truth about the world, just one that he happens to believe in. Daniel's comment allows for a similar interpretation: that his own belief in rationality (which I am conflating with science as a possible hearing) paradoxically excludes him from what could be, had he a belief in it, actually effective. Daniel spoke elsewhere of the power of illusion in western medicine:

AW: . . . I mean maybe that's got something to do with the expectations of people in the medical profession. . .
Daniel: Oh yes. . .
AW: . . . that we tend to believe that they can do miracles anyway.
Daniel: . . . and in some doctors it's certainly encouraged, that sort of witch-doctor attitude. Well. . . and again, the witch-doctor thing, the best doctor that I had any dealings with was the consultant in neurology at the UCH, a man called G, and he's a *real* witch-doctor man, full of shaman technique and so on, fostering the illusion that he actually *can* do something for you. Now is that really bad? Because as any witch-doctor will tell you, the illusion is all. And people are cured with illusions so. . .

This on the one hand implies a relativist view of medical knowledge rather than an absolute one; yet on the other, that unless the person has faith in the illusion – or rather sees it as real rather than as the illusion it really is – it is ineffective. So although there is an acknowledgement that knowledge is relative, that in principle there are many ways of knowing, the potential effectiveness of knowledge is made manifest only when the grounds for that knowledge in particular are also believed in – a belief that it is not possible to create at will.

We can see then that 'going to the doctor' is a course of action that is spoken of as simply arising from the fact of having symptoms; doctors were the obvious place to go for knowledge of what they signified, for expertise. By contrast, 'going to alternative medicine' was accounted for by the invocation of intervening factors – social pressures and temporary vulnerability. Although it was said that both alternative and scientific medicine required a person's faith in order for them to be effective, it must be noted that the necessity of having 'faith' in science was not invoked when people were speaking of the initial going to the doctor; only as part of accounting for their actions vis-a-vis medicine's alternatives.

None of the respondents claimed it would be sensible to have gone to alternative medicine to settle the matter of what was wrong with them.[10] Alternative medicine was portrayed only as a source of possible alternative treatment rather than of alternative diagnoses.

The distinctions between what was counted as medicine and what alternative medicine are themselves constituted through this analysis. That which is accounted for by the patients' invocation of the necessity of faith as a prior requisite for its effectiveness or by the invocation of intervening social or psychological factors is, by analyst's definition, what is countable *as* alternative medicine. That which is presented in the talk as requiring no elaboration beyond that implicit in the sequencing of symptoms-so-doctor becomes what alternative medicine is alternative to, viz. medicine. The possibility of distinguishing between two kinds of knowledge *and* the capabilities of those two kinds of knowledge are created by the process of this analysis: and demonstrated because they have been demonstrable.

At the same time, the grounds for the analyst's proposition of the possibility of there being two kinds of medicine relies on her member's knowledge of the possibility of this kind of distinction. She 'knows' that medicine means (in some sense unexplicated before the analysis but explicable through it) a coherent, identifiable, scientific body of knowledge and practices; and that there are alternative knowledges and practices which purport to be relevant to bodies and their illnesses but which are premissed on different, non-scientific, theoretical grounds. Thus the analysis and what is analysable – the phenomena of medicine and its alternatives – are reflexively bound together.

Doctors' 'Incorrect' Diagnoses

The fact of MS, taken as the fact of the matter, is for these people a fact only (and obviously) to be sought through doctors' knowledge. Given the exclusive power granted to scientific medicine to classify accurately what is wrong, how did patients account for the fact that they also said that their doctors had, in every case, initially made an 'incorrect' diagnosis?

Des: I saw the elder statesman of the practice and he diagnosed iron deficiency.
AW: Oh that's a good one! Southampton doctor was it?
Des: No it was a doctor up the road, Doctor G.
AW: So what did he give you for that?

Des: . . . I saw the other doctor, Doctor R, later on and he, he's got seventeen MS patients so he knows all about it.

Jane: . . . but they did lumbar punctures and tests like that and they were all clear, and they put it down to hysteria because [recounts her history of mental and physical stress at that time].

George: He [the doctor] said that probably I'd just overdone it you know, too much walking. But I'm not that sort of person that overdoes exercise and I I thought perhaps it was just me.

Although his first doctor made an 'incorrect' diagnosis, this was accounted for by Des by the fact that the doctor had lacked direct experience of MS. 'Lack of experience' works to limit the potential generalizability of this criticism of all doctors to just this one individual, Doctor G. With sufficient experience of MS (as 'Doctor R' had had) doctors were capable of knowing what was not iron deficiency. Doctor G's 'incorrect' diagnosis was not so much a mistake as a lack of relevant experience.

George also invoked experience as the grounds for his doctor's mistake, but in this case it was the doctor's insufficient experience of him, George, as a whole person in terms of his usual habits of physical activity. Since the doctor did not have (and could not have had, it is implied) this whole picture, he could not appreciate that the grounds for his diagnosis – 'over-doing things' – were unfounded. George recalled concluding that it was probably 'just him', which seems to mean that since his symptoms could not have been the result of over-exertion, and since the doctor had offered no other reason than that for them, they 'must' have been due not to disease but to some weakness in himself – somehow *he* had made a mistake. Significantly, the responsibility for the mistake comes to rest with him and not his doctor.

In Jane's case, the 'incorrect' diagnosis of hysteria was even less of a mistake on the doctor's part since, according to her account, given the symptoms she was displaying at that time, and her then recent history of stress, no doctor could have known that it was really MS. And 'the tests' (the lumbar puncture being a commonly used indicator of the condition) had in any case been done but had shown nothing. In the fullness of time, the doctors would know what had been wrong all along (as indeed had been proved to be the case three years later). Thus the diagnosis was not incorrect; but a reasonable conclusion given the circumstances.[11]

Accounting for 'incorrect' diagnoses, then, introduced intervening factors to do with deficiencies of a particular kind: an individual doctor's lack of direct experience of other cases of MS; insufficient (but understand-able) knowledge of the patient as an individual; the absence of unambiguous symptoms; an insufficient elapse of time for the disease to have developed clearly. These deficiencies are all presented as the upshot of mediating factors which (only temporarily) obscured the relation between the evidence and its true significance; they are not presented as grounds for regarding the misdiagnoses as really incorrect. And most critically, they are either deficiencies in the knowledge of specified individual doctors, or deficien-cies in the disease itself – in the sense of its notorious ambiguity. The mistakes are accounted for in a way that preserves the efficacy of doctors and medical knowledge in general.

The possibility of these diagnoses being erroneous comes from the knowledge that what was really wrong was MS, both at the time being recalled when the 'incorrect' diagnoses were being made and at the time of the interview. I selected these people for interview in the first place because they were 'people with MS'. Consequently their talk was understandable in terms of that basic fact. In the light of that knowledge, held by both of us, any other illness was known at the time of the interview not to have been the case. My response to Des, 'oh, that's a good one', speaks both to our knowledge that iron deficiency was not the correct diagnosis and to a wealth of other 'incorrect' diagnoses of which I had been told.

That there is 'something wrong'; that it is possible to 'know' what 'it' really is and therefore also that it is possible to be wrong about it, are all assumed unproblematically by both interviewer and interviewed – and now analyst. Arriving at a diagnosis comes off in this talk as a technical matter of, as in these extracts, achieving sufficiency of contextual knowledge to understand 'the facts' (the physical signs of something wrong) to make up for what was once lacking. The fact that, in the end, the right diagnosis was made provides, as a prefatory statement, for the possibility of this analysis which makes distinctions between 'incorrect' and incorrect, 'correct' and correct knowledge.

By means of their accounting practices, patients constituted doctors' mistaken diagnoses as not having been really incorrect. That category was reserved for patients' own attempts to find out what was wrong with them.

Patients' Incorrect Diagnoses

Daniel: I actually looked, somebody I've forgotten who, did it for me. It wasn't my wife, somebody else, read up something in a medical handbook thing. Some other mad disease. But I had a lot of the symptoms of it certainly and it was a very very nasty thing. And when I went to the doctors and asked if I had it they just laughed.

AW: Did they say/what you had then?

Daniel: /Yes they said stop reading those books!

George: I mean I hadn't gone into other illnesses at all. I hadn't even thought about. . .the only thing I'd heard before this, I mean I'd heard of MS, was muscular dystrophy and so I thought well, I wonder if it's muscular dystrophy. In my mind. . .

Meg: Oh no well I started off, I was absolutely I *knew* it was a brain tumour, I mean absolutely convinced.

AW: Yes, yes.

Meg: I was absolutely petrified. I mean I, and that sort of blocked everything else out because I was so sure I was going to have the, that awful brain scan they were going to say yes, it's a tumour, because because of the paralysis. . .

Each of the incorrect diagnoses mentioned here was of a disease which the person now viewed as worse than MS – a brain tumour, muscular dystrophy and even syphilis (extract not quoted)[12] – all frightening and terminal diseases.

Accounts of their own incorrect diagnoses were often produced in the context of speaking of their relief on eventually hearing from the doctor that it was MS that they had. Thus their own attempts at self-diagnoses acquired, from the context in which they were spoken of, a kind of added *frisson*, in that those imagined complaints had been more dire than the actual one – an exaggerated and now faintly silly over-dramatization of what was really wrong. By this contrast, medical knowledge gained both credibility and a kind of benignity, for its diagnostic pronouncements had always turned out to be more optimistic than those the patients had thought they could reach by themselves.

Although the sources from which patients had drawn their versions of what was wrong were still regarded as reliable – it was not that medical dictionaries contained untrue facts – they were acknowledged to be, in hindsight, an inadequate substitute for real medical knowledge. Medical knowledge was thus held to consist of something in addition to 'the facts', a something by definition not available to themselves as proven non-experts. Patients said they had sought the name of a disease which would explain the whole range of their symptoms, a disease of which their symptoms could be understood as sensible documents, based on their knowledge – crucially flawed as it had turned out – of physiology. It was the grounds which link facts and explanation together, the theories behind medicine that they had been unable to supply, and which had lead them, in spite of following the correct method, to draw their incorrect conclusions. The doctors' ability in the end to make the correct links – from the same facts – maintained and reinforced the patients' view of experts *qua* experts, and of themselves as mere amateurs.

George gave this version of ignorance an added twist. In our interview, he said he had very early on seen the letters 'DS' written on his physiotherapy card, but he had not understood that the initials stood for Disseminated Sclerosis (an earlier and now almost entirely superseded term for MS). Now, however, he could see that the true diagnosis had been available to him long before he had finally known that he had MS. This demonstrates that knowing also entails a prior understanding of what that knowledge could be – in order to recognize it *as* knowledge.

Arriving at the correct relationship between their symptoms and the disease of which they were the manifestation required, as the patients' accounts show, an underlying theoretical ground which would bind these two necessary but not sufficient elements of knowing. For the patients, though, there was in the end an independent external criterion by which to adjudge the accuracy of diagnostic attempts – the correct fact of MS.

There is no equivalent external criterion in sociology with the facticity of 'having MS' to settle the supremacy of one theory/account over another. Thus for me as analyst there is no way of knowing for sure whether the links made in analysis between the documents – the data – and the features noted in the analysis which have led the analyst to draw the conclusions she does, are correct.

It is possible to refute the contention that this is a handicap unique to sociological analysis. One way would be to argue that the 'disease MS' is not, actually, an external criterion independent of the discourse of its discovery but that it, too, is constituted by the discourse. The 'fact' that the symptoms and the disease, when matched by an expert, make sense is to say no more than that experts count these symptoms as indicating MS and that MS is the name given to that which is constituted by those symptoms. If these symptoms are not co-present then *ergo* it is not MS but something else. The certainty bestowed by the existence of an external criterion depends, according to this line of argument, on an externality which is in fact spurious. To argue this way would be then to say that medicine – one discipline within science – can really be no better than sociology at achieving certainty of knowledge. We appear to be less able to be certain only because science claims to be more so. Demonstrate that medicine is no more firmly grounded, and it will be stripped of its false facticity. A familiar argument.

But what about the current analysis? I am using patients' talk as raw data and, through the use of my expertise as analyst, demonstrating features not visible to the patients themselves, but claiming that they are features which the patients themselves rely on to produce their accounts. Only the analyst can 'see' what lies behind. I am implying, if not explicitly claiming, a special status for my own analysis.

But it is I who have proposed both that patients accord themselves lacking in the expertise necessary to do accurate diagnosis *and* that this 'expertise' is itself a closed reflexive loop. Both the analysis and that which is to be analysed are inescapably my creations through this text. Inescapable because there is no other way of writing. I have to speak for both the data and for myself.

Can I then also say that the patients themselves provide *their* raw data and their analysis of it? Is it possible to say anything? What cannot be said?

Patients' 'Correct' Diagnoses

Although, as I described earlier, patients admitted they had made mistakes, they did not portray themselves as altogether ignorant. They may have made incorrect diagnoses, but they were also capable of arriving at the 'correct' one by themselves.

George: I found out – I was watching a television programme and it wasn't a documentary or anything – and there was something on about MS in it and the, I thought these symptoms are very like mine. [Afterwards] in fact I went to a book, a medical dictionary, looked up to see what MS was and read all about it and thought that's me, definitely. So I went to my doctor and said have I got MS? And he said yes.

Meg: and the reason I switched to MS [as being what was wrong] was very simply I was on the private floor at the National and in the next ward was a woman with MS. And I wandered in to talk to her one day...and she started to tell me about her disease and I thought my god, that's what I've got. So that's why I asked her [Meg's GP] if I had MS.

John: I saw, one evening by chance I saw a programme on television and I saw these people I thought god, they look like *me*. And so it came to my mind that possibly I'd got this disease you see. So when I went to the hospital, confronted them with it, they said no, definitely not. They were really adamant about it in fact...This was about three years after I had had this lumbar puncture so they were adamant about it and I was, well what could I think other than the fact that it can't be then. And then after two years they decided that I might have it.

In these instances, the patients' source of knowledge was a direct comparison between themselves and people who they knew had MS. But these striking similarities were not thought sufficient to count as knowledge that they themselves had MS. They each went to their doctor for confirmation. In all three examples, the doctor's response was presented as an essential precondition of the factual status of their suppositions; the people themselves could only know the epistemological status of what they thought they knew by virtue of medical arbitration. John's account strengthens this point. He first accepted from the doctors that he had guessed wrongly; then subsequently that he might after all have been right all along. But this did not mean that the doctors had been wrong; merely 'wrong' (cf. previous section on doctors' 'incorrect' diagnoses).

There is, it should be noted, a striking contrast in the elaborate accounts people gave for how they themselves arrived at their 'correct' diagnoses and the verdicts the doctors produced: 'and he said yes' (George); 'they said no' (John); an asymmetry which works to bear witness to the stumbling and hesitant seeking after knowledge which was all that people themselves could manage in contrast to the precision of the doctor's verdict.

At one time I was very struck by a metaphoric resemblance between the idiosyncratic patterns of patients' figures of speech, the substance of their stories about their MS, and their personalities. I wondered if it would be possible to use such noticeable speech patterns as indicative evidence – good evidence because it was 'unintended witness' (Marwick, 1970) – of how each person dealt with their MS. The symmetry held convincingly in every case. For example, George's constant use of the phrase, 'you know' – appealing to a hearer's understanding and approval of his statements – tied in nicely with his readiness to admit his own misunderstanding of what his symptoms might indicate ('I thought it was just me') even when he had had clear evidence of what was really wrong with him (the 'DS' written on his medical card); and what seemed, throughout his talk, to be a particularly passive acceptance of his disease. I was able to produce for myself a highly detailed correspondence.

But now, given that my theoretical auspices have changed from an earlier 'interactionist' perspective (while I was collecting the data) to a concern with the 'methodological horrors' with which all knowing is ineluctably involved (the in-principle reflexivity, indexicality, inconcludeability and defeasibility of all statements) (Garfinkel, 1967; Woolgar, 1981), it is *obvious* that I would have noticed this symmetry. After all, I could find this symmetry *because* of the reflexive relationship between reality and what I took to be the documents of that reality. I was reading George's character from what he said, taking his talk as documentary evidence of what he, underlying those documents and giving rise to them, was like; understanding what he said in the light of what I deduced his character to be; noticing what was idiosyncratic about his talk *because* it expressed and revealed what he was. There were/are no independent criteria; they were/are all reflexively constituted by me as hearer/analyst.

The auspices for my theorizing when the symmetry first struck me, *and the different auspices for my theorizing now*, created both what was then and is now obviously discernible in the data.

My current theorizing auspices also provide grounds to account for the seductive quality of people's talk as data. Part of its immediately recognizable 'reality' is that we take talk to be the documents of the selves of others. The people talking on tape seem real because we are practised in the deduction of what people are from their talk. There may be other documents too – bodies, gestures, smells, textures – but no medium that is any more direct; no way unmediated. All we have to go on are the *documents* of selves – behind which to read the selves of others. And our own.[13]

Doctors' Correct Diagnoses

By comparison with the accounts of the other categories, the eventual achievement of the correct diagnosis is recounted as curiously matter of fact by those who at the time of the interviews were in possession of what they regarded as a definitive diagnosis of MS.[14] The *fact* of MS is as simply reported as 'going to the doctor' was in the first place.

George: So I went to my doctor and said have I got MS? And he said yes.

Bob: and so Professor F wasn't satisfied and he told me to come back in two days' time and see Doctor H and he diagnosed Disseminated Sclerosis.

Des: but I think he [his doctor] sussed what it was quite quickly . . . I think actually he told me on my birthday, what it was. We had to drag it out from the consultant at the hospital whose policy, both neurologists there, is not to tell the patients what they've got.

Anne: [I went to see] the doctor and he then arranged for me to go and see this consultant at UCH and by the time I got to see him, you know how long it takes to get an appointment, it [the symptoms] had gone. And he in fact diagnosed it then but he didn't tell me because you don't know whether it's going to come back again. And then about a couple of years later when I started getting symptoms and went back, and he told me.

However, crucial distinctions between 'doctors' (GPs) and consultants are being made here. The status of correct diagnosis was in every case in these accounts reserved for the pronouncements of specialists, made either face-to-face or conveyed via GPs to patients. The fact that the correct diagnosis was eventually made, and the facticity of what it was (MS) is merely reported, rather than 'justified'.

The only way in which 'consultants' are criticized is over the question of their telling or withholding the diagnosis from the patient: that is, not their knowledge per se but what they did about it; a criticism made of consultants not in terms of their expertise but *qua* persons.

How experts eventually decided that it was MS is not detailed here – but evidence of the expertise that decision involved is conveyed by recounting the length of time since the first symptoms; the different stages of hope and despair that had to be gone through; the visits to GPs, hospitals, etcetera. The sheer arduousness of the pursuit (which takes up long sections of the interview tapes) contrasts with the laconic reporting of the final verdict. The efforts of both patients and the medical profession also work to reaffirm that diagnosis is an expert skill.

These factors of time and effort are also involved in accounting for the *lack* of arrival at a diagnosis, so far, in two of the interviews.

John: [I have atypical symptoms] which has been a bit of a complex really, bit of a red herring to the hospital, what with having the polio of course [in childhood]: So they weren't quite sure what was the matter with me. It took them quite five or six years before they came to the conclusion that it might be MS because they can't find anything else. And in fact I still have to go back into hospital within a week or two for other tests. Although they confirmed it was MS, they still think there's an outside chance it may not be.

Meg: . . .and it's really only in the last, oh I should think in the last six months that I haven't cared that it doesn't have a name or that no one wants to give it a name or whatever, I mean because for me it just wasn't, it obviously *is* some sort of demyelination and I don't mind what they call it.

AW: So how do you feel about them not actually acknowledging that it is MS? I me-, are you a hundred per cent sure that it is?

Meg: No, no, because I think that MS has become 'how long is a piece of string' . . .

AW: Yeah.

Meg: . . .my own feeling is that in twenty years' time there won't be a diagnosis of MS – I mean I think it umbrellas a whole lot of things.

John's account provides for the reappraisal of the validity of the diagnosis by invoking his atypical symptoms and the confusing residues of his childhood polio. The doctors in any case, he said, had only concluded that it was MS, 'because they can't find anything else'; it was always a merely contingent diagnosis because of the intervening factors. So the reconsideration of his diagnosis due in a few weeks' time does not force him to characterize re-diagnosis as the correction of an error, a doctor's mistake, because 'they' had not been sure when they initially made it. Thus, this is not a questioning of a correct diagnosis: the epistemological validity of diagnosis is not undermined by his account, nor is the expertise of doctors. They had always known enough to know that they didn't know for sure.

Meg invokes the problem of taxonomy to account for her own case. She suspects that the term MS will be found to cover a number rather than a single condition. What the doctors had diagnosed – a 'demyelinating disease' – was both sensible and sufficient, and not incompatible with the possibility of it turning out in the end to have been MS all along whatever, she says, that means. Her scepticism thus addresses the question of redefinition of boundaries of what is to count as MS. She does not fundamentally question the basic conceptualization of the disease, nor the doctors' abilities to apply its taxonomy correctly.

These accounting practices portray what might seem to be a fundamental confusion on the part of doctors as merely the result of peculiar, non-typical circumstances in their own cases and of the long time period that has to elapse before certainty can be achieved. The doctors' not knowing becomes the result not of ignorance but another example of their expertise.

All the accounts concurred that the authoritative diagnosis of MS is merely the revelation of what truly is the matter. By means of their special expert abilities and knowledge, doctors are uniquely able to see clearly through the documents of appearance to what lies beneath – multiple sclerosis.

There are at least three ways in which MS is working as a prefatory statement here. First, the patients' accounts can be seen as pathing towards the known-at-the-time-of-the-talk-but-not-at-the-time-being-referred-to true fact of having MS (cf. Smith, 1978). The indexicality of what they say is contained by the eventual diagnosis, in the light of which everything else makes a particular sense and acquires a particular relevance from the tale of that pathing.

At the level of making sense during the interviews and on earlier re-hearings of the tapes, I as analyst knew I had made the same prefatory statement by my conducting the interviews with these people in particular, because I 'knew' them to have MS. Detailed attention to the data shows how much that could have been questioned on the grounds of its relevance to the story of having MS was passed over as interactionally, for the moment, adequate – because the talk, by definition, was 'about MS'.

At the level of this current analysis, the prefatory statement is available that this analysis is about people accounting for MS and for various versions of knowledge about what was wrong – in particular, knowing the diagnosis and differentiating it from guesses and mistakes.

This is additionally complicated by my references in the analysis to my recall of earlier, different, thoughts about this material; rememberings which cannot perhaps be 'counted' as themselves data for this paper because they were not recorded – a conventional prerequisite for what may be counted *as* data.[15]

And yet all that process too is an intrinsic component of how I am re-reading this material now; that and all my other knowledge about MS, medicine, sociology, research, the world and so forth – an inconcludeable list – and which are all unrecorded (invisible) yet constitutive grounds for my theorizing now.

All these levels reverberate together and are only arbitrarily distinguishable on the basis of chronology – this reading, my analysis, the conversations, the times the patients were recalling, and so on – for the purposes of this current writing.

Does this prefatory statement pre-empt or subsume all the others?

Belief in Science

But what of medicine beyond the point of diagnosis? There is no cure and precious little effective treatment available for MS.

Yet in the teeth of what their own experiences revealed to them of the inabilities of both doctors and medicine to grapple with their condition (even though, in the end, it had been named), the patients' talk retains a faith in a science which will save them. This is faith in a knowledge uncontaminated by the exigencies of the personalities of doctors or by mediating social factors: arising as a possibility through the apersonal, asocial power of pure scientific enquiry.

At least this was what I thought was in the data. Careful attention supplied something rather more complex.

AW: In terms of personal faith [I wondered] whether you have something like that that makes you able to understand or to put what's happened to you in a context beyond...
Anne: What, a religious context
AW: Well yes.
Anne: No I'm not a particularly religious person so I don't I put it much more on a sort of scientific than a religious.
AW: Yes I mean faith in a very general sort of belief system I mean really and I suppose you could say, the scientific way of looking at the world...is that your belief? Is that how...
Anne: I don't really know.
AW: I mean you feel it has um er a rational explanation, MS?
Anne: Yes.
AW: It's not random or...
Anne: At the moment it's pretty random, but I feel that ultimately the, it will be put on a much firmer scientific basis when more is known about the cause of it and how to combat it.

Meg: ...and I do respond to cortisone very well so that I suppose that my own sort of psychological defence is that every time I get ill I'm going to have cortisone, I'm going to get better and er that'll go on I suppose until they find a cure – is probably the way my mind thinks about it. I mean I've never thought it through but I suspect if I didn't respond to the cortisone I might feel quite differently.[16]

George: I'm reasonably optimistic, um not that I think they'll find a cure, I mean I'd like them to find a cure obviously but I don't think they'll find a cure but I do think they'll come up with something either to stop the progression of the illness or something in the next ten years or so. From what I've read, from what I've heard and the sort of general feeling, I mean, but you can't predict those sort of things, I mean I could be wrong, completely up the creek.

Daniel: I'm quite confident that medical science will...
AW: ...given more money, given more time and a few good ideas?
Daniel: Oh yes, they'll find it, they'll find it. I'm sure they will. But for example there was a doctor [that we met] by absolute chance. He worked for among other places the Bethesda Naval Hospital...
AW: Ah.[17]
Daniel: ...a big American and he was specialist in of all things MS...he later on in the evening said what er his research was based on and he said that well I don't think that er in our time – and he was fifty years old – we're likely

to see a discovering of what is the cause of it. Various possibilities but it's so difficult to work on because of the remissions and so on but anyway, he said, the most interesting one we're working on at the moment is this triact-something and I said what do you mean? And he said well your blood plasma...well he says we've had some striking results with that. Not yet, not that we could confidently suggest it for general use, but one of the problems is that our machine – and he *laughed* – blew up. One of the patients, killed him. Really, we can joke now. Well for the doctors it's a joke of course but for a hypothetical patient, not so funny. But anyway, as far as the MS is concerned yes I think MS, that medical science will...whether the atom bomb gets there first I don't know.

It is only Anne, herself a scientist, whose response expresses complete confidence in the power of science to cure MS – 'when more is known about the cause of it...'. For her it's just a matter of time. She appears not to register the possible relation between 'science' and 'belief'.

None of the others is so unequivocal. Meg refers to her expectation of a cure being found as part of her psychological defence against full recognition of her situation, made possible to sustain because medicine seems to be in control of her attacks. George's hopes are modest, for control rather than cure, but he simultaneously implies his own lack of qualification to make such a prediction ('I may be completely up the creek...'). Daniel's expectations of science are – with his story of the Bethesda experiment and his reference to the atom bomb – couched in the knowledge that what science can do may be too powerful: either at the expense of individuals or indeed of humanity.

Thus although they each declare a belief in the power of science, they also produce reasons why it may fail – but this is failure in the specific case of MS rather than an impotence of science per se. Yet the very faith they express in science they know is a faith grounded in their own hopes and their need to hope; and as such their predictions are biased by their desire for them to be true.

It is in this way that 'science' enters the epistemology of the everyday. It is according to science that subjective desires contaminate the development of pure knowledge. In the light of what they take to be an axiomatic dictum of science, people are unable to say for sure that science can save them.

Conclusion

These patients' accounts of the different categorizations into which knowledge may be divided are strikingly tautological. Beginning with the premiss that what is wrong with them is indeed MS, a knowledge which is the pronouncement of scientific medicine, any knowledge that resulted either in a different conclusion or that came from a different source was by definition either incorrect or required expert confirmation. Doctors were the natural people from whom to seek correct knowledge; knowledge had thereby been gained and ergo doctors had been the right resource from which to seek it.

What appeared prima facie to have been doctors' mistakes were accounted for as reasonable given the circumstances, and in any case were limited to failures of individual, specified doctors rather than doctors per se by the invocation of their inexperience of cases of MS, of patients as 'whole people' or of the atypicality or ambiguity of the presenting symptoms. The patients' own mistakes were a result of their own lack of knowledge – in particular their tendency to leap to conclusions because of their fundamental lack of the theoretical grounding which turns knowledge of individual facts into true knowledge. Doctors had been able, in the end, to deduce what was meant by those very same facts. The patients found it possible to make intelligent guesses, but in every case these needed expert confirmation before they could become accepted as the true fact of the matter. The experts were those who could make the correct diagnosis of MS – the 'specialists', the 'consultants' and those who could, as in the cases of Meg and John, knowledgeably state that they did not (yet) know what was wrong.

The axiomatic distinction between expertise and non-expertise enabled the maintenance of faith in a medical science disembodied as it were from both practitioners and its subjects. Their scepticism was confined to their own abilities to be expert, either about themselves or about what science could do. Although researchers could 'laugh' about the explosion of an experimental machine and be condemned, as persons, for so doing, the knowledge science was held capable of producing remained in these accounts both immune from mediating factors – and demonstrably potent. For science, and only science, had been able to describe 'what is', another case of MS.

But how has this analysis come to this conclusion?

The data I am using are part of a discourse about a disease, MS, but a discourse between lay people and a sociologist, myself, not between scientists or between scientists and researchers (as is more usual in the sociology of science).

A major interest in considering the data is, for me, how they can bear on researching the lay use of a concept of science. In looking for talk to use as data for that project, talk about science, how – since it is talk divorced from the persons and sites of scientific institutions – are certain sections of the talk discernible as being 'about' science? And what should that 'about' include – the methods, the data, the theories, the knowledge of science?

Although 'medical science' appears to feature strongly in the data, in the talk both of myself and the people with whom I was speaking – how can instances of it be picked out as being certain talk's topic without *pre*-supposing what is to count *as* 'talk about medical science'? Our talk seems to provide for a hearing that our topic is substantively about knowledge: what is known and by whom and from whom knowledge may be sought. One could say that all along we are displaying the project of research into MS.

The interviews were once criticized for my clearly not having known what to ask, the grounds for that 'knowing' being proposed as something *I should have already known*, given my training as a sociologist (my expertise): that is, the straight application of sociological interview methods to yet another topic – MS – would have told me what I needed, and ought, to have asked. That is to say, keep the form the same and the content will take care of itself. Indeed, keeping the form 'the same' *will* produce . . . another sociology of . . . To get away from the kind of product that is the result of the traditional forms involves paying attention to what form itself does: to the inherently reflexive relationship between form and content, theory and substance, method and findings.

The question of how it might be possible to escape from a priori assumptions about what medical science, multiple sclerosis are, is a question that requires an answer only if it is believed that such answers are both necessary and in-principle available. It is the pursuit of definitive answers that turns questions into problems. Questions though may also be an occasion not for angst, but for wonder.[18]

Notes

This chapter is a shortened and edited version of an earlier draft, first presented at the Discourse Analysis Workshop, Oxford Polytechnic in 1983, and subsequently at the George Sarton Centennial CC/EASST/SSSS Joint Conference, University of Ghent, Belgium, November 1984.

I am grateful to Ian Robinson, Director of the Brunel-ARMS Research unit, Department of Human Sciences, Brunel University, for permission to use the data; to the charity ARMS (Action for Research into Multiple Sclerosis), and to the people for their talk; to the members of the Discourse Analysis Workshops for their comments; to Steve Woolgar for his editorial advice and to Teri Walker.

1. In the research literature on MS, credit for the first detailed description of MS is usually given to Charcot (e.g. Charcot 1868, 1872, 1877). As is now familiar from the sociology of science, the history of 'the discovery' of MS is not a matter of simply tracing what happened. What has been claimed to be the first unwitting record of a case of MS comes in a diary, 'The Medical History of Augustus d'Este 1794–1848: By His Mother and Himself' (Firth, 1945, quoted in McAlpine et al., 1972).

2. 'For over a century, Multiple Sclerosis has intrigued workers in all the neural sciences, with perhaps more publications resulting than for any other neurological disorder. However we face today a situation little different from that of Charcot: it is still really a disease of unknown cause, inadequate treatment and unpredictable outcome' (Kurtzke, 1980: 170).

3. See Wynne (1987b) for a development of this observation.

4. There is a debt to be acknowledged here to readings of Barthes' *S/Z* (1975) and to Hofstadter's *Gödel, Escher, Bach* (1980). Cf. also Ashmore (1985); Mulkay (1985) and this volume.

5. To be more precise, two of the twelve people interviewed were relatives of people who had had MS and had died, and two at the time of interview had not been confirmed as having MS. The interview material from the former has been excluded here: the interview material from the latter has been used (and its status indicated in the text).

6. Cf. p. 120 and Note 10.

7. In the theoretical sense of Alan Dawe's (1978: 409) suggestion of, 'another metaphor for sociological analysis than that of science: the metaphor of the conversation'.

8. The names are changed.

9. An extrapolation from advice tendered to postgraduate research students in the Methodology Seminars of the Department of Human Sciences, Brunel University, and at the ESRC 'Post Graduate Summer School', University of Surrey, July 1983.

10. Although George had recalled that it was the faith healer who had told him he had MS, because, as will be seen below, he referred to his *doctor's* confirmation of the diagnosis as the end of his quest for knowing what was wrong, I am taking the status of the faith healer's knowledge as 'less than' that of the doctor even though 'greater than' George's own.

11. Cf. 'Discovering the Diagnosis of MS' (Brunel–ARMS Research Unit, 1983) for accounts of the distress sometimes caused by this not infrequent initial doctors' response to patients' presenting symptoms, interpreted sometimes by them as meaning their troubles were 'all in the mind'. There are three cases on record in the Unit where the early diagnosis of hysteria led to admission to psychiatric hospitals and in one case to electro-convulsive therapy. Whether these individuals would have regarded these as instances of 'incorrect' or incorrect diagnoses, and whether they would have accounted for them in a similar manner is a question that can only be raised here.

12. This person – Bob – had reported that he had understood his earliest symptoms – incontinence and blurred vision – to be connected with his practice of 'self-abuse' and somehow then with syphillis when an uncle, returning from the trenches in the First World War had told him of the lectures on VD given to the troops. This had prevented Bob from seeking treatment for twenty years, because he 'already knew' what was wrong.

13. Cf. Wynne (forthcoming) for a substantial redevelopment of this idea, in the light of literary theory.

14. See my brief discussion of the problem of diagnosis: also see Poser et al. (1984).

15. Cf. Wynne, 1987b.

16. The paradox of this knowing and not knowing between, as it were, the self speaking in the interview and the self being spoken of is pursued in Wynne (forthcoming).

17. The Clinical Epidemiology Branch, National Cancer Institute, Bethesda Naval Hospital was, I knew, one of the research bases for the highly cited series of epidemiological studies of MS which drew on the records of 5,305 veterans of the Second World War and the Korean Conflict (see for example, Kurtzke et al., 1979).

18. This is a reference to Alan Blum's paper on 'Theorizing': 'Theoretical life [to the Greeks] meant more than science because it was not conceived as arising from mere curiosity or from practical necessity, but out of wonder, as an attempt to escape from ignorance' (Blum, 1971: 303–4).

Cf. also Blum's later book of the same name (1974) in which he draws a fundamental distinction between the Aristotelian model of theorizing as a progression (through questions and answers) and the Platonic, for which the form is rather a continuous questioning of theorizing's own grounds (a form which Blum's own work exemplifies).

It is within this latter form of theorizing that the question of the writing-text-reading relationship and its implications for the discipline of sociology becomes increasingly central (Wynne, forthcoming; see also Ricoeur, 1981, 1984; de Man, 1979, 1983).

Reflexion on Wynne

Wynne's chapter experiments with a form of presentation to try to make visible, in the course of a text, some of the work (questions, doubts, anxieties) involved in producing that text. This work is usually concealed by standard empiricist forms of reportage or, at best, appears as a methodological appendix. These conventional approaches sustain and reinforce the notion that all such work is merely ancillary to the main business of reporting, and hence to the main news borne by the text. The text is organized so as to interweave the straight text and its alter ego. Does this amount to the use of a 'second voice device' as initially suggested by Woolgar and Ashmore? For one thing, the voices do not seem to talk to each other in the usual dialogic manner. We might be tempted to think of the 'second voice' as an 'intervention', but perhaps this results from our commitment to the idea that only 'the first voice' provides real news. The straight text clearly does not participate in a dialogue; at no point does it comment on the musings of 'second voice'. Notice also that, by contrast with what we shall see in Pinch and Pinch (Chapter 9), the 'voices' are not differently weighted in their typescript. All this suggests that these are better construed, not as 'two voices', but as one voice operating in two modes.

The organization of the text here addresses the challenge of making visible the work of the text without it appearing a mere distraction for the provision of news or an over-indulgent concern with technical difficulties of method. The tactic adopted by Wynne is to suggest an isomorphism between the work of producing a (mere?) text and the work of producing the world (in this case, that aspect of it known as MS). The suggestion is that issues in certainty, time, asymmetry of accounting for correct and incorrect versions, the influence of presuppositions and so on are all as much available in the diagnosis of a disease as they are in the diagnosis of the diagnosis. In this way, Wynne welcomes the self-referential character of analysis. The implication is that fundamental questions of epistemology can be addressed through bringing this isomorphism to observation, by way of realizing the similarity in one's own practices.

But does this isomorphism pre-exist its accounting? Are we suggesting that here (at last) is one aspect of reflexivity which enjoys an objective pre-existence? My answer is (again) no! Just as Wynne's reflective 'voice' constitutes its own troubles, so too this Reflexion produces 'isomorphism'. There is no alternative. What a text comprises is its commentary (use, reading). Which is why these Reflexions are so helpful in bringing to observation what the reader may have missed.

Reflexion on Mulkay

It clearly wasn't appropriate to offer a reflexion on Mulkay at the expected position, given his closing reference to 'the chapter which follows'. We have already asked whether or not Wynne's chapter meets the notion that 'the self-referential character of the sociological analysis of discourse is...to be welcomed and celebrated'. But in what sense does Mulkay's chapter re-present something we already know (cf. Walker, this volume)? A cursory reading of Mulkay (1985) tempts one to conclude that his chapter in this collection is remarkably similar to Chapter 4 of *The Word and the World*. But 'Mulkay of 1985' is clearly a different author from 'Mulkay of 1988'. This is evident both from a whole series of changes in 'extraneous' circumstances (too numerous to mention) and, more importantly, from changes in the text itself. Compare, for example, the Mulkay of 1985: 'I have tried to emphasize in this final section that the analysis presented in this chapter is self-referential and self-exemplifying.' (Mulkay, 1985: 154) with the later version: 'I have tried to emphasize in this final section that the analysis presented in this chapter is self-referential and self-exemplifying.' (Mulkay, this volume, pp. 99–100). The irony of the latter, the reappearance of the very same lexical sequence that appeared three years before, is wholly absent from the former. Indeed, the 1985 remark appears utterly flat-footed by comparison with the lyrical reference to its new setting, this volume, in 1988. It is, of course, one thing for the author merely to change his mind, but to do it by *retaining the very same form of words* is a major achievement. It is also apparent that the second text contains a subtle indictment of the earlier argument: whereas 'Mulkay of 1985' insists that his chapter can be read in any of three ways (the same as Collins [1981a]; the same but also different from Collins; and as fundamentally incompatible with Collins), 'Mulkay of 1988' rejects this simplistic conclusion. Instead, he now introduces a clever nine-fold option. For example, 'the same as Collins' (this volume, p. 98) alerts us to the way in which this is either the same as, or the same but also different from, or fundamentally incompatible with, 'the same as Collins' (Mulkay, 1985: 154). And so on.

But where do we now stand? Can we yet conclude on the nature and utility of different approaches to reflexivity? Although 'Mulkay of 1988' is a substantial improvement on 'Mulkay of 1985', and although Wynne has pointed the way towards constitutive reflexivity, are we still left with the feeling that reflexivity is just a distraction, or should we regard it as something to be welcomed and celebrated as in the chapter which follows?

7

The Life and Opinions of a Replication Claim: Reflexivity and Symmetry in the Sociology of Scientific Knowledge

Malcolm Ashmore

> When a scientific finding is said to be demonstrable by its
> replicability, this claim needs close analysis.
> (Collins, 1982c: 372)

Introductory Dialogue of the Replication Analysts

A: This chapter is part of a larger project [Ashmore, 1985] in which I attempt to use the resources of the sociology of scientific knowledge (SSK) to illuminate its practice. This project is predicated on the assumption that SSK can be profitably treated as a self-exemplifying discourse. Harry Collins, my partner in this dialogue and the main actor of this chapter, has suggested encouragingly that a major objective of a 'putative' sociology of SSK would be to provide an answer to the non-trivial and non-obvious question of whether it is possible to treat SSK in this way [Collins, 1981a: 216]. Of course, readers must judge the results for themselves, but...

C: Now hold on! You really shouldn't use this dialogic format as a justification for quoting out of context [Pinch and Pinch, this volume]. I certainly did not mean to imply in that flight of fancy that I was *recommending* the sociology of SSK as an interesting and worthwhile research project. I take it that we agree that any demonstration of self-exemplification requires that SSK's knowledge be treated in the same way as SSK treats scientific knowledge?

A: Certainly. And that's what I try to do in this chapter.

C: Well, I have stated in print that to treat sociological knowledge as being like scientific knowledge is an arbitrary, unnecessary and undesirable prescription [Collins and Pinch, 1982: 190]...

A: Naturally I entirely disagree with that.

C: ...and furthermore, I have also written that questions of sociological methodology and questions of the construction of natural scientific knowledge can be kept separate [Collins, 1982a: 142].

A: Yes, but then you go on to say, and I quote: 'The findings of the sociology of scientific knowledge *need*' – which you emphasize – '*need* only inform sociology when the attempt is made to justify certain sociological methods by reference to canonical versions of scientific method' (Collins, 1982a: 142)

C: So?

A: So! I am claiming that your own practice stands as a prime example of this very pathology!

C: You're missing the point. 'Here is a definitive statement that you can use if you wish:
It is clear that in some sense there is a contradiction between discussing the permeability of replicability in natural science and claiming replicability as a justification for my own claims. It is hardly a contradiction that I overlooked. One couldn't really miss it. On the contrary, in making such strong claims about the replicability of the replication studies I was trying to show in dramatic form that the permeability of replication does not mean that it is still not the only criterion of what is to count as a natural regularity (or social regularity). It is the only one we have' [Collins, Letter: March 1983].
(*Pause*)

C: Did you hear what I said?

A: Your treatment of replication in natural science depicts it as the most canonical element of scientific method and *your* method is designed to destroy its canonical status by irony. Fair enough. But then you 'change hats' and proceed non-ironically to (re-)claim the canonical status of replication *for the very studies that destroy it!* Surely, you must see that in a case of this sort the sociology of scientific knowledge may have a salutary effect, as your own conclusion puts it [Collins, 1982a: 142]. Don't you agree that in this case at least my reflexive approach is absolutely relevant, entirely necessary and totally desirable?
(*Pause*)

A: Did you hear what I said?

The Substance of the Claim

In this chapter I examine the credibility of a particular replication claim with the aid of a 'recognition schema' originally developed by H. M. Collins (1976, 1978b, 1985).[1] The reflexive interest of the exercise lies in the fact that the claim, made by Collins himself, is that his own original SSK studies of scientific replication in physics (1975) and parapsychology (1976) have themselves been replicated by other work: 'One of the most well *replicated* outcomes of [SSK] concerns the social negotiation of reproducibility' (Collins, 1982b: 304). The other work responsible for achieving this state of affairs includes the five papers in the special issue of *Social Studies of Science* (edited by Collins) entitled *Knowledge and Controversy: Studies in Modern Natural Science* (Collins, 1981b). As Collins puts it in his introduction, in these papers '. . . the socially-negotiated character of experimental replication is further documented' (1981c: 4). Collins repeats the claim in a recent review of his 'empirical programme of relativism': '. . . the sociology of scientific knowledge offers unusually good opportunities for replication. . . and much has been independently confirmed [such as] the replication studies (e.g. Collins 1981b)' (Collins, 1983a: 92, 108, n. 8).

The Meaning of the Claim:
Two Versions of Replication

In Collins's studies of, and writings on, scientific replication (1975, 1976, 1978a, 1978b, 1982c, 1984, 1985, 1987) he puts forward a version of replication in opposition to what he treats as the 'standard view' of the phenomenon. In this standard version, the reproducibility of scientists' findings is seen as the major epistemological guarantor of scientific validity while the institutionalization of replication as a behavioural norm acts as an effective mechanism of social control (Zuckerman, 1977). Collins's version, in contrast, treats replication as a problematic and complex phenomenon, the meaning of any particular instance of which is subject to social negotiation over the relevance of perceived similarities or differences between the events (e.g. experiments) concerned. As no two events can be totally identical, there is always a 'space' for this negotiation of sameness/difference. The success or lack of success of any replication claim can never, therefore, rest on the way the world is; rather it must rest on social agreement in the relevant community.[2]

As a starting point for our analysis of the status of Collins's replication claim, we need to understand which of these two versions of replication is implicated in the claim. Here is how Collins formulated and attended to this question in interview:[3]

C: Is your question this: you're asking me this: when I say that sociology – the replication studies have been replicated, do I mean that they have been replicated in the way that a scientist would say, 'this observation has been replicated', or do I mean that the replication studies are self-exemplifying?
A: Well, I wasn't going to ask you whether you thought they were [self-exemplifying] because I imagined you thought they weren't.
C: That's right.
A: Right. So it's in the first sense in the . . .
C: Yeah.
A: . . . sense of the scientist.
C: Yeah.
A: Um. I'm just wondering how, how you can live with those two things at the same . . .
C: Well, no problem at all. I just ban reflexivity![4]
A: [*Laughs*]

(HC 1509–14)

The consequence of banning reflexivity in this context is a principled refusal to connect claims *about* replication with claims *for* replication. In the following two quotations, the first from a general discussion of the sociology of scientific method and the second from a review of his own programme, Collins presents the standard view of replication in very similar and yet very different terms:

> The objectivity of science and its insulation from social and political biases are supposed to be ensured by... above all, the possibility of replication of... work by independent parties. (1981e: 7)

> Ultimately the argument for all these things rests... above all on independent replication of the findings. (1983a: 92)

In the first quotation, where the topic is *others'* scientific work, the standard view that quality is dependent 'above all' on independent replication is presented ironically (Woolgar, 1983); here, this is merely 'supposed to be' the case. In the second quotation, however, where the topic is the methods and findings of Collins's *own* work, this note of irony vanishes. When it comes to replication in *SSK*, Collins himself seems to be among those holding the 'widespread view that replicability is essential in science' (Collins, 1982c: 372) and among those who insist that replicability guarantees the validity of their own knowledge-claims.

The Schema of the Six Stages

Replication claims can be considered claims for the sameness of (at least two) sets of findings. As Collins tells us that the problem of sameness is 'the topic of the replication studies' (Collins, 1983a: 108), I shall use certain findings and methods of these studies in assessing the credibility of Collins's particular claim-for-sameness. The chief tool used for the analysis is an adaptation of a schema from Collins's study of replication in parapsychology that consists of 'a series of stages of demarcation [that] are generated... by asking how a series of replications might be recognised' (Collins, 1976: 4).

The warrant for using this schema outside its original application is given in the several invitations for comparative analysis in the article.[5] For instance, the schema 'might be suggestive in the analysis of areas of science not dealt with here' (Collins, 1976: 4) and 'comparative analysis of a similar type in other fields of science might be illuminating' (1976: 5). It could be objected that 'science' here is only meant to include the hard or physical or natural or experimental varieties. However, it would seem that sociology, at least, should not be excluded:

> *Belief* in replicability is of constitutively vital importance in science [which] is reflected in the theoretical and practical adherence to the criterion of replicability by those in less well established fields who wish to claim scientific legitimacy... (Collins, 1976: 2)

One such 'less well established' field would appear to be sociology as evidenced by the citation at this point of a paper about replication in sociology (Bell, 1974).

I also make some use of the idea, originally put forward in 'The Seven Sexes' (Collins, 1975) that it is in negotiations over what is to count as the set of competent experiments (or 'studies' – see Stage Two below) that the existence and characteristics of the phenomena with which they deal are established.

My strategy is as follows. First I set out an adapted version of the schema with appropriate alternatives to fit the sociological context. Then, sticking closely to Collins's analyses, I go through the stages showing in each case the difficulty of making an unambiguous decision about whether the candidate-replicators 'pass' on each criterion.

> Imagine there has been some...experiment E ['study' X] performed by scientist S [undertaken by researcher C] at time t. After time t the life of the world goes on, and is filled with multifarious activities. How can it be decided if some subset of those activities render E [X] a 'successfully replicated experiment ("study")?' Imagine a search is to be conducted through all the post-t activities in order to find a set of replications of E [X] and make the appropriate decision, and suppose that the procedure adopted is to remove from consideration all activities that could not count as replications of E [X] for one reason or another, so that in the end all that is left is a residue which consists of the appropriate set. A series of decisions would be required such as the following:
>
> *Stage 1* Reject all activities that are not to do with the phenomenon [under investigation i.e. replication].
>
> *Stage 2* From the remaining set of activities, reject all those which aren't experiments ['studies'].
>
> *Stage 3* From the set of experiments ['studies'], reject all those where the identity of the experimenter [researcher] is inappropriate.
>
> *Stage 4* From what remains reject all experiments ['studies'] that were not competent copies of E [X].
>
> *Stage 5* Divide the remaining set into those which generated negative results [produced different findings] and those which generated positive results [produced the same findings].
>
> *Stage 6* Decide whether E [X] has been replicated.[6]
>
> (Collins, 1976: 4–5; see also Collins, 1978b: 2–3, 1985: 38–9)

In what follows, Collins (1975) and (1976) play the role of the original study 'X'. (See Ashmore, 1985: fig. 2, for a quantitative justification for this selection.) The five contributions to *Knowledge and Controversy* (Collins, 1981a) play the candidate-replicators. These are (by) Travis (1981), Collins (1981d), Pickering (1981), Harvey (1981) and Pinch (1981).

Stage One: Do the Candidate-replicators deal with the Phenomenon of Replication?

A fundamental aspect of Collins's replication claim is his use of the term 'replication studies' to characterize the five candidate-replicators. This implies, of course, that replication is, at least in part, the topic of these studies. I have shown elsewhere that these studies, sometimes collectively and sometimes independently, have indeed been cited as such in the SSK literature (Ashmore, 1985: fig. 2).

However, as Collins (1981e) has argued, such consensual character-izations tend to be unstable in the 'core-set' itself. And indeed, in interview, Pinch claimed that only one of the five papers was a genuine replication study:

A: Harry [Collins] claims that the replication studies are mutually replicating.
P: Yeah, that's – there's only one of those isn't there? That's, uh, Dave Travis's.

(TP 0517–18)

Bibliographic services working on keyword classification would be likely to endorse this assessment. Travis's article is the only one, whether in the title or the abstract, that contains the word 'replication' – and what is more it occurs three times!

My own reading of the position is this: 'replication' is a central topic in Travis, a marginal topic in Collins and Pickering, a less-than-central but more-than-marginal topic in Harvey and a non-existent topic in Pinch. I say 'non-existent' with unusual confidence because in the solar-neutrino field (according to Pinch, 1981: 132), 'only one experiment has been completed so far'. I have been unable to invent a version of replication that fails to include at least two such events.

Now it might be argued that raising this question is merely splitting hairs on the grounds that the label 'replication studies' is really only meant to be a convenient shorthand method of collecting this particular set of writings and writers. However, Collins often wants to claim more than this. When we read (again) that 'One of the most well-*replicated* outcomes of [Collins's] programme is the social negotiation of reproducibility' (Collins, 1982b: 304) it is hard to avoid the impression that this is a claim for the existence of a (presumably fairly large – see Stage Six for a discussion of 'well replicated') number of studies, all of which demonstrate or find 'social negotiation of reproducibility'. That is, that there exists a set of *accurately described* replication studies.

Following the argument in Collins (1975), the question of whether the replication studies are accurately described or not is one of the issues that is settled (for all practical purposes) by the fate of the replication claim itself. Its acceptance, and thus its success, would entail membership of the set of 'studies of replication' for the five papers in question. (To my knowledge, Collins's claim has not been seriously contested. The question of the ambiguous role of the present chapter in this regard is dealt with later.)

Stage Two: Are the Candidate-replicators 'Studies'?

The quotation marks around the word 'study' designate the technical meaning of the word as used here: 'studies' are simply those pieces of sociological work that consist of empirical research. For sociology to be in *any* sense replicable it must be in *some* sense empirical. The task at this stage would thus appear to be fairly unproblematic: all we have to do is to distinguish empirical work from other kinds and to remove the latter from consideration. Work could thus be rejected if it were programmatic, theoretical, methodological, a review of the literature, a reply to criticism, a polemic and so on. Put simply, the difference appears to be between 'doing...sociology...as opposed to talking about it' (Collins, 1983a: 102). But what could be the criteria involved in such decisions? Any particular paper, whether based on empirical research or not, will tend to contain a measure of theoretical discussion, a review of the relevant literature and suggestions for further research. Demarcation based on the rejection of all candidate-'studies' that include elements of the non-empirical would reject virtually all sociological work.

The alternative decision – to reject candidate-'studies' if they contain *no* empirical element – might seem to be more productive. However, this procedure would rest on criteria for recognizing the empirical that are far from easy to apply (in theory). If 'empiricality' consists essentially of a method for going out and looking, it could be argued that *all* scholarly or academic work consists of some form of looking, if (merely) at documents. After all, this is what (perfectly respectable) historians do and according to some participants/commentators much historical work is considered constitutive of SSK (Shapin, 1982; Bloor, 1982).

If a strict distinction between work that is unequivocally empirical and work that is not may be difficult to justify, in SSK the distinction is regularly applied in practice. Mulkay, for instance, in a review of sociology of science in the West distinguishes 'work based upon close examination of original empirical material...in which particular aspects of knowledge production have been explored in depth [from] abstract discussions...or attempts to provide some...conceptual apparatus' (Mulkay, 1980: 81). Concluding this section of his review, Mulkay remarks that 'the relatively few empirical studies have taught us significantly more...than has the large body of general discussion' (Mulkay, 1980: 93).

This tendency to categorize writings as empirical or non-empirical is widespread in SSK participants' reviewing practices (Shapin, 1982; Collins, 1983a). It appears to be linked with and perhaps to be dependent upon an equally widespread evaluation of the 'empirical case study' as the ideal form of work. Pinch's comments in interview are typical:

P: I think it's very dangerous once you get away from empirical work because the whole, this whole field is characterized by good solid empirical work. A lot of people have done it and that's one of the things that made it a better field than most fields of sociology.

(TP 0816–19)

With such unanimity from practitioners I can only repeat that this agreement can have no unassailable formal grounds. Luckily, this kind of conclusion seems to constitute a general finding of SSK empirical work. (See, for example, Mulkay, 1980: 89.)

A second dimension of ambiguity at Stage Two concerns the appropriate 'size' of an experiment or a 'study'. In the case of parapsychology: 'Demarcation at this stage demands that an experiment be distinguished from, for instance, a preliminary observation' (Collins, 1976: 6).

A 'study', then, could be taken to be either a complete research project or any particular paper arising from it. Moreover, if a particular paper is concerned with only the early stages of a project it could be treated as analogous to a 'preliminary observation'. Such ambiguity seems to be evident in Collins's various comments on the candidate-replicators. In the replication claim from Collins (1983a), the items referred to were specific papers, i.e. those appearing in *Knowledge and Controversy*. However in his (1981e) 'Core-Set' article Collins refers to the same authors dealing with the same topics in terms of research projects. Although no specific replication claim is made in this article it is difficult to be sure whether Collins is claiming a replication of projects or a replication of papers. This ambiguity becomes relevant when one considers that moving from one position to the other could be significant in negotiations over the claim. For instance, if a critic were to point out that a paper that was claimed to be a replication study did not appear to deal with the topic of replication (see Stage One) the claimant could reply that the larger project, of which the paper was only a (perhaps preliminary) part did indeed deal with this topic.

Stage Three: Have the Candidate-replicators Appropriate Identities?

> [Researchers] might be 'inappropriate' because of the relationship they have with the original [researcher C]. Thus one might look at the relative value of [studies undertaken] by students of [C], members of the same group, known sympathisers, known sceptics and so on. It might be hypothesised that the greater the social and cognitive separation of [C] and a repeating [researcher], the greater the value of a positive replication, and vice versa. (Collins, 1976: 7)

This implies that: 'critics will question the outcome if most results come from one "socio-academic" camp' (Collins, 1978a: 391).

David Travis 'is a Research Fellow at the Polytechnic of North London. He is completing a thesis, begun at the University of Bath, on the "memory transfer" controversy' (Collins, 1981b: 32).[7]

> T: Harry gave a seminar [. . .] which was an early version of 'The Seven Sexes' paper and that was just sort of 'click' you know, 'bang, here we are.' And then I came to, you know, to do some research, wanting to do research in sociology of science, it was basically wanting to do the degree at Bath. Harry said, you know, 'stay at Bath'. That was how I came to it.
> (DT 1603–6)

T: When I first started out as a [graduate] student, I mean I was the first one to start anything that looked like Harry's research, and I chose the area because it was a scientific controversy and there were arguments about the facts of the matter.

(DT 0706–9)

Collins comments thus on the problem of student replications:

A single positive replication by an academic archenemy would provide more evidence, as far as neutral parties were concerned, than any number of replications by a proponent's own graduate students. (1978a: 391–2)

We would seem to have here an unproblematic case of a candidate-replicator with an 'inappropriate identity'. On the basis of Collins's own criteria, Travis appears far too close to '*C*' socio-cognitively speaking, to be able to play the role of an independent replicator to the satisfaction of a critic of the replication claim.

However, it could be argued that because Travis had ceased to be Collins's graduate student at the time of the production and publication of the specific *paper* that is the subject of Collins's replication claim, Travis's independence is thereby analytically increased. (An example of the use of Stage Two's project/paper argument.) But I think it doubtful that this would greatly deter a determined critic. Perhaps, then, an argument could be put forward stressing the simplistic nature of the supervisor–graduate student relationship implied in the independence criterion. However, despite the fact that Travis does sometimes claim to be 'doing something different' from Collins (see Stage Four), having experienced the difficulty of convincing people in SSK that my having been Mike Mulkay's graduate student does not make me a discourse analyst,[8] again I doubt that an argument on these lines would be very convincing to a critic.

Harry Collins 'is Lecturer in Sociology at the University of Bath and Convener of the Sociology of Science Study Group of the British Sociological Association. He is the author of a number of papers in the area of sociology of scientific knowledge, most using case material from physics and from parapsychology' (Collins, 1981b: 62).[9]

We would seem to have here an obvious example of 'the special case where the relationship of the replicating [researcher to *C*] is one of identity' (Collins, 1976: 7). In this case, presumably, independence from the originator is by definition zero. Alternatively, Collins comments that self-replication may be treated as a different kind of phenomenon altogether: 'critics do not count a series of positive results by the same [researcher] as a positive series of *replications*' (1976: 7).

Although the paper in question – 'Son of Seven Sexes: the Social Destruction of a Physical Phenomenon' (1981d) – is implicitly included in the replication claim, when Collins discusses its particular relationship to 'The Seven Sexes' his claims are of a different character. For instance: 'Collins's paper is a *development* of earlier work on replication in gravity-wave experiments. It deals with a more recent 'chronological cut' of material' (1981c: 5); 'as its title implies, it *builds directly* upon . . . "The Seven Sexes"' (1981d: 33); 'In this paper I *continue* the documentation of the history of the detection of gravitational radiation' (1981d: 34) (my emphases). In these comments Collins is treating both papers as two stages of the one project; in fact as a (two-element) series. In this case the *claimant himself* seems to be unwilling to count such a series as constituting a replication relationship.

The situation would appear to be this: either Collins is ruled out as a candidate-replicator because his relationship to the originator is rather too close or because he never claimed to be a candidate in the first place. Either way, it is clear that the schema, and especially the independence criterion, works efficiently for critical purposes.

Andrew Pickering 'is a Research Fellow at the University of Edinburgh [Science Studies Unit], where his current research concerns the development of elementary particle physics' (Collins, 1981b: 93).[10]

On the face of it, Pickering's independence would seem greater than, for instance, Travis's merely because he has always worked at a different institution than Collins. This impression is strengthened by his connection to the Science Studies Unit at Edinburgh. My 'SSK native competence' tells me that the Unit is the home of the Strong Programme and Interest Theory together with their various originators/perpetrators including Barnes and Bloor, both of whom Collins has criticized in print (anti-Barnes: Collins and Cox, 1976, 1977; anti-Bloor: Collins 1981a). More recently, however, Collins has depicted both 'Schools' – the Bath and the Edinburgh – as being defined by a common characteristic:

C: The crucial description that binds all this sort of work together is probably less 'relativism' and more 'symmetry' – and there I think we see exactly eye-to-eye.

(HC 2701–3)

What is more, the things that are different are unimportant: 'The differences are on small points of methodology and on minor philosophical issues' (Collins, 1983a: 108).

The following interview selections are concerned with how Pickering treats the relationships: Edinburgh/Bath and Pickering/Collins:

P: What people in Edinburgh are doing is, I suppose, what sociologists of science in general are doing; the relativist programme, if you like.
A: Right. Do you think there's a difference between what goes on at Edinburgh and what goes on at Bath?
P: Yes, in a way, I mean when you talk about Bath you think especially of Harry and Harry's work is single-mindedly devoted to . . . showing that any piece of

knowledge can be deconstructed. I guess up here we're more concerned with understanding how . . . pieces of knowledge actually do get put together [. . .] But I think basically we're all doing the same thing. I've never managed to have a proper argument with Harry about anything at all – I've often tried to. It usually ends up in just saying 'Yes, you're right.' [*Laughs*]

(AP 0211–0303)

P: I tried to express as clearly as I could what I felt to be the difference between my approach and Harry's, and Harry just said there's nothing to argue about. And I think we generally end up agreeing that what he wants to do is to show that all knowledge is deconstructible and what I want to do is to show how this is papered over in practice. So is it the same or is it different?

(AP 0809–13)

The last selection can be glossed as an agreement to differ. Such essentially ambiguous formulations can be used for critical or for friendly purposes simply by emphasizing one or other of the elements. For instance, for the purpose of supporting Collins's replication claim the element of difference should be emphasized in order to produce appropriate independence. Despite such subtleties, an informed critic would no doubt insist that Pickering is far from being an 'academic archenemy' or a 'known sceptic'; however, in interview Pickering states that he used to be highly sceptical of SSK ideas:

P: When I first came up here I was, well, completely against people like Kuhn. I thought his *Structure of Scientific Revolutions* was talking through the back of his head, and I was also extremely perplexed about Harry Collins's own work. I remember when I first went to Bath before I came here, he showed me a copy of 'The Seven Sexes' . . . I remember I asked him whether it was a joke . . . I thought I'd look at a couple of controversies just to see how I would make sense of them for myself. Yeah, and with the idea of probably refuting what Harry was saying. And, uh, the more I looked into it and the more I studied what Harry had written . . . in 'The Seven Sexes', I was – that was one of the things that started me agreeing with the whole programme of the sociology of knowledge, and I tended to agree with him.

(AP 0703–12)

Have we after all got a case of an appropriate replicator here? Someone who set out to 'probably refute' and after 'looking into it' and studying the original text, ended up 'agreeing with the whole programme'? Such a conclusion, a critic might argue, would depend on the *time* at which such a conversion took place. If Pickering was already converted by the time he wrote his contribution to *Knowledge and Controversy*, he would remain an inappropriate replicator. However, in the following interview extract, Pickering displays the essentially equivocal nature of such judgments:

P: I always saw all my work on theory development as being an argument against Harry. At that time I felt that I'd discovered something new [...] So at the time I would have said that, although Harry claimed that my monopole paper [1981] was like his work [1975, 1981d], I would claim that it wasn't [*Laughs*]...It proves that I reached the conclusions that I wanted to even though Harry claims that I agree with him.

A: Yes. Yes that's right, he does. So you're claiming that there's no way in which your work could be seen as a replication of the main [drift] of Harry's?

P: Well, I suppose if reflexivity is the topic of this conversation then I will have to say it can be glossed either way.

(AP 0715–808)

Exactly!

Bill Harvey 'is a lecturer at Napier College, Edinburgh where he is currently completing a sociological study of the quantum physics community, for which most of the research was done at the Science Studies Unit, University of Edinburgh' (Collins, 1981b: 130).[11]

Everything said about Edinburgh and the Unit in the Pickering section also applies here, of course. Harvey's move away from the Unit might well imply more independence from *that* institution but it says little about his independence from Collins. Here is Harvey on the latter relationship:

A: Do you ally yourself with...either the strong programme or the Edinburgh School? How do you sort of place yourself?

H: Well, I suppose if I had to align myself with a group it would be the Bath group, in so far as there is a Bath group, rather than with what's going on within the Unit.

(BH 1105–09)

H: It's possible to do the stuff that Collins does without having prior sociological theory, and really just by being hyper-critical of what people tell you the contingencies and so on, emerge. So that's why – if you like to think of a single paper that influenced me, it would be Collins' 'Seven Sexes' and I saw this could be done.

(BH 1117–202)

Here again then Harvey provides ample ammunition with which a critic may conclude that he has an inappropriate identity. Nevertheless, a 'friend of the replication claim' would be able to argue that his institutional remoteness from the originator counts considerably towards his independence as does the fact that he has never studied under, or worked with, Collins.

Trevor Pinch 'is a Research Fellow in the School of Humanities and Social Sciences, University of Bath. His specialist area is the sociology of scientific controversy. He...has collaborated with H. M. Collins on research in the sociology of parapsychology. He is currently completing a sociological study of the development of solar-neutrino astronomy. He is the co-author (with H. M. Collins) of *Frames of Meaning: The*

Social Construction of Extraordinary Science' (Collins, 1981b: 158).[12]

After graduating in physics, Pinch did a Masters degree in the sociology of science at Manchester:

> *P:* When I used to work in Manchester, I used to find out all these things about this controversy [see Pinch, 1977] and it seemed really exciting. Um, you know, lots of things in the sociology of science, scientific knowledge which were then – the ideas were just up for grabs, were star[ting], star[ting] – actually appeared to be true. You could, you know, you could see scientists actually fighting over technical arguments and – because at that stage I still had a lingering, like most people in this area at first, sort of Lakatosian methodology [. . .] And I think Andy Pickering was the same [. . .] I stood out for scientific rationality against relativism for quite a long while. Um. But eventually Lakatos went by the board.
>
> (TP 0101–10)

Interrupted Dialogue – Concerning Symmetry – Between a Friend and a Critic

Friend of the Replication Claim: Aha! It looks as if Pinch might be an appropriate replicator. We seem to have evidence here of the same kind of 'conversion' as Pickering underwent. Pinch's mention of Pickering in this context is definitely significant.

Critic of the Replication Claim: I don't think that kind of consideration can outweigh the extremely close socio-cognitive relationship between Pinch and Collins. And besides, the conversion factor is only significant for your position if the timing is right. I think we had better hear some more.

Then Pinch went to Bath as research officer on the 'spoon-bending' project, directed by Collins, that resulted in the joint-authored *Frames of Meaning* (Collins and Pinch, 1982):

> *P:* By the time I finished the research I agreed entirely with Harry that this was the best approach. Um, and I wouldn't distance myself from Harry at that stage on any issues at all. I think we saw eye to eye on most things in the field.
>
> (TP 0712–14)

Critic: There you are! What did I tell you! You can't get a much clearer statement than that!

Friend: Aren't you being a bit premature? I thought you said that timing was everything. The period Pinch is discussing in this extract is prior to his research on solar neutrinos which is the topic of the paper in question. I think we had better hear some more.

After this Pinch carried out research for a PhD supervised by Collins. His paper in *Knowledge and Controversy* – 'The Sun-Set' (Pinch, 1981) – is a report from that research:

> *P:* Now, in my PhD I take that second stage [of the empirical programme of relativism] I think further than Harry would like in the sense that I actually

use interests models to explain what went on in the solar neutrino field [. . .]
So I am separated from Harry in the sense that I'm pushing for interests
models and Harry doesn't have any interest himself in interests models.

(TP 0808–14)

Friend: You see! At the relevant time, Pinch has retreated from his earlier total
agreement with Collins and is evidently at serious odds with him on the crucial
question of methodology.

Critic: I'm afraid you are reading far too much into this 'small point of
methodology' as Collins [1983a: 108] himself describes his differences with
the Edinburgh 'interests' theorists. And at the time, remember, Pinch was
Collins's graduate student. Such a relationship plays havoc with a candidate-
replicator's independence, as we know. But maybe our Author has some more
evidence, though I cannot believe it will help your case very much.

P: I mean for me, I was originally a physicist and actually find the thing about
actually studying science of interest and I don't think Harry – for Harry
science is, it doesn't really matter that much.

(TP 0906–7)

Friend: Your confidence is obviously unjustified. Here, Pinch is expressing a
major disagreement with Collins about the entire rationale of the whole
enterprise.

Critic: You're wrong in two important ways. First, this kind of disagreement
is unimportant on a practical level: the programme is pursued regardless.
Secondly, I have reason to believe that Pinch has simply misunderstood Collins's
actual opinion on this one. Author, if you would oblige us with a quote from
Collins's interview?

C: I happen to find physics the most interesting of the sciences and I'm bound
to like researching on it.

(HC 0208)

Critic: I think that's conclusive.

Friend: You are mistaken. The point is not the relative intrinsic interest of
particular sciences; it is, as I have said, the *aim* of the work that is at issue
here. Author, another quote from Collins, if you will.

Relativists typically choose to study science only because it is generally counted
as the canonical example of knowledge, or because it is a readily accessible
knowledge-producing institution [. . .] The relativists' *constitutive* question
is. . .about knowledge in general, not about scientific knowledge in particular.
(1982b: 300)

Friend: It would seem that Pinch is not a 'typical relativist' after all. One to
me, I think!

Critic: I think not. Why not let our candidate speak for himself?

P: I think, you know, it's like natural scientists, I think to a large extent I'm
working within a research programme, a relativist programme that's been
mapped out in Harry's empirical programme of relativism. . .

Critic: I rest my case.

Friend: I hadn't expected dishonesty from you, or collusion from our Author,
come to that. There's more to come, obviously: notice the three little dots and
the absence of any reference? So if we could continue. . .

> . . .and I've got a few quibbles with that but roughly it says – if you want
> to know what my quibbles are you should photocopy the first chapter of
> my PhD. . .It sets out what, where I disagree with Harry's programme. . .

Friend: . . .we can see that disagreement is still rife.

Critic: You must be really desperate to insist on displaying an extract that explicitly refers to 'a few quibbles'. A quibble is just a quibble, and should be of no concern in such a learned disputation as this. If this is the best you can do, even with the obvious assistance of our Author who quite clearly is on *your* side – notice how he cuts it off immediately after the relatively strong 'disagree' phrase – well, I think you should admit that you're beaten. I must insist that our corrupt Author finally completes this extract.

> . . .and it says at the start I'm doing essentially a piece of normal relativism
> and there's no need to get into the philosophical issues again, so I'm not
> going to defend relativism, I'm just going to go on ahead and do empirical
> studies and that they'll stand or fall on the empirical work, whether it's
> telling us anything interesting about science.

> (TP 2312–402)

Critic: I was right! This is the kind of thing Collins says all the time.[13] And I was right about our so-called Author too. His feeble attempt to withhold such a damning piece of evidence for Pinch's lack of independence is contemptible!

Friend: On the contrary, he has in fact been biased in your favour throughout Stage Three. If another Friend [?] hadn't interceded on behalf of justice and symmetry and persuaded our Author to revise his first draft of this chapter, we wouldn't have had our say.

Critic: *You* wouldn't, you mean.

Friend: Exactly! This section on Pinch might well have consisted in its entirety of the following kind of asymmetrical comment which is typical of that first draft:

> Documentation of agreements, relationships or even 'quibbles' with Collins
> seem quite unnecessary for a candidate whose socio-cognitive distance from
> the originator is clearly so small; indeed the smallest of all, with the exception
> of Collins himself. (Ashmore, 1983: 39)

Critic: Well, what's wrong with that? I can't fault it and I don't see how Collins can either. After all, it seems to follow as a straightforward application of his own analytic apparatus. Is it our Author's fault if Collins is hoist with his own petard? Surely not; any more than it is if our Author's original conclusion happened to coincide with my own. He should have had the courage of his convictions. He should have stuck to his guns. And then, at least he could have kept it short!

Friend: That last remark is about the only thing we seem to be able to agree on! But Ashmore certainly could not have retained his original reference to horse racing. . .

Critic: Horse racing?

Friend: Yes. In his first version he wrote this as his conclusion to Stage Three:

> There is a sense in which the Schema is like a steeple-chase with each Stage
> as a fence. . .all our candidate-replicators. . .appear to have fallen

at the third (with the possible exception of Pickering, who might, or might not, have picked himself up and Collins who might have refused!). (Ashmore, 1983: 39)

Now, this is simply the wrong approach. 'The point of the whole schema is never to say who has passed through each stage but to show that there is ambiguity in deciding who has got through each stage. The main point is to show that it is not possible to come to an unambiguous conclusion about whether [X] has been replicated at time *t*, *not* to provide an algorithm for reaching that conclusion! The horse race, therefore, has different outcomes for different people. Everyone will claim that it is they who have won the money.'[14]

Critic: That speech sounds terribly like Collins. I realize, of course, that you support his replication claim on the participant level, but surely it is unjustified to enrol his particular *analytic* position on your side.

Friend: But by its very nature, relativist analysis is *symmetrical* and therefore does not 'take sides' in the controversies it examines. Its whole point is to be disinterested and neutral in such disputes. The distinctly *non*-relativist analysis of our Author's earlier draft, on the other hand, clearly did come down on one side: the side of the Critic.

Critic: But that wasn't a matter of taking sides. That was a coincidental outcome of using the form of analysis recommended *by* the originator *on* the originator. Ironic, no doubt, but hardly biased. Your analytical recommendations, however, clearly let Collins off the hook. No wonder you are so keen on them.

If I might interrupt this dialogue, I may be able to settle this dispute. The problem here seems to revolve around the ambiguous status of the schema itself which is at once an external-analysts' resource for SSK research and an internal-participants' resource in controversies over replication. Now, in this dispute between the Friend and the Critic both of the protagonists clearly *recognize* this ambiguity and both of them equally clearly *deplore* it. The consequence is that they each accuse me of being on the other's side (i.e. of using the schema as a participants' resource) while recommending as the alternative that I should (and therefore could) remain neutral by using the schema only as a pure analysts' resource. Thus, the Friend sees the old Stage Three (Ashmore, 1983) as illegitimately biased towards the Critic and assumes that the new version has solved the problem of bias altogether. And the Critic sees the new Stage Three as taking sides with the Friend's position and thus recommends a return to the old unbiased version.

In his commentary on Ashmore (1983), Collins writes:

My hypotheses about who is inappropriate as a replicator give a *possible* set of criteria but not a definitive set. My hypotheses would probably be argued as necessary by a critic but not by the originator. Thus, if I put on my non-reflexive hat again, I would say that all the replicators are appropriate. (Letter, March 1983)

It seems to me that Collins here admits that his 'hypotheses' are not neutral and, moreover, that they can be appropriated, as we have seen in the

Dialogue, *only* by the Critic. The originator (and the Friend) can have no use for them. They would have to invent a different set of 'criteria of researcher-appropriateness'[15]; or at least they would have to show how, in this particular case, Collins's 'hypotheses' are inappropriate. This has been attempted (on their behalf) in this present version in the discussion of the contingent nature of student replications (Travis), the ambiguity of self-replication (Collins), the problematic timing of conversions (Pickering), the uncertainties of indirect influence (Harvey), and in the hardest case of all (Pinch) the nuances of agreement. Thus I have tried here, as I should, to 'gloss it either way'. *But*, and this is what the Dialogue and this present commentary have been about, such an analytic procedure does *not* result in a symmetrical text, but only (in this case at least) in a Friend-lier one.

Stage Four: Are the Candidate-replicators Competent Copies of (*X*)?

We are concerned at this stage with the question of the similarity/difference of the candidates' *research areas* and *methods* with respect to those of the originals. However, addressing this question is only a preliminary exercise; decisions about whether the candidates are competent copies involve assessing in what way particular degrees of similarity or difference affect the candidates' 'consensus forming value' (Collins, 1978a). It is clear, as Collins (1976: 8) notes, that this stage 'involves the most complex web of arbitration'. Unfortunately, I have no space to do more than sketch some of the strands of the web.

Triangulation and generality arguments suggest that when a researcher sets out to confirm previous work too much similarity in methodology ('copy-catting') or in research area (re-researching) may be of little value. The credibility of the phenomenon under investigation is enhanced in such cases by demonstrating its existence with different methods (triangulation) and/or in a different area of research (generality). Moreover, the value to the secondary researcher of exact repetition (or 'mere replicaton') is also low because originality is difficult to attribute to such work (Mulkay, 1985; Mulkay and Gilbert, 1984). Consequently, secondary researchers will attempt to avoid their own work being labelled 'mere replication' (Ashmore, 1985: 257–9).

In keeping with these considerations, none of the candidate-replicators claims to have engaged in exact repetition of the original replication studies. For most of the candidates, the absence of any such claim may be simply due to the absence of any such intention (see Stage Three). Travis, however, would appear to be a bona fide intentional replicator. After all, the title of his paper is 'Replicating Replication?' and Collins (1981c: 4) describes it as 'in the main, a replication of earlier work on replication!' [16] However, Travis's own characterization of the relationship between his paper and 'The Seven Sexes' is in much looser terms: 'the perspective on the replication of experiments which informs...this discussion...is taken from a paper by Collins (1975)' (Travis, 1981: 12). Asked in interview whether he had intended to replicate Collins's original studies, Travis replied that as his chosen area of research involved controversies over replication

T: ...in that sense, yes it was a replication of Harry's study but only in the very loose sense of which 'The Seven Sexes' probably was a kind of examplar. I wasn't going out and replicating it in any *strict* sense because it was a different area of science, but obviously it was very much in that kind of line.

(DT 0714–16)

So for Travis, 'strict' replication involves the kind of exact copying which by definition cannot take place in a 'different area of science'. 'Loose' replication on the other hand seems to involve characterizations of the original as an 'informing perspective', a 'kind of exemplar', or a 'kind of line'. In the conclusion to his paper Travis details the ways in which his research area differs from the gravitational radiation field examined in Collins (1975). After glossing the findings of his study – which he claims are 'in effect' the same as those of 'The Seven Sexes' – he writes:

These similarities with Collins' study have been found in a field which differs from gravitational radiation in a number of ways. 1. ...it is a quite different area of science. 2. Worm running experiments are vastly less expensive. 3. ...there were only some half-dozen experiments in gravitational radiation whereas [in worm running there were] at least ten times as many studies. 4. ...learning in planarians, though rejected in the early stages is now virtually accepted knowledge. 5. [In the worm running field] some actors were explicitly conscious...of the ambiguity of the notion of replication. (Travis, 1981: 26) (my numbering)

This elucidation of five distinctive differences in research area can be seen to serve the rhetorical purpose of making the claimed-sameness of the findings more significant; the passage is saying: *In spite of* all these differences the same processes (as described in the findings) are at work. Thus, by a display of generality the credibility of the knowledge claim is increased.

In a general discussion of the prospects for replication in SSK Collins endorses this view and even incorporates it into another expression of his replication claim:

Of course, any sociologist who wants to replicate previous work must develop *the same native competencies* as the original investigator. (Of course it will be unusual for *the very same passage of scientific activity* to be researched in this degree of detail by any two researchers. But, there is no need for *the same area* to be looked at in order that confirmatory findings be generated.

Findings ought to be expressed at a level of generality such that research on *similar passages of scientific activity* can confirm them – this has been the case with the 'replication studies'). (Collins, 1983a: 92–3) (my emphases)

While Collins seems to be more than content to invoke the generality argument here, he does not make use of the formally similar triangulation argument. Differences in method, that is, the non-development of the same native competencies appear to be entirely credibility-detracting to this originator.

In a recent reply to a critic, Collins's interpretative methods seem to fit his own analysis of the strategy of an originator faced with the challenge of a negative replication. This analysis, suitably modified, is as follows:

[Researchers] who claim to find effects will not accept negative results arising out of [studies] which were not 'identical' to their own. Non-identity may be claimed by questioning the 'competence' of secondary [researchers] or pointing out technical differences between a primary [study] and the others. (Collins, 1976: 9)

The criticism (Gieryn, 1982) to which Collins responds is of Collins's originality-claim rather than his replication-claim. It takes the form of an accusation of 'redundance' (mere replication) and in so doing utilizes a triangulation argument to account for the production of similar findings from different methods:

The relativist/constructivist programme[17] is neither new nor preferable to other theoretical orientations in the sociology of science. Its empirical conclusions are consistent with, and occasionally anticipated by, at least one voice from the past (Merton) [. . .] More importantly, the distinctive epistemological premises and methodological imperatives of the . . . programme are not essential to reach these empirical conclusions. (Gieryn, 1982: 292–3)

In response to this charge of mere replication, Collins's strategy is rhetorically to increase the distance between Mertonian research and relativist research. To do this he first selects a particular paper for a Mertonian exemplar. Then he contrasts its findings with relativist findings on the same topic. Thirdly, he argues that the Mertonian conclusions are not only entirely different but are also wrong. Finally he offers an explanation, in terms of a lack of competence, to account for their inadequacy. By these means he not only rebuts Gieryn's charge of redundance; but more importantly, in establishing the 'non-identity' of the Mertonian exemplar in this way, Collins is also rejecting an implied negative replication of his own work. This is because his chosen exemplar is a Mertonian study of *replication*, namely Zuckerman's (1977) 'Deviant Behavior and Social Control in Science'. The following extract from Collins's reply to Gieryn starts with a quote from Zuckerman's paper:

'In science, the institutionalized requirement that new contributions be reproducible is the cornerstone of the system of social control [. . .] The requirement of reproducibility. . .serves not only to deter departures from cognitive and moral norms but also makes for the detection of error and deviance.'
. . .it is the epistemology – the reproducibility of scientific contributions – that is supposed to be the very *cornerstone* of the norms. Seeing this, it is quite remarkable that Gieryn should say that the norms precipitate views about science which are similar to those which emerge out of the relativist programme. One of the most well *replicated* outcomes of that programme concerns the social negotiation of reproducibility. One thing that the programme has shown above all, is that reproducibility is not the 'epistemologists' stone', nor the Mertonian's cornerstone. A more marked difference in two programmes would be hard to find. (Collins, 1982b: 304)

To Gieryn, Collins is saying, How when we are clearly so different can you possibly maintain we are the same? To Zuckerman he is saying, We differ; the difference is that I am right, as evidenced by my findings being 'well replicated' and you are wrong, as evidenced by what these same right-because-replicated findings say, that is 'reproducibility is not. . .the Mertonian's cornerstone.' Collins's next step is to address the problem of *how* Zuckerman came to be so wrong. In other words, what is responsible for her 'non-competence'?

It is a question of the integrity of one's approach to the data of science and the vigour with which sociological analysis should be pursued [. . .] It seems likely that Merton and Zuckerman find themselves making their sort of references to reproducibility as an unproblematic mechanism of social control precisely because of the common-sense interpretation of science that underlies their outlook [. . .] appropriate vigour requires. . .that [reproducibility] be seen as problematic. . .(Collins, 1982b: 304)

Having established the source of Zuckerman's negative result – the non-competence of 'analytical lethargy' brought on by an overly commonsensical attitude to science – Collins has effectively achieved a state of non-identity between Zuckerman's paper and his own replication studies. This state is expressed in practice as distinctive 'schools' or 'programmes' that are incommensurable: 'Through their *practice* it is easy to see that the differences in origin, focus and philosophy between the Mertonian school and the relativist school are not only apparent but real' (Collins, 1982b: 304).

Another way to appreciate this interpretation of Collins's argument is to compare it to his own prediction of how he would react to a claim for negative replication, as given in interview:

C: Anybody who goes and looks will see the same things; and if you find that they do that's really great and if you find that they don't then I'd be happy to say that they didn't look properly although I haven't actually come to that point yet, because nobody seems to have wanted to say the opposite yet when they've actually gone and looked.

(HC 1718–802)

Collins certainly seems to have been happy to say that Zuckerman 'didn't look properly'. However his perception of nobody, including Zuckerman, having yet 'wanted to say the opposite' is possibly more fundamental. It is easy to overlook work that *could* represent a (competitive) negative result, if it can be implicitly written off as non-identical.[18]

Stage Five: Have the Candidate-replicators the Same Findings as [X]?

In the present context, Collins's original distinction between positive and negative results (1976) can be reformulated in terms of the similarity/difference of the findings. In these terms, it can be seen that we are dealing here with a version of Collins's replication claim itself: in its essentials, the claim is precisely that the candidate-replicators have the same findings as the original studies. As an answer to this question is clearly dependent on answers at earlier stages – especially stages One and Four – readers may review the material presented there if they wish to come to either empirically-informed conclusion. It seems more in the spirit of the replication studies, however, to examine how any similarity-claim can credibly be made (and be made credible) given the 'obvious fact' of such differences as the use of different arrangements of varying words. How is it that the originals and the candidate-replicators can all be read as saying the same thing when, quite clearly, they do *not* say (exactly) the same thing? The answer, of course, is that common-sense–empirical differences are continually overruled in those efforts at sense-making which consist of methods for investing dissimilar entities with similar meanings.[19] Collins makes a similar point in 'The Seven Sexes' with the example of two 'heteromorphic' heat measuring activities:

> Dipping a glass tube filled with mercury into a liquid, and dipping two dissimilar metals linked by a voltmeter (a thermo-couple) into it, may be the same experiment – measuring the temperature of the liquid. In seeing these experiments as the same and competent many of the characteristics of heat are implied, for instance it is neither spontaneously generated by glass, nor say 'repelled by voltmeters'. (Collins, 1975: 216)

Collins calls this consequence of seeing things as the same, 'negotiating the character of phenomena'.

The phenomena we are concerned with here are the findings of the replication studies. Their character is, as I have interpreted and glossed it, the non-standard view of replication. How does it come about that I and other commentators have no difficulty in producing one such gloss for (all) the replication studies? Collins, in another passage from 'The Seven Sexes', maintains that such credible glosses become culturally available as a result of *successful replication claims*. (I have adapted the passage to suit the context.)

> When a [researcher] claims that [a study] has been properly replicated...he is claiming that all [studies] which are to be included in the set of competent [studies] settles [the gloss of the findings]. (Collins, 1975: 216)

It could be argued that it is a process of this kind that makes perceived differences in findings seem either major or minor. Collins, as we have seen, excludes Zuckerman's study from the 'set of competent studies'. As a result the perceived differences between Zuckerman's and Collins's findings are construed as extremely large; as 'not only apparent but real...differences in origin, focus and philosophy' (Collins, 1982b: 304). On the other hand, when commenting on a perceived difference between two of the *Knowledge and Controversy* papers, Collins writes:

> According to Harvey...experimental activity need not produce data to change the pre-existing plausibility of an idea; the activity itself is sufficient. This suggestion seems to contrast in an interesting way with Pickering's conclusions about the power of pre-existing theory. (Collins, 1981b: 6)

In this case, the difference is between two claimed *members* of 'the set of competent studies'. The interpretative task thus becomes one of not letting perceived differences count against that membership. This is done here by characterizing the difference in question as (merely) an 'interesting contrast'.[20]

Another way in which competent membership may be maintained in the face of perceived difference is to characterize all the work of the competent members as contributions to a coherent research programme with distinct phases. Collins's empirical programme of relativism has three such phases, the first being to show the potential local interpretative flexibility in science and the second being to show the mechanisms which *limit* this flexibility. Thus, for instance, Pickering's (1981) findings – which as we have seen at Stage Three, the author describes as 'an argument against Harry' – can be interpreted unproblematically as a contribution to a further stage of the same programme: potential contra-dictions are translated into extensions.

Another example of the utility of 'research programme construction' for dissolving problematic differences can be seen in an unprecedented 'Authors' Preface' (Collins et al., 1984) to a pair of papers in the November 1984 edition of *Social Studies of Science*. The papers are Shapin (1984a) and Pinch and Collins (1984). The Authors' Preface states that the '...papers were conceived and written independently: their focus on the relationship between language and knowledge, and their methodological orientations are similar, yet their findings are seemingly opposed.' A case then of topic-sameness, method-sameness but findings-difference. Is this a paradox, they ask themselves? Certainly not, they reply. Their 'seemingly opposed' findings are actually two aspects of the same thing. 'The two papers *exhibit different ways* of displaying private activity as a generator of collective property.' The task ahead is to discover more about this problematic phenomenon: '...this is a *research programme* rather than a paradox' (Collins et al., 1984: ii) (my emphases). Thus, we can understand the rhetoric of research programme construction as a form of 'difference-accounting' which projects current differences into the future as potentially solvable intra-paradigmatic puzzles (as Kuhn might say) in order to preserve the overall sameness of the programme and its competent membership.

We can see then that findings-sameness as well as topic-sameness, methods-sameness, and researcher-sameness is subject to interpretation and negotiation. This conclusion is, I claim, entirely consistent with the usual SSK gloss on the non-standard view of replication, as given here by Mulkay: 'The requirement of reproducibility is...the negotiated and contingent outcome of variable social processes' (Mulkay, 1980: 55).

Stage Six: Has [X] been replicated?

> It is...possible to argue about the required length of a series [of replications] for it to be taken as definitive...it must always be possible to ask that more [studies] be done, to 'make absolutely certain'. (Collins, 1976: 11)

The claim that the existence of a certain number of empirical studies makes the phenomenon in question 'trustworthy' is common. Unfortunately the desirable number is never specified. Researchers often use as a variant designed to express their modesty which goes something like this: 'Such results are, of course, only tentative. Much more research will have to be done before phenomenon Z can be considered to be established.' Reviewers and commentators use another variant, perhaps to justify their particular selections. For example, from Mulkay's discussion of SSK work on replication we read: 'I do not intend to suggest that these few studies enable us to generalise about the whole of science or that their conclusions must be accepted without demur' (Mulkay, 1980: 55). The replication claimant, on the other hand, is saying that the critical number has already been reached. Thus, when Collins claims that the phenomenon of the social negotiation of reproducibility has been 'well replicated', this can be read as a claim for the existence of a *large enough* number of studies to have done the job. That number appears to be five.

The Dialogue between a Friend and a Critic Revisited

Friend: It is now clear that Collins's original replication studies have indeed been replicated.

Critic: I am now convinced that Collins's conclusions remain unsupported by the candidate-replicators.

Friend: But the studies *have* been replicated!

Critic: They certainly have not!

(Etcetera)

Let us leave this unedifying, but highly symmetrical, dramatization of the 'interpretative flexibility' of our enquiry in order to spell out some of the interesting consequences entailed in coming to either the Friend's positive decision or the Critic's negative one. The Friend's decision would seem to produce the following series of claims:

1   the originals have indeed been the subject of bona fide replications, namely the papers in *Knowledge and Controversy*:

2   all these studies now form the set of SSK replication studies which means that they all say the same thing;

3   the thing that they all say can be taken to be the case *because* its original demonstration has been replicated;

4   the thing that is the case is the non-standard view of replication which can be glossed as the claim that replication *cannot* demonstrate what is the case.

On the face of it, a similar paradoxical difficulty is not involved in the Critic's negative decision. If the epistemological status of findings rests 'above all' on replication, then the findings of the originals must be considered (by the Critic) to be 'suspended'. However, the Critic faces a problem arising from the fact that the decision procedure itself (the schema) has been taken from the methods and findings of one of these 'suspended' studies. Thus we have a decision, arrived at by following the original analyses, that rejects (or at least 'suspends') their findings.

The Replication-candidacy of 'The Life and Opinions'

What is implied here, and indeed what has been implied throughout, is that this present text (hereafter LO) must itself be a further candidate-replicator.[21] Let us apply, briefly, the schema of the six stages to it.

1   *Does LO deal with the phenomenon of replication?*
I would like to claim that it does. However, as it deals with the practical interaction of two versions of replication while Collins's original studies do not, it could be argued that LO is therefore dealing with a significantly different phenomenon.

2 Is LO a 'study'?

I want to claim that it is on the grounds of its undeniable use of empirical materials including interview transcripts. However, because of its concern with reflexivity – a concern which is commonly seen as distracting SSK researchers from 'good solid empirical work' – it may therefore be treated as insufficiently imbued with the empirical spirit. As I have argued at Stage Two, whether it legitimately may be described as a 'study' must remain formally undecidable.

3 Has the author/researcher an appropriate identity?

I am not and I have never been a 'Bath relativist'; I therefore claim an appropriate identity. However, non-members of SSK would be more likely to see SSK-membership itself as the relevant category, in which case I would seem an inappropriate replicator. In as much as my positive reflexive strategy has led me to attempt to follow Collins's method as a competent native member (see below), my appropriateness may thereby be reduced; however, simply because I have a positive reflexive strategy while Collins's approach to reflexivity is negative, this difference should increase my appropriateness as a candidate-replicator.

4 Is LO a competent copy of the Originals?

Again, I claim that it is. The grounds on which I do so are that I have used a similar methodology by following the directions for good SSK practice given by Collins. For instance, I have tried to use interviews 'to tap the body of rules and understandings that comprise the individual as a scientist' (Collins, 1983a: 93), and I have tried hard to treat the claims at issue as problematic. However, it could be argued that by extending SSK's area of research into a non-natural science I am displaying a form of non-competence: if the strong version of Special Relativism[22] is held then a study that necessarily ignores the existence of a boundary between the natural and the social must be a 'non-copy'. However, the generality argument would suggest that this difference in research area (SSK rather than physics or parapsychology) is credibility-enhancing.

5 Has LO the same findings as the Originals?

I certainly think it has: LO shows how a standard-view replication claim can be deconstructed and translated into non-standard terms. This is exactly what Collins's original studies show. However, perception of the similarity of findings seems to be dependent on prior decisions about membership of the set of competent studies, as both Collins's work and my own clearly demonstrate.

6 Has LO replicated the Originals?

On the argument from numbers it would seem unlikely that just one study would be enough to achieve replication. However, if we assume that the

Friend-ly arguments prevail and that all the candidate-replicators are successful, what would it mean for 'The Life and Opinions' to be in this position?

If LO were to be accepted as a bona fide replication of Collins's original replication studies, it would find itself saying one thing (the standard view is 'wrong'; the non-standard is 'right') while doing another (becoming a standard-view replication). If such paradoxes are to be avoided then it would be as well not to make a replication claim or to accept one being made on its behalf. However, I imagine this an unlikely fate for LO. If it 'will be read for its purpose and function rather than as "just another" "neutral" description' (Woolgar, 1983: 253–4), then we can speculate on likely readings. If we disregard the (highly likely!) possibility that LO will have no impact whatsoever, I would argue that because of its focus on Collins and because of the way it is ironically structured as a *tu quoque* or 'you too' argument (though with a positive self-reflexive twist) it is most likely to be read as an attempted 'refutation' of his work.

Concluding Dialogue of the Replication Analysts

C: I read your work 'as a confirmation of the studies. I found it quite sympathetic! I would not have known that it was an attempt to refute Collins unless you had implied as much.'[23]

A: I hope I haven't implied as much. *I* certainly don't understand it as a refutation, whether attempted or achieved. Were it to 'become' so, it would presumably also 'become' a refutation of itself in as much as it would then be a competent copy of the work that it refutes. And besides, I was merely talking in terms of Woolgar's argument about the way that the very *form* of ironic discourses such as SSK tend to precipitate such a critical reading despite authors' disclaimers.

C: So I should ignore the disclaimer you have just made then?

A: Definitely! And by the same token you should also ignore all my own Friend-ly arguments on behalf of LO's own replication-candidacy. Which would be just as well considering the problematic result of the success of such replication claims. But of course, as I have also pointed out, a 'refutation claim' is equally problematic.

C: I see. You seem to have got yourself into a bit of a fix. If this is the result of being reflexive I am obviously right to ban it!

A: On the contrary, it is you who are in a fix. The problematic nature of your claim is the result of your decision to ban reflexivity. By doing so, you felt 'safe' from self-reference – so safe, in fact, that you felt able to make the replication claim in the way that you did.

C: If this is your conclusion, you haven't got very far have you? I told you at the beginning that I was quite aware of what I was doing and since then you have consistently avoided any discussion of my purposes. I made the point, if you recall, that 'the permeability of replication does not mean that it is still not the only criterion of what is to count as a natural regularity (or social regularity). It is the only one we have'.

A: Well, if you are right in saying that the 'permeability of replication' – or what I call the non-standard view – does *not* affect its ability to act as the criterion of empirical regularity, then you could have achieved a regular fact-like status for the findings of the studies in question by being reflexive and simply claiming that the process whereby the findings were produced exemplified those findings. It seems to me that that would have been a far more credible claim to make in the circumstances. It would have avoided all these problems and. . .

C: But that would not have been nearly so interesting or so dramatic! And had I done so, you wouldn't have had anything to study!

A: Luckily, that's not entirely true.[24] And as I was saying. . .

C: It's about time it was finished. There can't be much more to say.

A: Well, not *much* more, no. Now, in conclusion. . .

Notes

1. The research on which this chapter is based was supported by the UK SSRC/ESRC and forms the basis of my DPhil thesis (Ashmore, 1985). This work examines the nature and relevance of reflexivity (self-reference) in metascientific practice and argument. Chapter 3 is an extended treatment of the themes of the present chapter.

2. Both of these versions of replication are often represented as far more complex and differentiated than they appear here. For instance, Collins's SSK version has been expanded to take account of the degree to which replicability is perceived as problematic in different areas of scientific activity. In non-controversial areas (such as TEA laser building) replication works in much the way it is supposed to work in the standard version while in controversial areas (such as gravity-wave detection or parapsychology), where the nature or even the existence of the phenomena are in doubt, replication becomes problematized (Collins, 1978b, 1984, 1985). However, when Collins's version of replication is used as a resource in didactic texts (e.g. Collins, 1982c, 1983a; Mulkay, 1979) or in polemics (e.g. Collins, 1982b), the kind of gloss I have given, which emphasizes the problematic nature of replication *as a contrast to* the 'naivety' of the standard version, is generally used.

3. In 1982 I interviewed all the people most closely associated with the claim. The interviews were of the 'depth' variety, being focused on the technical details of the case while being conducted in an unstructured manner. They were all recorded and transcribed verbatim. The following conventions of transcription and presentation are used here. 1. Speakers are represented by their initial. 2. Speech is represented in the manner of play scripts or novels rather than the manner of conversation analysis. Thus, when I hear an interrogative on the tape, I mark it in the transcript with the conventional sign '?'. I do this to make the reader's task of sense-making as easy as possible. Moreover, as nearly everyone who reads this text is likely to be extremely familiar with these conventions, their use does not restrict its readability to those few initiates who can cope with the complexities of certain other modes of transcription.

4. Although this paper is not concerned specifically with Collins's views on reflexivity which I examine elsewhere (Ashmore, 1985: 86–97; see also Oehler, 1983), this comment can fairly be taken as a summary of these views. See for instance, Collins, 1981a: 216, 1982a: 140, 1983a: 101; Collins and Pinch, 1982: 190.

5. Collins himself has subsequently used the schema in a generalized fashion as the basis for comments on 'the rule of replication' in science (1978b) and as part of his recent 'empirical model of replication' (1985: ch. 2).

6. The particular number and order of these stages of demarcation are not, it seems, crucial: 'This search procedure could be divided up in a number of different ways, and more or less steps might be involved' (Collins, 1978b: 2); 'The exact number and nature of the stages would be arbitrary to some extent, but any sensible scheme would filter down from general to more specific sorting criteria' (Collins, 1985: 38).

In his (1985) Collins demonstrates this arbitrariness by adding a new second stage concerning scientificity and moving the previous stage two (about experiments) to fourth place. In the analysis which follows I take some advantage of this potential for flexibility.

7. As these biographical details, here and throughout Stage Three, are quotations from a 1981 publication they are, of course, out of date. Travis is now once again working with Collins at Bath as a research fellow on a project in the UK ESRC's current initiative on Science Studies and Science Policy. He has very nearly completed his thesis. (Note dated February 1987.)

8. My attendance at the series of (inaccurately described) 'Discourse Analysis Workshops' initiated by Mulkay has no doubt helped to foster this inaccurate impression.

9. Collins is no longer the Convener, is now a Senior Lecturer, and has also written a book 'using case material from physics and from parapsychology' (Collings, 1985). (Note dated February 1987.)

10. Pickering has since been temporarily employed at MIT and is now at the Institute for Advanced Study, Princeton. His research on elementary particle physics has been published (Pickering, 1984). (Note dated February 1987).

11. Harvey's study is now complete. (Note dated December 1984.)

12. Pinch is now a Lecturer in sociology at the University of York. He has long since completed his study of solar-neutrino astronomy which has recently been published (Pinch, 1986). (Note dated February 1987.)

13. For instance in the introduction to *Knowledge and Controversy*: 'This collection, it is hoped, in addition to its substantive contribution, will reveal clearly the flourishing empirical programme associated with relativism and thereby obviate the necessity for further defenses and reaffirmations' (Collins, 1981c: 4).

14. Collins, Letter (March 1983).

15. It is interesting that neither in his commentary (Letter, March 1983) nor elsewhere does Collins give any indication of what these might be. Thus, when he indicates that Ashmore (1983) is *not* a 'proper reflexive copy of SSK relativist work' he seems to be saying that it fails because it treats his (mere) 'hypotheses' as a definitive set of criteria, i.e. it is not a competent copy because it copies the original too closely. This would seem to imply that this present version is a (more) competent copy because it does not follow the original so closely. However, as this 'looseness' is precisely what Collins (1978b, 1985; see note 6) stresses in his later adaptations of the schema, my attempt to do the same may suggest, once again, that I am guilty of 'over-copying' and thus of non-competence. See Stage Four for further discussion of the problematic nature of copies.

16. The significance of this interesting punctuation is examined in detail elsewhere (Ashmore, 1985: 279–80). Briefly, both Travis's question mark and Collins's exclamation mark are devices for the recognition of the paradoxical nature of replicating replication, but where Travis's punctuation displays a certain openness to the phenomenon, Collins's attempts to achieve closure.

17. Gieryn (1982) is a general critique of what the author calls the 'relativist/constructivist' programme. The specific targets are two collections of papers (Knorr et al., 1980; and Collins, 1981b).

18. As far as I know, Zuckerman has not claimed (or even 'wanted to' claim) that her 'Deviance' paper represents a negative replication of Collins's work. The argument does

not require explicit claims to be made, however. It is perceptions of similarity/difference that are at issue. A plausible account for Zuckerman's 'silence' is that, like Collins, she perceives their work as so totally dissimilar that the possibility of competitive results simply does not arise.

19. Jorge Luis Borges, in his story 'Pierre Menard, author of the Quixote' (1970), inverts this sequence of interpretation. Borges shows how morphologically *identical* entities (Cervantes' 'Quixote' and Menard's 'Quixote') can be subject to radically different interpretations: 'Cervantes' text and Menard's are verbally identical, but the second is almost infinitely richer' (1970: 69). For two texts that analyse replication by way of an analysis of Borges' analysis of Menard's and Cervantes' 'identical but different' texts, see Mulkay (this volume) 'Don Quixote's Double', and Mulkay (1985: ch. 4), 'Don Quixote's Double'.

20. The reader should note the reflexive self-exemplification on the meta-level in this paragraph. In perceiving a difference between Collins's perceptions of difference in the cases of 1. Collins's findings and Zuckerman's findings ('extremely major'); and 2. Pickering's findings and Harvey's findings ('interesting contrast') I set up an 'interesting contrast' of my own between 1. and 2. So, my interpretative practice in this paragraph provides for my continued membership of SSK, just as Collins's interpretation of the differences at 2. provides for their (Collins, Pickering, Harvey) unproblematic memberships.

21. Another candidate-replicator of Collins's replication studies is Mulkay's (this volume, ch. 5 and 1985: ch. 4) 'Don Quixote's Double: a Self-exemplifying Text'. The final section of Mulkay's text discusses the ways in which it is itself an example of which it speaks in that it too utilizes similarity/difference attributions and it too can be considered a 'candidate-replicator' (though Mulkay does not use this term) of Collins's work. Clearly, this self-referential attention makes it a suspiciously similar piece of work to the text you are reading. Moreover, the authors' socio-cognitive relationship is obviously far too close for either of them to be able interpretatively to achieve the mutual independence necessary for the work of the one to be able to validate the work of the other. Unfortunately, we seem doomed to the ignominious relationship of mere replication. The only question, of course, is where each of us stands in this relationship. Should we come to blows over this, it is nice to know that our deteriorating relationship should improve the value of our work.

22. 'My prescription is to treat the social world as real, and as something about which we can have sound data, whereas we should treat the natural world as something problematic – a social construct rather than something real' (Collins, 1981a: 216). For other similar expositions of Special Relativism, see the works by Collins cited in note 4. For critical examinations of this doctrine see the works by Ashmore and Oehler cited in note 4.

23. Collins, Letter (March 1983).

24. See Ashmore (1985: chs 4 and 5) for analyses of the work of advocates of a positive approach to reflexivity.

Reflexion on Ashmore

Ashmore's work thus provides further support for the idea that readings of sameness and difference are essentially open-ended and interpretively flexible. This conclusion is reached in a rather different manner from Mulkay, Collins and other authors, by extraordinarily detailed attention to the arguments and claims of the sociology of scientific knowledge (SSK) itself. This means, of course, that the claims of SSK to have produced a corpus of well-replicated findings about science must be regarded with some scepticism. Ashmore provides independent confirmation of the way in which SSK has insufficiently acknowledged the interpretive flexibility of the very concepts and categories at the heart of its own practice.

Alternatively, we see that Ashmore's work is so centrally situated within the SSK tradition that we can hardly take it as independent confirmation. Given his intellectual origins and, more especially, the immediate context of his work at the University of York, it is fairly predictable that he would reach the same conclusion as Mulkay and the rest. Ashmore is therefore merely a reiteration of a familiar view. Nothing that can be said about 'bringing to observation what we already know' (Walker, this volume) can save him. This means, of course, that Ashmore does not provide any significant challenge to SSK.

Of course, these two alternative interpretations of Ashmore merely replicate the point which the author himself makes: namely that on any specific criterion of similarity/difference (in this case, the putative independence of a candidate-replicator), claims to replication can be either credited or faulted. Of course, for reasons which there is no (longer) sufficient space to go into, these two alternative interpretations of Ashmore also make a point rather different from that made by the author himself.

The point, then, (*this* 'new' and 'different' point) is that alternative interpretations are always available. The richness of this situation generates *openness* in the sense that further questions and paradoxes are raised by exploring reflexive relationships. This contrasts with (is different from) the *closure* entailed by attempts to solve paradoxes and to avoid or banish reflexivity.

So can we at last agree, at least in a general way, on the benefits of reflexive exploration as exemplified by Ashmore? Fortunately (or unfortunately, depending on your point of view) the answer is again no. For an argument which agrees with the starting point of the 'celebratory' attitude to reflexivity, but which seeks an alternative to what is seen as the 'counter-productive' results of these 'celebrations', we turn to Latour.

8

The Politics of Explanation:
an Alternative

Bruno Latour

From more ashmore the phoenix will rise.
(proverb from Yorkshire)

Reflexivity is necessarily at the heart of social studies of science because it is often argued that relativist sociologists are sawing the branch upon which they sit (Woolgar, 1982, 1983; Hollis and Lukes, 1982; Ashmore, 1985; Lawson, 1985). By making social explanations of the behaviour of natural scientists they make it impossible for their own explanations to be seriously believed by anyone. Their arguments in feeding back on themselves nullify their own claims. They are in effect self-contradictory, or at least entangled in a sort of aporia similar to the famous 'all Cretans are liars', aporia from which they cannot escape except by indefinite navel-gazing, dangerous solipsism, insanity and probably death.

The Accusation of Self-contradiction

Such a critique levelled at the work done during the last ten years in the social studies of science implies the following.

1   The strength of (natural) sciences comes not only from their somehow getting in contact with extra-human objects (no matter through how many mediations) but also from *not* being limited by the human, historical or local point of view; this ideal should be imitated by the social sciences and this is, historically, what they have tried to do. Thus, asking the social sciences to study the natural *sciences* – or, worse, asking them to study themselves – is a logical, moral, political and even aesthetic impossibility, since it means abandoning the only safeguard and source of certainty, which is offered by the non-local, non-historical, non-human contact with objects; the sky will fall on our heads if it is not firmly propped up by at least a few pillars much stronger than our weak forces or those of our contingent, local and historical societies.

2   *Self-contradiction* is so bad that if someone can be convicted of being self-contradictory this is the end of all his or her serious claims; the principle of non-contradiction is somehow necessary for all legitimate

explanations in both human and natural sciences as it is for daily life in general.

3   Providing a *social* explanation of knowledge (in the natural as well as in the human sciences) is, in effect, to nullify or at least to weaken the claims involved; if someone can be accused of being influenced by social factors, this means that he or she no longer needs to be taken seriously (Barnes and Bloor, 1982).

4   The *relativist* sociologist of science is supposed to offer social explanations of something, as this is what is expected of him or her; the 'something' comprises an infinitely long repertoire of objects which are admitted to be non-social; 'social' denotes a long but finite repertoire of elements that tie men and women together; a social explanation thus occurs when an element of the list of objects ('wrongly' thought by natural scientists to be 'only objective') is related to or replaced by one of the elements from the list of social factors; this relation is a one-to-many rather than a one-to-one type, that is, the *same* social factors are used to explain many natural or objective elements (see below).

5   Providing an *explanation* (in either natural or social sciences) is inherently good; thus accusing someone of providing no explanation puts an end to the dispute; the opponent is just story-telling and may be stopped by a simple question like 'so what?'; to answer the 'so what?' question entails proving that he or she is doing *more* than just telling stories, that he or she is really also offering some explanation.

6   A further point which is implicit in all the preceding: everyone is looking for who or what is *responsible* for some state of affairs; 'accusation' is thus implicated in all attempts at explaining something; the accusation made against relativists of being self-contradictory is a mirror-image of the accusation made by social scientists against natural scientists who are said 'wrongly' to believe that they are dealing 'only' with a repertoire of objective elements (see Figure 1).

In order to understand the importance and place of reflexivity in our field, and then to define our own policy of explanation, it is first necessary to criticize each of these common-sense arguments implied in the accusation of self-contradiction.

1   Relativist sociologists are not sawing the branch upon which they sit because they are not seated on it, and no one is or has ever been: the strength of any science, and indeed of any argumentation, has never come from non-local, non-human and non-historical allies; denying rationality does not mean that the sky is going to fall on our heads (as my Gallic ancestors used to believe), because the sky is supported by many other firmer pillars.

2   The principle of non-contradiction is far from the necessary condition of any explanation (be it in natural or in social sciences); on the contrary, the basis of anthropology of science, the principle of *translation* (Callon,

1986; Latour, 1987, 1988) makes the idea of non-contradiction a belated end-product of the practice of science.

3   Providing a social explanation of something has nothing to do with weakening or nullifying a position provided that...

4   ...it is made clear that the notion of a 'social' explanation is entirely reshuffled; it must no longer be seen as a replacement of several elements in the infinite repertoire of natural objects by one or two factors taken from the list of social objects.

5   This in turn is possible only if we abandon the idea that offering an explanation is good for your health and inherently better than 'just story-telling'.

6   This in turn becomes possible only on the condition that the accusation process and the search for responsibility – which shapes the development of the social sciences – is brought to a stop.

The Politics of Explanation

To criticize the notions that form the basis of the accusation of being self-contradictory, we first have to define explanation. In its simplest form (see Figure 1) it means establishing some sort of relation between two lists, one comprising an inventory of elements to be explained (B) and the other a repertoire of elements said to provide the explanation (A).

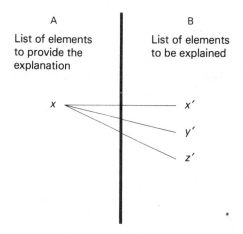

Figure 1   *The two repertoires:* explanans *and* ad explananda

It is generally admitted that if there is a one-to-one connection, nothing is explained since there are as many elements in one list as in the other. Thus, an explanation is said to be provided only when *more than one* element in list B is related to one element of list A. In this general form the politics of explanation can be described like this: when you hold *x* element of A, you also hold the *x'*, *y'* elements of B. It is in effect a general definition of power, power being understood in both its political and logical senses. The corollary of this 'holding of' several elements by one, is a general feeling of strength, economy and aesthetic satisfaction: the one element may 'replace', 'represent', 'stand for' all the others, which are in effect made secondary, deducible, subservient or negligible.

This simple definition allows us to measure the *power of an explanation*. An explanation becomes more powerful by relating more elements of B to a single element of A. This scale makes it possible to calibrate variations in explanatory power (see Figure 2).

The maximum on this scale is set when you can say that all the elements of B, including those which are *not yet* present in it, can be *deduced* from one element of A. In this case holding an element of A is holding *in potentia* the rest of the list. Traditionally, a mathematical demonstration is considered to offer this best form of explanation. The belief in the existence of a demonstration or deduction explains most of the enthusiasm characteristic of the classical age.

Scale of powerful explanations

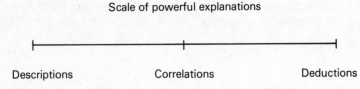

Figure 2 *The scale of explanatory power*

The centre of this scale of explanatory power occurs when several elements of B are said to be often (always, frequently, significantly) related to one another. In this case no element of A can replace elements of B. What can be done, however, is to write down in list A the constant relation recognized among elements of B. Column A is thus made up of a list of constant correlations. The belief in the possibility of various structures, correlations, statistical laws does not trigger as much enthusiasm as the former belief in deduction but is better adapted to our sceptical age. What could be called a disappointed scientism runs through most of the natural sciences and all of the human sciences (apart from ethnography, exegesis and psychoanalysis).

The other extremity on the scale of explanatory power is when no deduction or correlation of any sort can be established. The list of elements in A is simply the repetition of several elements of B, arranged and summarized in such a way that, for a few practical ends, holding list A is provisionally equivalent to holding list B. This kind of explanation most often has the literary character of a *story*. This is what is called a 'description', and is often associated with the work of historians.

This account of explanations is all very well but, apart from the sociological use of the word 'power', is still very much in keeping with classic discussions in epistemology. To go further and define our own policy of explanation we should understand why there are two lists in the first place. In other words, why should we want to explain anything? In what sort of peculiar situation is an explanation necessary and when is a powerful explanation seen as inherently better than a weak one?

A strong explanation becomes necessary when someone wishes to *act at a distance* (Latour, 1987). If you are in the setting x' you do not need to explain it – practice and weak accounts will be sufficient. If you are away from the setting and indifferent to it, you do not need to explain it either – practice in the new setting x will do. If you are away and simply remembering how it was when you were in setting x' you still do not need powerful explanations – story-telling will do the job much better. You start to need a stronger explanation when you are away and still wish to act on the setting x'. Why? Because you now have to be in two settings x and x' at once. You need to hold in the setting x some elements or features of x'. 'Information' is the word often used to describe all the elements of x' that can be mobilized, transferred, accumulated in x. Information is the go-between, the mediation, the translator, the *metaxu* that constantly oscillates between the presence of x' and its absence.

The Greek offer, as usual, the best mythology of the action at a distance, through the use of carefully designed forms. After all, Thales is credited with inventing geometry when, not wishing to climb on Kheops' pyramid, he 'simply' measured the shadows of a stick firmly stuck in the ground (Serres, 1983). His theorem (the epitome of powerful explanations) resulted in the possibility of holding all the pyramids (existing, to be built and never to be built) through the little calculations held in the hands. What we so much admire in the Greek miracle is a reversal of power relations: the weakest, that is, a tiny people holding only shadows and paper-forms become stronger than the ancient and powerful Egyptians with their heavy stone pyramids. Holding the forms is tantamount to holding, in addition, everything else. Platonism, through its many avatars, is the philosophy of this fantastic enthusiasm for a reversal of the order of priority between 'shadows' and 'things'. But the same process is at work for weaker explanations as well. Theorems are not the only technics that allow these moves. All sciences are defined first of all by the sort of elements they extract from the settings, and then mobilize, accumulate, combine and display: fossils, stuffed animals, photographs, trophies, questionnaires; everything which, in one way or another, solves the problem of action at a distance, fills the gap, through the production of information, between the presence of x' and its absence (Latour, 1986; Latour and de Noblet, 1985).

This definition of an explanation as a *measure of a distance between contexts* has three important consequences that I shall use later in the argument. First, it creates the very distinction between practice on the one hand, and knowledge on the other: practice becomes whatever people do in the setting acted upon; knowledge becomes whatever is mobilized in x to act upon the other setting. It also establishes the distinction between form and matter: form becomes whatever is transferable from x' to x; matter is whatever cannot stand the trip. Finally, it is also what produces the very separation between the 'outside world' and our 'interpretation of' what the world is like. Rationalists and relativists debate endlessly on whether or not our ideas have to be in correspondence or not with the world 'out there', without ever raising this simple question: how come that the world is '*out* there', in the first place, instead of being '*in* there'? The answer is simple enough. The problem of correspondence between the forms mobilized and the settings from which they have been extracted, becomes crucial only for those who want to act at a distance. If you are not at a distance, or do not wish to act upon other settings, the notion of correspondence vanishes, and so does the problem of the referent.

If you now wish, from the setting x, to hold not only x', but many other settings, x'' and so on . . ., you start to need more and more powerful explanations. This need does not arise from any psychological, political or metaphysical lust for power, it is simply the consequence of solving the practical problems of acting at a distance. Since the mobilized forms are not the settings themselves mobilized, it is perfectly possible for someone who holds the forms to hold nothing at all but shadows. Thus, something additional has to be done to (re)gain, in the setting x, the superiority which is lost by being away from x', x'', etcetera. In other words, the notion of a powerful explanation cannot be dissociated from the slow establishment of what I have called *centres of calculation* for acting at a distance. The two lists above and their various connections were an epistemological rendering of a very practical activity: *network-building*, that is, how we can tie as many settings as possible to as few elements as possible through as few intermediaries as possible (Latour, 1986, 1987).

This problem should not be seen as just a formal, technical, economical, aesthetic, or political endeavour. The same problems have to be solved no matter if one wishes to invent a new theorem, a telephone network, a trade route, an elegant theory, or an empire. More exactly, none of these separate endeavours is possible without simultaneously engaging in the others. This is why we had, in our studies of network-building, to replace distinct political, economic, technical and intellectual questions by one common task, namely how to build centres of calculation and extended networks (Hughes, 1983; Callon et al. 1986). The differences between realms of activity are less important than the possibility of them all conspiring to reverse the order of priority or the relations of strength between centres and periphery.

Such a point of view has one important consequence for the present argument. There is no reason to believe that there should be a list of social elements which can be related, in a one-to-many connection, to provide the explanation of some natural science elements. The possibility, indeed the very existence of two homogeneous lists, one of social elements, the other of non-social ones, is fanciful. What we see, on the contrary, is how settings strive to become centres by mobilizing everything at hand and tying their claims to as many resources as possible. Is this social or natural or technical? Good luck to the person who tries to carve out this kind of distinction from the imbroglio that holds together precisely because it associates as many heterogeneous elements as possible in one centre. To be sure, social factors are still there, but they are one of the things to be studied, not elements which allow us to understand. 'Social factors' are the particular product of professional social scientists striving to establish new types of calculations in their institutions. They define, in many various ways, what holds us all together. They call this 'society', and try to render their definitions indispensable to as many other people as possible, by insinuating themselves in as many other trades as possible (business, politics, academic life, journalism, the publishing industry, and so on). No matter how interesting their work, it is no different in form and purpose from that of all the others engaged in network-building. In other words, the social sciences are part of the problem, not of the solution. To expect an explanation of the natural sciences from them, is a bit like expecting the water distribution companies to 'explain' the telephone networks.

The main consequence of focusing on centres of calculation and on the many practical ways in which they extract and combine information, is a strong rejection of arguments in terms of cause and effect. No matter how much the notion of cause has been criticized (and now replaced by more modest variants such as correlation, correspondence, structure, pattern) there remains, in the back of our minds, the idea that a story is incomplete if it does not conclude with a set of words (or concepts, or sentences) endowed with the ability to trigger (generate, influence or produce) the events or occurrences which have been studied. All the debates about internal and external factors are based on the possibility of having something like 'factors' or 'determinants'. Even those who are sceptical about the possibility of finding a cause for phenomena (especially in the social sciences) do not dispute that some elements (*explanans*) should occupy the position of a cause while others (*ad explananda*) should play the role of effects. There is always something of a tribunal in these trials that settle responsibilities, decide on who will be accused and who will be innocent – the cause is always literally a cause; some of them like capitalism have even be turned into a '*cause célèbre*' (Girard, 1978).

The very existence of these two lists, or of these two sets, one of causes, the other of effects, becomes very doubtful in the work of building centres of calculation is considered. Paradoxically, the cause appears as *the consequence* of expanding the networks and of reinforcing the centres. This is very beautifully expounded by Fernand Braudel (1985). You cannot explain the development of the world economy by invoking a force of some sort (for instance, capitalism) because this cause is itself helpless as long as centres do not exist which are able to capitalize, on a larger scale, on whatever is produced and sold. The heterogeneous association of many elements (which was supposed to be explained) is precisely what, *in the end*, gives strength to this capitalism which was supposed to offer an explanation. In more philosophical terms, it means that a cause (factor, determinant, pattern, or correlate) is the outcome of a trial of responsibility through which a few elements of the network are taken to be the impetus behind the whole business. It is, in practice, very much an election of representatives or, depending on the outcome, an accusation made against a scapegoat (Girard, 1978). The belief in causes and effect is always, in some sense, the admiration for a chain of command or the hatred of a mob looking for someone to stone.

Providing an explanation is, in a nutshell, working at empire-building; the more powerful an explanation, the larger the empire and the stronger the material in which it is built. What we admire in powerful theories we should also admire in freeways, multinational corporations, satellite networks, weapon systems, international banking and data banks. If we do not admire these achievements, there is no basis for using a double standard and letting the 'powerful theories' stand apart and alone be worshipped. What we mean by a 'powerful explanation' in the social sciences is most often an imitation of a simplified version of a combative interpretation of some hard sciences of the past when they were politically at their weakest and when they were dealing with their simplest objects (Shapin and Schaffer, 1985; Prigogine and Stengers: 1979)! Although such an explanation has been given of only a very few simple laws in some parts of mechanics and astronomy, philosophers of science have made of this *apax* a general rule.

Should We Explain Anything?

The issue is not to explain the natural sciences by using social sciences, nor to substitute 'centres of calculation' for 'capitalism', nor to replace the search for causes by empire-building. This would be to replace one scapegoat by another and again to leave our argument open to the accusation of being self-contradictory. As Girard (1978) suggests, the point is to modify the whole regime of accusation.

There are two ways of displaying powerful explanations, and thus two ways of solving the problem of the *distance* between the setting that offers the explanation and those that are explained. The first is common to all disciplines: hold the elements of A and deduce – correlate, produce, predict, reorganize, comment or enlighten – as many elements of B as possible. The second has just been alluded to: *display the work* of extracting elements from B, the *work* of bringing it to A, the *work* of making up explanations inside A, the *work* of acting back on B from A. The first way tries to abolish distance, the second feeds on it. In the first, power is reinforced and the represented elements disappear in their representatives. In the second, power is weakened and the initial elements are maintained in full view. The first is reductionist, because holding a single element of A is tantamount to holding all the elements of B. The second I call non-reductionist or 'irreductionist' because it *adds* the work of reduction to the rest, instead of subtracting the rest once the reduction has been achieved. The first creates a power, that is the impression that having one element involves having all the others 'in potentia'. The second creates what I call a gradient of force (Latour, 1988: part II). In other words, the first starts with *equivalences* without telling through which instruments and through which metrology these equivalences are obtained; the second starts from translations and tries to present the work of *rendering elements equivalent* by setting up new instruments and keeping long metrological chains in alignment. In still other words, the first tradition accuses and allocates responsibilities, while the second regards accusations as unfair because they always fall back on an innocent scapegoat. The first is on the side of the knowing, the second is also on the side of the known.

This distinction makes clear that relativist sociologists are far from trying to emulate the natural sciences they study – an emulation which, as we saw earlier, provides the basis for the accusation of being self-contradictory. Social studies of science are not an inferior breed of science, unable to offer explanations as powerful as those of the natural sciences. No science, be it natural or social, has ever offered a powerful explanation of that sort. As well as they can, they all strive to tie their claims in as many ways as possible to a sufficient number of elements to establish an effective two-way connection with the settings on which they want to act from a distance. In this game, the social sciences fare no worse than many natural sciences.

The aporia from which I started is thus completely modified: the first question is no longer 'Since you do not believe that science comprises of non-human, non-historial, non-contingent elements, how can you, relativist sociologists of science claim to explain anything?' No explanation, no matter how abstract the science, no matter how powerful the regime, has ever consisted of anything more than a disproportionate amount of heterogeneous, historical, contingent elements. *We do not deprive ourselves of allies* when we show that these are the only allies that have ever been on the side of the hard natural sciences. We, the soft and critical sciences, have the same type of resources, although, I admit, *less of them*. The second question is no longer 'How can you, without contradiction, appeal to social factors in order to explain the development of natural sciences?' Social sciences are not a reservoir of notions and entities from which we would draw our resources. They are part and parcel of the very activity we want to study, part of our problem, not of our solution. In the course of our work we have irreversibly altered the meaning of the word social. Thus, to the seemingly tricky question: 'What is left for a relativist to explain' the only possible answer is: 'Everything'.

This reformulation, however, does not bring the issue of self-contradiction to an end. We now have to raise a new question, a moral quandary much more difficult than the simple trap inside which rationalists tried to corner us. (It is also much more difficult because we raise it against ourselves.) If the work of explaining something is that of empire-building, *should we* explain something? Do we really want to participate in network-building? Do we want to add yet another discipline and profession to the many that we study? Do we wish to offer more powerful explanations, that is, to transfer the power relations from the setting studied to the centre of calculation studying them? Do we lust for power and recognition? Do we want to imitate the ethos and styles of science? Do we want to dominate the natural scientists by evaluating, explaining and judging their behaviour? (This is not a spurious question since, in at least a few sub-disciplines like science policy, evaluation or management of R&D, we have some of the means to produce evaluations and judgements, and we can therefore be dangerous.)

The answer is a qualified *no*. In other words, now that I have freed my enquiry from the false accusation of being self-contradictory, I have immediately to limit its newly-obtained freedom and turn this time not against the rationalists – who are no longer any match for us – but against my own trade. The ideal of an explanation is not to be reached, not only because it is unreachable, but *because it is not a desirable goal anyway*.

Figure 3 may help us to understand this new quandary. The disciplines we study are taken to be either really fictitious or really scientific; our own explanation of their development may also be taken as really ficti-tious or as really scientific. The four boxes obtained represent four un-acceptable ways of continuing our social studies of science. Boxes 2 and 3 are rivals in arrogance, the first because it dismisses all attempts at studying science as being unscientific and the second because it grants itself privileges it denies to the sciences it studies. Box 1 drowns everything, including oneself, in a cynical and derisive regression. Box 4, on the contrary, extends a pompous, uncritical and scientific belief in science to everything, even going so far as to generate the monster known as science of science!

Disciplines studied

		Fictitious	Scientific
		1	**2**
Our own explanation	Fictitious	Coherent; anarchist version; our own account is as fictitious and no more serious	Incoherent; our own account is ridiculous and does not threaten science (version often held by scientists)
		3	**4**
	Scientific	Incoherent; our own account is privileged since social science is firmer; asymmetric sociologism	Coherent; scientistic version; no threat to science

Figure 3   *Four unacceptable ways of doing social studies of science*

Reflexivity, Yes, but Which Sort?

Let us square the circle: we are looking for an explanation of the natural sciences quite different from what is usually called a scientific explanation; we strongly reject the helping hands offered us by the social sciences; on the contrary, we consider them all part of the networks we want to explain; we try to establish a space which is neither above nor inside those networks; we want to describe and expose the politics of explanation, but without replication and without adding another discipline to the plethora already striving for existence; we want to be at once *more* scientific than the sciences – since we try to escape from their struggles – and much *less* scientific – since we do not wish to fight with their weapons. Our quandary is similar to that of a non-violent pacifist who still wishes to be 'stronger' than a violent militarist. We are looking for weaker, rather than stronger, explanations, but we still would like these weak accounts to defeat the strong ones...

This problem is so difficult because it entails simultaneously resolving three paradoxes. The first paradox is common to all forms of writing: how to be at once here (in a setting x) and there (in another setting y); the second is common to all sciences: how to be at once here (in x), there (in y) and *in between* managing the network that ties the two together; the third is common to all texts that try to escape the alternative between fiction and science: how to steer a course between being believed *too much* by the readers and *not enough*. Resolving the first paradox would enable us to write stories; resolving the second would make us remain scientists; resolving the third would enable us to write *reflexive* accounts. I use 'reflexive' to denote any text that takes into account its own production and which, by doing so, claims to undo the deleterious effects upon its readers of being believed too little or too much. Resolving all the three paradoxes simultaneously would mean that we could write texts which would at once be craftily written, scrupulously true, which would not make the readers believe that what is reported is exact and which would still be interesting. Such texts would in effect abolish the distinction between science and fiction.

In order to develop this alternative policy of explanation let us assess the advantages and disadvantages of reflexivity. To do so I shall distinguish two kinds of reflexivity which correspond to the kind of deleterious effects writers wish to overcome. Meta-reflexivity is the term for the attempt to avoid a text being believed by its readers, and infra-reflexivity the attempt to avoid a text *not* being believed by its readers.

Meta-reflexivity

For many writers the main deleterious effect of a text is to be naively believed by readers. Readers have this bad habit, they say, of being immediately taken-in by any story and being led to believe that there is something 'out there' which is the referent of the text and which is in correspondence with the text. Many ancient and modern writers, wishing to point the attention of the reader away from the referent have tried to add reflexive elements that operate in the manner of so many caveats: do not believe me, something else is at stake which is more important.

When they try to shift the attention of the reader to the *text* these writers are called 'deconstructionists' and are often associated with Derrida. When writers try to sway the attention of the reader to the very activity of believing and making sense of something, they are sometimes called 'ethnomethodologists' and have Garfinkel as symbol. The deconstructionists try to write texts in such a way that they neither refer to anything nor give the impression of presenting or representing anything. Ethnomethodologists aim at just the opposite, they write texts that, although by necessity distant from the setting they describe, aim to give the impression of being still present out there in the lived world of their subjects, without deformation or transport. The stylistic goal is similar in both cases: render the text unreadable so that the usual two-way link between the account and the referent be interrupted and suspended.

In spite of their claims to novelty and post-modernism, these writers too often forget that a third way of creating reflexive texts has been practised for centuries by writers who try to direct attention to the reader himself, to his own life and fate. This redirection is obtained by many religious texts, especially the New Testament, and implies a radical rejection of the whole business of explanation (Péguy, 1914; Latour, 1975). For instance, the story of the empty tomb in the Gospel of St Mark (Mark 16) is not to be read as information about the distant empirical tomb in the outskirts of Jerusalem sometime around Easter, AD 30, but about the reader of the Gospel and the kind of signs he needs in order to understand for himself that Jesus is alive, that he has risen from the dead. The silly empirical question of the women 'Who will roll the stone away from the entrance of the tomb?' (Mark 16:5) is replaced by the angel's admonishment, 'He has risen, he is not here. See the places where they laid him.' The good reader of such a text is not the one who asks the silly question 'What *really* happened there? Would I find traces of the empty tomb if I were to go to that place in Jerusalem and dig the ground?', but the one who asks the question: 'What is happening to me, now, hearing the angel's voice? Jesus is not really there, out there, any more. This is, indeed, what the angel means. Stops asking silly questions. He has risen. He lives now.' And in the process, the reader becomes the writer or the commentator, or the preacher of *another* text that transforms, translates, embroiders and adds to the unbroken chain of commentaries. For hundreds of years (until the seventeenth century) every effort had been made to make a normal 'linear' matter-of-factual reading of the Bible impossible. Not surprisingly, when scientifically-trained exegets started to read the Bible in their new way most of the stories fell apart.

In terms of reflexivity, translation, cunning and cleverness, I am not convinced that the post-modern deconstructionists are any match for the Evangelists and Fathers of the Church. In comparison they play with very few tools. Their meta-reflexivity is obtained by *adding* specific parts about the way texts or discourses should or should not be written (as I am doing now). This is what is usually called methodology. In the end the only way of writing a text that does not run the risk of being naively believed is to write methodologically. The dire result of such a tack is visible in the prose of Derrida and Garfinkel. If the prose was just unreadable, not much harm would be done. But there is something worse in it; worse, that is, from their own reflexive point of view. Deconstructionists and ethnomethodologists consider that if enough methodological precautions are taken, then better texts (better, that is, in the sense of texts which solve the absence–presence quandary) can be written. Derrida really believes that by all his tricks, cunning and entrapments, the texts he writes are more deconstructed than the column of a *New York Times* journalist writing about the latest plane crash. Some of the followers of Garfinkel really believe that once all the methodological precautions have been carried out, the lived-in world of the competent members can be presented truer to life than in the gloss of a classical sociologist such as Merton. Derrida believes that a text can escape from the fate of presence, whereas Garfinkel seems to believe that a report may eventually escape from the fate of absence. Beneath these opposite reflexive claims there is a naive and irrepressible belief in the possibility of writing truer texts. Ashmore's marvellously funny PhD thesis (1985), ridicules all these claims to meta-reflexivity by pushing them to their ultimate dead ends. As we could say in French: 'Plus réflexif que moi, tu meurs.'

Meta-reflexivity is based on the idea that the most deleterious effect of a text is to be naively believed by the reader as in some way relating to a referent out there. Reflexivity is supposed to counteract this effect by rendering the text unfit for normal consumption (which often means unreadable). This accepts as given that the readers are naive believers, that there is such a thing as normal consumption, that people easily believe what they read, finally, that believing is always to relate an account to some referent 'out there'. This is a very naive set of beliefs in the naive beliefs of readers. I suspect this post-modern view of what it is to be modern is the result of a naive and uncritical version of what it is to offer a scientific explanation of something. Our experience in studying the scientific literature makes me seriously doubt these four assumptions (Callon et al., 1986). Readers seem to be much more devious, much harder to take in, much cleverer at deconstruction, much faster in fiction-making than is assumed by those writers who, with some arrogance, believe that others believe. Here, too, 'we need to play down the exoticism of the other'. Scientific texts prepare themselves against a much more likely outcome: that of *not* being believed by their readers, or worse, that of not *interesting* anyone.

But the most bizarre belief involved in meta-reflexivity comes when you study 'self-reference'. Woolgar (this volume, Chapter 2) for instance, assumes that an ethnographic text by Malinowski that talks about the way ethnography is produced is more reflexive than an ethnographic text about, say, the Balinese. Moreover, Malinowski's reflexivity could be, for Woolgar, a naive way of telling us a true story of how ethnography is reported. So he devises, along the same line, a truly third degree reflexive text that shows how Malinowski naively believed that being reflexive (in the second degree) he could escape from the accusation of being a naive story-teller. But Woolgar does not want us to believe that this third degree would be 'truly' reflexive, so he is very happy to imagine many other rungs on this Jacob's ladder — the top of which does indeed disappear in the sky but fails to promise an endless fecundity. Unfortunately, no amount of degrees, layers and Hofstadter's tricks, will make a very simple semiotic argument go away. A text about Malinowski's way of writing about the Balinese is no more and no less reflexive than Malinowski's text about the Balinese and this is no less and no more reflexive than what the Balinese themselves say; and Woolgar's *n*th degree account of the whole thing is no more and no less reflexive than any of the others in the chain. Why can't they be ordered in a pile of reflexive layers? Because they are all texts or stories bearing on *something else*. There is no way to order texts in layers because they are all equal. Texts, so to speak, live in a democracy, as far as semiotics is concerned. The whole vertigo of self-reference stems from the very naive belief that the *same* actor appears in both the first (down below) and last text (up there). Conversely, reflexivists believe that when the text does *not* have the author as one of its characters it is *less* reflexive than when it does, as if these were not, in semiotic terms, two similar ways of building the enunciation (Greimas and Courtes, 1983; Bastide, 1985). Semiotically, the role played by the Balinese in the first text is exactly that of Woolgar in his fifth degree account. Instead of riding piggy-back on one another, the accounts simply stand side by side.

When Woolgar shows a photograph of himself writing a caption for this same photograph in an article about a book on the observation of observers, he seems to suggest that he is several loops of reflexivity above a 'naive' and 'unproblematic' photograph of a naked native. Semiotically he has not moved an inch; the two pictures, side by side, just show different actors and things. Woolgar's picture fails to abolish the problem of distance in the slightest. This also means that the original picture is in no way more naive or less reflexive than his. The pictures are on equal grounds, since they both show things at a distance and they both play with this distance. There is no difference between showing a woman planting rice in a paddy-field, and a sociologist writing a caption for his own photograph. The first is no simpler than the second, any more than 'once upon a time' is more unproblematic than 'this is the first sentence of the story'. The surrealists delighted in little tricks like 'ceci n'est pas une pipe' and such aporia, not because these broke away from common sense, as was claimed, but because they believed that common sense was naively believing. If Woolgar is right, then 'playing down the exoticism of the other' (this volume) means we have to get rid of all these loops, not because they are useless, but because everyone else makes use of them as well.

Infra-reflexivity

Meta-reflexivity is counter-productive since it makes texts less interesting, less rich and less believable; like all others, these texts already suffer from being uninteresting, poor, disputable or discredited! To think that social studies of science can benefit from this form of reflexivity is, in my view, a suicidal attitude, similar (in spite of the contrary impression one might have) to the older idea that a sociological account full of statistics and methodological commitments can defend itself better than a 'plain' journalistic account.

Fortunately, there is another direction which allows us to maintain the

necessary reflexivity without whirling helplessly in our efforts to outdo
and outwit each other in proving that the other is a naive believer. I call
this other tack infra-reflexivity because instead of writing about how (not)
to write, it just writes. 'Just'? Well, not exactly. Let us detail this sounder
policy of explanation.

A deflation in methodology. Since no amount of methodology will ever
bring a text closer to the distant setting about which it writes, no amount
of ignorance of deconstruction will take a text farther away from it either.
I much prefer reading the *New York Times* to Derrida, and between
Garfinkel and Merton I would hesitate for more than a minute (and
probably would pick up the latest copy of the *New Scientist* instead – see
why below). If many critieria, other than the extent of its meta-reflexivity,
define the quality of a text, why not do away with all the paraphernalia
of methodological precautions altogether? If meta-reflexivity is marked
by an inflation of methods, infra-reflexivity is characterized by their
deflation. Instead of piling layer upon layer of self-consciousness to no
avail, why not have just one layer, the story, and obtain the necessary
amount of reflexivity from somewhere else? After all, journalists, poets
and novelists are not naive make-believe constructionists. They are much
more subtle, devious and clever than self-conscious methodologists. They
did not have to wait for post-modern writing to tell stories; they are as
self-conscious as those who naively believe they are *more* self-conscious.
Instead of saying that precautions should be taken either to recover the
lived world of the competent member or to render the text unusable for
make-believe consumption, just offer the lived world and write. Isn't this
what novelists have done for three centuries?

Replacing methodology by style. This is especially clear if the main problem
for any text is, as I claim, not to be too much but to be *too little* believed.
What is merely signalled by methodological warnings should be done by
style. (Amateurs of self-reference will have noted with delight that these
last two paragraphs are self-contradictory: I am glad to offer them this
delight.) All the literary resources that can be mustered to render an account
lively, interesting, perceptive, suggestive and so on have to be present.
Probably a better model is offered by English and French eighteenth-
century philosophers and natural scientists, than by nineteenth- and
twentieth-century German or French writers. It is true that to use the
resources offered by such authors it means abandoning the naive idea that
there is such a thing as post-modernism and such a thing as modernism
(Latour, 1988: part II). This means abandoning the cherished idea (cherished
in academic circles) that other people, before or elsewhere or down there
below, believe in things and behave without consciousness. 'Forgive them,
Father, for they know not what they do.'

Self-exemplification instead of self-reference. A much simpler way of obtaining the necessary reflexivity is to stick to principles of analysis which are self-exemplifying. This means that no privilege is asked for the account at hand. This main difference between meta- and infra-reflexivity is an ethical as well as a methodological or a stylistic commitment. Deep in the minds of (meta) reflexive writers there is the possiblility of reaching a meta-language, in terms of which all the infra-languages could be evaluated. Their passion for a meta-meta-level that would judge all the others (or render them harmless) is the best indication of this. The reductionism of this position suggests that reflexive writers share the belief in the possiblity of a final level. Infra-reflexivity goes against this common belief in asking no privilege for the account at hand. When I portray scientific literature as in risk of not being believed and as bracing itself against such an outcome by mustering all possible allies at hand (Latour, 1987), I do not require for this account any more than this very process: my own text is in your hands and lives or dies through what you will do to it. In my efforts to forestall certain outcomes and encourage others, I too muster all available allies, all linguistic possibilities (if only, God – or Mammon – willing, I could write in my own mother tongue!).

Writing non-scientific texts. We each use a touch-stone to evaluate analyses of science in the making. Marxists, for instance, say that we need a powerful alternative theory that allows us to reject entirely the existing sciences; this is what reflexivity means to them. The meta-reflexivists say we need to stop saying anything about the world or about the way sciences talk about the world. All factions require *specific words, signs* and genres to decide whether or not an analysis is acceptable (see the disclaimer at the end of this paper and the editor's final word). For instance, Marxists (and other social scientists) accept the findings of a case study only if it shows the larger framework within which the case study is situated and by which it is in the last instance determined. Without the *words* 'larger framework' (or some equivalent), self-righteous readers consider that the 'case study' is misconceived, perhaps even dangerous since it leads to the 'pit-falls of empiricism' (Russell, 1986). A reflexivist of the Woolgar denomination considers a text naive if it describes only how life goes on in a biological laboratory (Woolgar, 1982). Without the presence in the story of the *character* 'author telling the story', the text is considered dangerously close to following the well-trodden path of scientism. Such reactions imply that these writers are fascinated by the presence or absence of certain words as a tool for evaluating texts. They suppose that by including characters like 'the framework' or 'the author', they can escape the terrible fate of being just a story, just another story. They would like to force us to limit our repertoire of literary tricks because they think their stories are somehow more than just a story. In effect they reject the semiotic turn.

The same puritanism is evident in attitudes as diverse as those of ethno-methodologists and deconstructionists. The latter scream if a text just tells a story because it might persuade the reader that the fiction is somehow true. The former scream if a text just tells a story about someone because, by representing them as what the text is 'about', it betrays those members truly responsible for the text. They too would like their texts to escape the terrible fate of being just another story about absent things. They too reject the semiotic turn.

All texts need somehow to solve the problem of being about absent elements (whatever the various reasons for this absence), that is, of being written in A about B. In most cases, a text tries to establish safe, two-way connections between A and B and to present (or represent) in A as many elements as possible of B. This is done so as to forget what happens in B as quickly as possible; for all practical purposes, B is now 'in A'. To fight this scientistic way of delegating representants and forgetting about the distance, the other solution consists in *interrupting* the two-way connection. The text becomes unreadable. This solution may be implemented in either A or B. Phenomenologists and ethnomethodologists solve the absence problem and try to stay in the setting B. The deconstructionists and reflexivists try to solve the presence problem by staying in A, without saying anything about anything.

The irony comes from the following observation. Each of these three solutions implies that the complete network must be *constantly maintained, surveyed and kept up*. No matter how scientific you are, you need constantly to move back and forth betweeen A and B, from the knower to the known, always afraid of being interrupted, unfaithful or wrong. No matter how ethnomethodological you are, you still write books in A about mathematicians (Livingston, 1986) or about biologists (Lynch, 1985) in B, but these are neither mathematical nor biological books. No matter how devious you are at writing about nothing, readers still assume you are at least saying something, about deconstruction. I do not point this out to ridicule these endeavours or to show, as reflexivists might, that they are all self-contradictory. The point is that they are all doing each other's job. Since everyone is in any case moving back and forth between A and B, and is worried about how to establish (or not to establish) the ties and how to represent (or not to represent) one setting in another, why don't we take this activity as the name of our game: displaying the knower and the known and the work needed to interrupt or create connections between A and B? I take this as the *non-scientific* way of studying both natural and social sciences; I also take it as a possible definition of infra-reflexivity.

The consequence of this position is that many more *marks* of a good story become available compared to the few insisted upon by the reflexivists. Since no amount of reflexivity, methodology, deconstruction, seriousness or statistics will turn our stories into non-stories, there is no reason for our field to imitate those few genres that have gained hegemony in recent time. To the few wooden tongues developed in academic journals, we should add the many genres and styles of narration invented by novelists, journalists, artists, cartoonists, scientists and philosophers. The reflexive character of our domain will be recognized in the future by the multiplicity of genres, not by the tedious presence of 'reflexive loops'. As Chairman Mao said 'Let a hundred flowers bloom...' (although he had them cut rather short afterwards).

On the side of the known. The reflexivists spend an enormous amount of energy on the side of the knowing, and almost none on the side of the known. They think that any attempt to get at the things themselves is proof of naive empiricism. Even those from Yorkshire who claim to use literary tools to pursue social sciences (Ashmore, 1985; Mulkay, 1985) do so only to expose reflexive claims, never to talk *about* something. Talking 'about something' is anathema to every one of them. This horror, the fear of contamination with empiricism is amusing, because it is exactly the counter-part of the empiricist position. They all think that objects, things-in-themselves, are somehow out of reach. As if any access to the world was for ever in the hands of the empiricist programme. As if the world in which we live was the property of scientistic accounts of science. Reflexivists fully endorse the scientistic agenda when they believe there is no other way out of empiricism than language, words and self-reference. This hidden Kantism is unnecessary. There is another way: that of the world, not the word.

Tracy Kidder's (1981) marvellous, 'unreflexive' – 'merely' journalistic – account of the building of the Eagle computer, tells us more about reflexivity than piles of Hofstadter's tricks, because it is the computer *itself*, yes, the *thing* itself that appears as a reflexive, sentient and historical event. Callon's (1986) account of the scallops' harsh life deep in St Brieuc's bay in Brittany is completely unreflexive. It talks about scallops, fishermen and scientists, not about social scientists and self-reference. But are these scallops the same as those portrayed in oceanographers' struggles? No. No more than Kidder's computer in any way resembles the black-boxes displayed in computer showrooms. Are these objects in the same way as an empiricist would like them to be? Not a bit. They are freed, active and anthropological *projects*, full of life, and ready to take place in a dramatic story. I claim that there is more reflexivity in one account that makes the world alive than in one hundred self-reference loops that return the boring thinking mind to the stage. Infra-reflexivity is the programme followed by Serres (1983) that pushes the knower off-stage. Down with Kant! Down with the Critique! Let us go back to the world, still unknown and despised. If you sneer at this claim and say 'this is going back to realism', yes it is. A little relativism takes one away from realism; a lot brings one back.

Throw-away explanations. The belief in the existence of a framework inside which events are inserted in order to be explained is the hallmark of non-reflexive social sciences. This is the basis of the process of *denunciation* that allows social scientists to allocate responsibilities, to accuse, expose, unveil or to prove innocent (Boltanski, 1984). No one should conclude from this that reflexive studies of science should either say nothing or be limited to case studies (or to historians' narrative genres). Actors have the peculiar ability to tie together many heterogenous elements. They have very strong ideas about what framework is, who is responsible, what counts as an explanation and who is innocent. Once rid of the general framework, we are not back at the micro-level; we are instead introduced to a world in which actors have only *relative* size and are fighting hard to vary the size of everyone else (Callon and Latour, 1981). In order to do this, they need to recruit as many heterogeneous allies as possible. The stylistic conclusion is that we have to write stories that do not start with a framework but that end up with local and provisional variations of scale. The achievement of such stories is a new relationship between historical detail and the grand picture. Since the latter is produced by the former, the reader will always want *more details*, not less, and will never wish to leave details in favour of getting at the general trend. This also means that stories which ignore cause and effect, responsibilities and accusations, will be unfit for the normal mode of denunciation, exposition and unveiling. Our way of being reflexive will be to render our texts unfit for the deadly proof race over who is right. The paradox is that we shall always look for weak explanations rather than for general stronger ones. Every time we deal with a new topic, with a new field, with a new object, the explanation should be wholly different. Instead of explaining everything with the same cause and framework, and instead of abstaining from explanation in fear of breaking the reflexive game, we shall provide a one-off explanation, using a tailor-made cause. I am all for throw-away causes and for one-off explanations.

Cross-over instead of meta-language. One other way of displaying infra-reflexivity is by avoiding building a meta-language. If the ideal of an explanation, as I showed at the beginning, is to subsume the thing to be explained under a new account, this subsumption is precisely what we, social students of science, should abstain from. It would be absurd to develop a meta-language of say, two hundred specific words, and then to test whether such a vocabulary is able to replace the hundreds of thousands of terms and practices of the sciences we study. The worst outcome would be to be successful at this little game, thereby substituting the boring rote of the sociologists' repertoire for the rich work of the natural sciences. Lynch (1985) has provided us with the ultimate critique of such an ambition. There is no sociology to be done, he argues, other than the technical work of the scientists themselves. They already have their sociology. Our work is to extract it. Unfortunately, Lynch failed to present an elegant solution to the problem because he was still embarrassed by Garfinkel's hopeless rejection of the semiotic turn. One possible formulation of Lynch's marvellous insight is that we strive for *equality* with the discipline we study. Instead of explaining it we want to *cross-over* it – as in a genetic cross-over. We want to learn our sociology from the scientists and we want to teach the scientists their science from our own sociology. This programme seems ambitious, even arrogant, but it simply means equal status for those who explain and those who are explained. This is 'affirmative action' extended to the social sciences; they have suffered discrimination for so long and they should not dream of an impossible revenge by trying to *dominate* the sciences through the use of a metalanguage.

Hybridization instead of disciplinary boundaries. Displaying the work of achieving an explanation is possible only if the display is not restricted to one location. If the work in our domain ends up generating a specific, distinct field of scholarship – defined as such perhaps in curricula – it means all our work has been by definition unreflexive. The criterion of our reflexivity is our ability to have our work distributed among the networks. This may be achieved by co-authorship with scientists (to abolish the meta-linguistic attitude of observers observing observers), but also by blurring the distinction between the study of science and the production of other sciences (thus showing how hegemony can be practically challenged). This in turn requires the ability to get out of academic circles and to tie our work to the many current struggles to resist being known, explained, studied, mobilized or represented. The shibboleth of reflexivity is not 'Do you include the author in your study?' but 'Can you make good your promise not to remain within the academic boundary?' Our domain will eventually be judged by its capacity to invent a technical and scientific democracy by showing how this relation between representant and represented can be altered. To propose an alternative policy of explanation is necessarily to define some new politics.

Conclusion

I have very briefly outlined some of the politics of explanation. I have freed our enterprise from the simple-minded argument levelled against us (by rationalists) that it is self-contradictory. I then tackled the crucial problem raised by reflexive writers such as Woolgar: we cannot innocently develop still another social science. Although these writers have rightly recognized the importance of the problem, their solution, meta-reflexivity, is too narrow and in the end sterile. I have argued for an alternative, infra-reflexivity, and sketched a few of its possible definitions. The reflexive trend is inescapable: otherwise our field would indeed be self-contradictory, not in the sense propounded by the rationalists as a way of trying to get rid of us, but in our own sense. The worst outcome would be to get rid of ourselves by imitating the sciences and attempting to offer stronger explanations of their development. If the proposed alternative – the search for non-scientific and weaker explanations – seems daunting, let us remember that the sciences are still young and so are we – provided the rhetorical style of some star warrior does not bring the whole story to an abrupt end.

Disclaimer

This is not a self-exemplifying text. My subtle referee asked me to explain why. I have no answer except this: 'Why does this generation ask for a miraculous sign? I tell you the truth, *no sign will be given to it*' (Mark 8:12).

Note

A version of this paper was read at Baillol College, Oxford, in June 1986 (S. Lukes and W. Newton-Smith's seminar on Explanation in the Social Sciences). I thank two eminent reflexivists who had the fairness to correct my English rather than my arguments.

Reflexion on Latour

I do not think the referee's point was very subtle. 'Correct' perhaps, but hardly subtle. On the other hand, Latour's response is *extremely* subtle. (But perhaps not 'correct'. Although this is probably less important.) For he reminds us that our scepticism about the relationship between signifier and signified (representation and object, form and content) is seriously compromised by insisting on trying to discern the actual meaning of a text. Is this text reflexive? Is Latour's chapter an instance of infra- rather than meta-reflexivity? Latour's response to the referee suggests such questions are misguided. They reintroduce the obsession with the adequacy of representation, an obsession which belies the practical character of interpretive action and saddles it with the unnecessary burden of philosophical investigation. The achievement of infra-reflexivity, says Latour, is that the meaning of the text is just evident: the 'truth' has no sign. Or, at least, I think this is what Latour means.

Latour also reinforces the important consequences of distancing the Editor's Voice from other voices in this text. The important point about this kind of 'action at a distance' (cf. Latour, 1986) is not just that the Editor's Voice can exercise 'power' over other voices, but that the illusion of distance constitutes these other texts as separate objects. The editor further constitutes these textual objects by denying contributors the opportunity of answering back (no reference to, nor comment upon, Reflexions has been allowed in this volume), by implying that the *same* Editor's Voice reappears each time (many different textual objects are thus united/'acted upon' by a singular editorial commentary) and by giving him/herself the last word. Once constituted, these textual objects are ripe for 'study', 'analysis', 'explanation', 'reflexion' and so on, part of which activity can involve the assignation of the texts to persons, as evidence of their position (viewpoint, circumstances, collectivity) (cf. Sharrock, 1974). This, of course, is what makes it possible to speak with confidence about 'Latour's argument'.

Latour's argument ends with a subtle evasion of the query about what counts as reflexivity. By contrast, our concluding chapter attempts to utilize a 'new literary form' as a way of both engaging in and criticizing reflexivity.

9

Reservations about Reflexivity and New Literary Forms or Why Let the Devil have All the Good Tunes?

Trevor Pinch and Trevor Pinch

This paper is perhaps somewhat unusual in a volume concerned to elaborate such exotica as reflexivity and New Literary Forms. It is designedly written as a text which is critical of both these recent developments in the sociology of science.

No, I beg to disagree! In the first place, there is nothing unusual in having a critical text in such a volume, but, more importantly, the text is not even critical. This is because it is clearly written in an unconventional fashion and thereby supports the move towards New Literary Forms.

I knew I should never have agreed to joint-authorship!

Yes, you were reluctant to put both our names on the paper. As I recall, however, I overcame your objections that a jointly-authored paper would only count for 'half' on your curriculum vitae, by pointing out that by collaborating with your namesake you would avoid your usual difficulty of writing papers with the likes of Ashmore, Bijker, Collins and even Mulkay – names that all come before you in alphabetical order. You will now not only get full recognition in the Science Citation Index, but also you will continue to get all the advantages of joint-authorship – such as having to put in only half the work.

Well if you believe that you will believe anything. But let me just say a bit about authorship. I agree that in this case it is somewhat unconventional. However, in having two authors and agreeing to let you interrupt me throughout the text I wanted to construct a text which was not that dissimilar from others to be found in the rest of this volume. My goals in doing this are, however, rather different from those who are advocates of these so-called New Literary Forms. Although I want my text to be self-exemplifying, I want it to be self-exemplifying as a criticism of this whole way of going about things.

Well that is fine by me and, as you say, it seems to fit in well with the rest of the papers – even 'so-called' criticisms can benefit from being presented in new textual forms, especially when those criticisms are of those self-same forms.

I am glad we agree that our common purpose is to make our critique as effective as possible; now on to the introduction.

Okay, but it is actually on *with* the introduction.

Introduction

In this paper I want to take the opportunity offered by the editor of this volume to examine critically the recent turns (both reflexive and New Literary Forms) taken within the sociology of scientific knowledge (SSK). I shall summarize in as straightforward a way as possible what the proponents of such new developments are trying to do; why they are doing it; and whether they really add anything new. He is encroaching into my space. I knew there would be problems collaborating with someone using one of these new-fangled word-processors. When he used that 'Right Hand Margin Justification' facility the 'new' which had previously been happily seated on the line above jumped down into my section of the text. It is not the sort of thing that happens with a good old-fashioned typewriter. But notice the neat way I dealt with it.

As I said, in case you have lost track of the flow because of that silly interruption, 'whether they really add anything new'. Take for instance, my co-author's last interruption. A neat device for drawing attention to our own textuality it may be, but it seems to me that he has wasted the few lines which I have allowed him – a missed opportunity to make some substantive points if I may say so.

Quite. And also my interruption serves to support your point about the insignificance of New Literary Forms, so in this case a New Literary Form actually helps make your criticism for you.

You are merely confirming that such forms waste space and distract from the main flow of the text. But at the risk of spoiling the flow of my introduction yet again and since these self-referential textual 'tricks' · on which you are so keen seem to be the flagship of the New Literary Forms movement (see Ashmore, 1985, Mulkay, 1985, Woolgar, 1984), I would just like to take this opportunity to make a quick observation about their use.

Yes, you had better 'take' that opportunity while you can, and do make it a 'quick observation'.

Thank you. The use of 'tricks' in these unconventional texts to draw attention to their own textuality is at best trivial and at worst distracting. After all, one wants to get on to the 'news' in a paper without having to keep pausing to admire the latest New Literary circus act. And in case you think I am just an unsympathetic reader who is unfamiliar with these sorts of texts, let me quote from one of these new literary performers themselves. Anna Wynne confessed the following at one of the much trumpeted Discourse Analysis Workshops where I believe a lot of this kind of 'work' goes on:

Perhaps strangely, as a reader I have severe problems with that kind of playful writing. For one thing I find the tone of some of it – including my own – too 'arch', lacking in seriousness however seriously it is written...the problem of such texts' readability applies for me also to many fictional texts which explore the possibility of form...I found, as reader, that those pieces I could 'translate back' into 'proper writing' I read: those I could not, I skipped over. (Wynne, 1986: 2)

HEAR, HEAR!

Thank you, readers.

Thank you, readers.

Although Wynne goes on to confess that she may be an unadventurous reader it is clear that the potential annoyance and distraction which some of the these 'tricks' elicit can be counter-productive – especially if all that happens is that such points are translated back into a conventional form.

I must say that was far from 'quick', even though you were interrupted by the readers and myself. Also it was a bit unfair; indeed it is a bit of a 'trick' in itself to quote the reservations of someone who is well-known as a proponent of a particular position. If you had quoted from some of Wynne's other texts (this volume) it would not have added weight to your comment at all – moreover you would have found some exciting New Literary Forms-style writing. You have employed a common trick found in conventional texts, known as 'to quote out of context'.[1] For instance, I have heard you complain on numerous occasions that most of the (conventional) literature is 'badly written, tedious and unimaginative' – to quote you, out of context.[2]

Well, I shall happily continue to quote from the Wynne paper so we can get more of the context, rather than having to rely upon undocumented sources.

What Wynne goes on to say actually bears out a point I made a few years ago in that little critique of reflexivity I published in the *EASST Newsletter*. If I may quote from my actual writings, and presumably this is 'in context':

I...think that there is a very good practical reason for researchers not to be self-conscious about their own social constructions...reflexivity can be debilitating to the carrying out of empirical research. (Pinch, 1983: 6–7)

By this I meant that a continual obsession with one's own intellectual production leads to introspection and ultimately it becomes impossible to write anything because one is continually aware that one's own writing is arbitrary and that there is always more to say. Let us read what Wynne has to offer on this topic:

One of the things that stopped me writing for so long – a year or more...was a conviction that to write, in whatever form, was at the same time always to have to leave things unsaid; a feeling that there was 'something about' writing sociology that did violence; that however one tried to escape it, denied the reflexive tie between analysis and the data. (Wynne, 1986: 2)

Well it seems to me that a little bit (sic) of Pinch could have saved her all that heart-searching.

Jolly generous of you, and you should know by now that I hate jokes about my name.[3] But what about all that heart-searching you went through when you first encountered the relativist programme in the sociology of scientific knowledge? No doubt you have conveniently forgotten about that.

That was, of course, quite different. But let us keep such irrelevant biographical details out of this. That is one of the troubles with these New Literary Forms – to make it fun you have to get personal. So let me get serious again.

Good, I prefer it when you are serious.

I take it we can both agree that the next section has one sub-heading?

Agreed.

And can we agree on my title?

The Move towards Reflexivity

It seems fine, but of course the 'move' started at my first interruption. However, please go ahead.

Those who advocate reflexivity and/or new types of literary forms (I shall show later that that the two need not necessarily be conflated) can be seen to be making a general argument of the following type:

> Proposition 1: Sociology of Scientific Knowledge has shown that X (where X is a body of knowledge) is actually Y (where Y is a body of socially constructed knowledge).

A corollary of the above is:

> Corollary 1: Y must be different from X in some significant respect.

this corollary is needed because if X and Y are not significantly different then SSK would not have shown anything much at all (Latour, this volume). This process of showing that something is different to what it was taken to be is often referred to as a process of 'deconstruction'. In other words, by showing that say, solar-neutrino science, is socially constructed, we (and I do mean 'we') have thereby deconstructed solar-neutrino science.

Most SSKers would probably subscribe to some version of the above. The new twist in the argument provided by reflexivity is to claim that X must include SSK's own findings. After all, this is a body of knowledge like any other X. In which case applying SSK to SSK means SSK is not what we thought it was (it is now socially constructed SSK, that is not-X but Y), and we are into a familiar self-referential paradox. If SSK is no longer what we thought it was then Proposition 1 no longer holds. In which case we do not have to worry that X is Y and SSK is just good old SSK and we can go on doing it as before. This immediately takes us back to Proposition 1, and if we include SSK itself within X, we get caught in the loop of the same reasoning.

I think I agree with all that, indeed it seems to me you have just summarized what Steve (Woolgar, 1983) has written on the topic. He refers to this process within SSK as constructing an 'irony'. If I may continue for you?

Woolgar took a whole article to make that point? It just shows you what can happen when you stop doing empirical work. But, anyway, if we are agreed I see no reason why you should not use up some of your allotted space making my points for me.

Actually Steve [4] made many other points in his article as, of course, for him SSK is his topic; and thus his work, since it addresses the textual practices of SSK is as deserving of the accolade 'empirical' as any other work in SSK. I shall continue, but please don't hesitate to interrupt me if I get it wrong.

Those who are proponents of reflexivity, and who wish to deny SSK any privileged position, argue that because of the above self-referential paradox one needs to replace SSK with a version which takes its reflexive potential seriously. Rather than trying to escape from the paradox, which is, of course, inescapable, it should be celebrated. The use of unconventional textual forms which draw attention to their own constructed nature is one means by which the self-referential paradox can be celebrated.

Hold on! Hold on! I knew I could not rely on you to get it completely right. You have moved too quickly from SSK to these 'new' developments. After all this paradox is rather obvious and could hardly have been overlooked. To take one early example, Bloor (1976) actually advocates explicitly that SSK be reflexive. It was, as I am sure you will recall, one of the tenets of his 'Strong Programme'. He writes of his programme that: 'In principle its patterns of explanation would have to be applicable to sociology itself.' (Bloor, 1976: 5)

Quite right, but I thought I was the one who was meant to be doing the interrupting in this paper. In any case you need to go back to your Steve (Woolgar, 1983). You will find there the claim that Bloor's version of reflexivity is less than adequate to the purposes of producing a truly self-referential SSK. Steve (Woolgar, 1984) refers to it as 'post-hoc reflexivity' or 'disengaged reflexivity'. Reflexivity is the one tenet of Bloor's programme which no one (including Bloor himself) takes seriously. As he admits it is 'an obvious requirement of principle' (Bloor, 1976: 5). But it does not seem to be a requirement of practice and he does not, for instance, demonstrate how his own work in SSK is socially produced. Indeed, he could not give reflexivity the same status as other tenets in his programme such as 'impartiality' or 'symmetry' because he would soon get into an infinite regress if he did. As Steve puts it:

> Authors like Bloor (1976) acknowledge and even encourage the possibility that constructivist irony can be turned back on itself (the 'reflexivity' tenet), but seek to avoid the infinite regress by declarations that irony is not intended as critical (the 'impartiality' tenet). (Woolgar, 1983: 154–5)

Thus, in short, what is needed is a strong programme of reflexivity?

Yes, but I think Steve (Woolgar, 1984) prefers the term 'constitutive' reflexivity, and of course he would deny that this was a programme in any conventional sense. [5]

Well, of course he would, that is Steve for you! But you really are being quite helpful now, and I am starting to feel encouraged that we can work together after all. If I may summarize. There are at least two versions of reflexivity within SSK and Bloor's version, according to Woolgar, is inadequate.

Woolgar might have said that, but I am sure Steve would have put it differently.

More multi-voiced obscurity, no doubt – please at least try to keep the ball on the ground; this is not one of your Discourse Analysis Workshops. We are out here in the public world. By the way, I take it that we do not have to mention here[6] the third form of reflexivity alluded to by Woolgar – the 'benign-introspection' version? I know that neither you nor I would ever take that sort of psychological talk seriously.

Quite – no need to mention that here.

Good. Back to self-reference. I was commenting on how SSKers such as Bloor had actually attended to the paradox, even if Woolgar does not like this particular way of dealing with it. What about other SSKers, such as our mutual friend Harry Collins? I remember Collins, in response to Ashmore's perpetual question, 'How can you be so deliberately unreflexive?' saying: 'I could hardly have overlooked that!'

Hee hee!

Indeed Collins (1981a) seems to be even more hard line than Bloor – he simply bans reflexivity. He argues that it is important to draw a distinction between the Natural and Social World when doing SSK. In other words, he treats claims about the Natural World in a different way from the way in which he treats claims about the Social World. It is legitimate for SSK to deconstruct scientists' claims about Nature but the Social World is to be treated as real and hence is not to be deconstructed. To put it another way: he advocates that SSKers approach the Social World in the same realist spirit that natural scientists approach the Natural World. Collins has no objections to an SSK of SSK, he just does not think it can be self-exemplifying. As he recently put it to me: 'That's the way knowledge is. You can shine a torch on someone else, and someone else can shine a torch on you, what you cannot do is shine a torch on yourself at the same time as shining it on someone else.'

The Torchlight Theory of Knowledge? I myself prefer the Light Bulb Theory where switching on the light illuminates everyone, including the bulb itself.[7]

[*Ignoring interruption*] Thus Collins, like Bloor, does have a way of dealing with the potential paradoxes, but unlike Bloor he is more straightforward on the reflexivity issue by having no truck with it at all.

He has even gone into print rejecting Bloor's reflexive tenet (Collins, 1981a). I suppose it's lucky Bloor did not respond in turn to Collins because then we would have had one of those classic end of *Social Studies of Science* 'go arounds', with Collins replying to Bloor, some American getting in on the act, and then with Woolgar coming in saying that everyone was missing the point anyway. Finally, Mulkay could have written a play about it all!

You seem to be picking up the flavour of things pretty well. It must be all those Discourse Analysis Workshops you attended – the culture has finally rubbed off on you.

And, of course, Collins presumably does not satisfy the proponents of constitutive reflexivity on other grounds, because to elevate the Social World, and thus social science, to the place where reality is to be found is to occupy an epistemologically privileged position – something which seems to be in blatant contradiction with the postulates of Impartiality and Symmetry in the Strong Programme of the Sociology of Scientific Knowledge, or of Stage One of Collins's Empirical Programme of Relativism (Collins, 1981b).

That's right. I must say we really do appear to be reaching a surprising amount of agreement. No doubt you have some twist to the argument lined up, whereby your 'straightforward' portrayal of all these arguments will lead you to 'discover' some inconsistency in, let me guess – I've got it – the reflexive position?

Well we have been working together for a number of years now, and you ought to have picked up a thing or two about my style.

Just to bolster the point about the Collins approach to reflexivity, there is even that unpublished paper sitting in a green battered folder in our offices with the words 'Early Thoughts on an Anti-Bath Reflexive Critique' scribbled on it. As I seem to recall, you wrote that paper after an unsatisfactory lunch-time argument with Harry Collins and Graham Cox soon after Harry first introduced the notion of a distinction between the Social and Natural Worlds. In that paper you have a nice argument where two scientists are disputing an experiment and one says he does not believe in the other's results because he is a Marxist. You then ask whether this claim is part of the Social World or the Natural World. Of course, within Collins's programme if your answer is 'Natural World' you treat the claim in terms of symmetry and impartiality. On the other hand, if it is part of the Social World then the claim can be unproblematically evaluated by the sociologist. The difficulty with Collins's distinction, of course, which you were well aware of at the time, is that what counts as 'Social' and what counts as 'Natural' in itself varies in different circumstances. That led you on to a general critique of Collins's programme – to quote from your paper (and here I must confess that I had some difficulty reading your writing, since as I recall you wrote this one up on a train, so please forgive me if I do not have it completely correct):

The achilles heel of all relativist thought from Mannheim onwards has been that some areas of knowledge are deemed to be immune to the relativist's argument. The most radical school of relativism – the Bath School – as advocated by H. M. Collins is no exception.[8] [8]

I must object. You are quoting from undocumented sources again. What evidence have you got that this paper – sorry, scribbled ramblings – exists? In any case if it does exist it was clearly written by you rather than me.

Well apart from having that green folder in front of me, the existence of such a paper is suggested by Ashmore in his thesis – he points out that 'Pinch' confessed in an interview to have written a paper on reflexivity which he was keeping on the 'back burner'.[9] [9] Also, he actually cites you as the originator of the argument about the problem posed by the scientist who disbelieves in a particular natural phenomenon because the proponent is a Marxist.[10] [10] So putting two and two together...

I knew that I could not trust Ashmore with that information, it was most unethical of him to mention that point in his thesis; indeed it may even be litigious. But in any case how do you know the 'paper' was written by me? I still maintain that it must have been you.

Well it seems more like your modus operandi – mentioning it to Ashmore was, I am certain, a calculated move on your part. You knew by that stage that you could comment on the most irrelevant things and Ashmore would treat them as data. I am certain that you just wanted to get some acknowledgement for a paper which you dared not publish since at that time you were going into print saying how misguided the whole reflexive turn was. [11]

This has gone quite far enough.

Interrupting me again?

Shut up! Indeed if you pursue this line any longer I may have to get litigious with you. But I must say that I have learnt my lesson. Despite our seeming agreement I now know never to trust you. These voices created in these new textual forms are perfectly capable of being Machiavellian and working as agents for some undisclosed purposes of the author behind the text. They are presented merely as being 'voices' but they are, of course, not to be trusted.

Surely it all depends upon which voice you think is dominant, if indeed there is a dominant voice? Also as senior author you have the right to remove the above passages. By having these squabbles out in the open, in the text itself, rather than, like most joint authors, hiding behind some common line, we are being more honest and making available to the readers the normally hidden politics of producing a text.

But at the same time a genuine multi-voiced dialogue must have the voices disagreeing or in tension. Thus I have let you keep in the above passages in order to make this a pukka dialogic text. But as you will see later, I do have a surprise in store for you, dear junior author – some voices will be more equal than others.

I must say I find all these threats rather tiresome, and you are merely playing into the hands of the putative feminist wing of the New Literary Forms movement. Many voices are not enough when they are still aggressive male voices! I do find your reaction to my point about that earlier unpublished paper of ours most surprising. I certainly did not mean to cause you offence since I was merely offering support to back up your argument about what Steve saw as the inadequacies of the Collins response to reflexivity. I was actually trying to help you clarify matters, in preparation for the deconstruction of Steve's position which I see coming, and who better to cite than you? Or was it me?

Help like that I could do without. Anyway, to return to matters of substance, and for the benefit of any readers who are still with us, I will summarize what we have been saying about the response of SSKers to reflexivity.

The means adopted by SSKers to cope with the reflexive potential of SSK are seen by proponents of 'practical' (Ashmore, 1985) or 'constitutive' (Woolgar, 1984) reflexivity – the strongest versions of reflexivity – as being insufficiently radical or even inconsistent. What is needed according to them is not SSK, but SSK + Z, where Z is discourse analysis – sorry *was* discourse analysis (as there do not appear to be many discourse analysts left on the Island of Britain these days) [12] – and/or reflexivity and/or New Literary Forms.

That is certainly one version of the position I have heard expressed, but please go on. You are now getting very serious indeed with all these algebraic-type characters, propositions, corollaries and postulates, and then to cap it all a little joke about Discourse Analysis. Ever noticed how people when they are being really serious often signal it with an obvious joke that acts as a contrast with the really serious points? It displays that they can tell what humour is all about and that therefore they also know what being serious is all about.[13] So I assume we now really are getting to the 'substance' of the matter.

Of course I am getting serious. There is surely no more serious issue to discuss in intellectual circles these days than the possibility that the Natural World is socially constructed. How wonderfully counter-intuitive it is that sociology, the 'softest' of all the scientific disciplines, should make claims to be able to account for physics – the Queen of the Sciences. Furthermore, we even seem to be succeeding to the extent that some philosophers and historians of science are taking the findings of SSK increasingly seriously. [14] And this brings me to the nub of many of the reservations felt about reflexivity, New Literary Forms and so on. SSK is a broad church and certainly no one is opposed to anyone having a little bit of fun, and there is no doubt that some of the New Literary Forms are quite enjoyable. Indeed, as I shall argue later in this paper, unconventional texts have always had their place within our discipline. For example, Lakatos (1963–4) was experimenting with Socratic dialogues while Ashmore and Woolgar

were still in kindergarten and while Mulkay was busy distinguishing cognitive and social norms in science. However, the particular twist which the reflexive argument has recently taken within SSK has the inevitable and inescapable consequence of threatening to undermine all the serious findings which SSKers have worked so hard to achieve over the last decade and a half.

Tell me more.

Well, if you accept what I have said previously you can see that the structure of the argument put forward by the proponents of reflexivity is just the same old critical irony – only in this case it is carried out on the topic of SSK. Rather than SSK being allowed to remain the same it is argued that it should become something different – namely SSK + Z. Why do we need SSK + Z? Because of lack of thorough-goingness and so on within SSK. In short, the proponents of reflexivity in arguing for their position first have to deconstruct SSK. They seem to be 'guilty', if that is the right word, of just the same sorts of moves which they object to within SSK.

Hold on! Hold on! I knew I could not rely on you to get it completely right. You have moved too quickly from SSK to these 'new' developments. After all, this paradox is rather obvious and could hardly have been overlooked.

Good, I'm glad you have seen the irony of being forced to reply with exactly the same words I used earlier on. Also, because this textual form allows me to make that point – that is, allows me to draw attention to our own textuality as we produce it – I have managed to escape from one of those silly textual loops of which New Literary Performers are so proud (Mulkay, 1984; Ashmore, 1985; Woolgar 1984). That seems to me to be a perfectly appropriate and proper usage of such forms. Also, by the way, a word-processor is much more suited for New Literary Forms than a typewriter. If you had used a word-processor all you would have needed to do was block mark my earlier passage and copy it to your section of the text. And if you were still stuck in the loop the word-processor could have churned out copies for ever, or at least until the paper ran out. Perhaps, on the other hand it is just as well that you have not discovered the word-processor.

Thanks for getting me out of the loop, and thanks for the advice about word-processors. I would like to point out, however, that you have wasted just as much time keying in your above point as it took me to type my last section. [15] Also, while we are on the topic of word-processors why are all your footnotes in those funny square brackets? I heard the 'micro monitor' muttering something about an 'interface compatibility problem'.

There you go being irrelevant again. I knew these damn New Literary Forms would get in the way. And just when I had worked up a good head of steam. As I was saying, the proponents of reflexivity in arguing for their position deconstruct SSK and, furthermore, of course, they have noticed this irony and have elaborate means to deal with the problem. New Literary Forms are actually the latest way of dealing with it. Not saying anything seriously; revelling in paradox; contradictions all round; and just plain (sic) obscurity are other tactics I noticed when I attended those Discourse Analysis Workshops. And, when pressed, the proponents of reflexivity always deny the critical ironic reading of SSK which their position entails. They say that it is a sign of recognition to have your text deconstructed – even a privilege! At least that is what they said to Harry Collins and I when we complained about the paper by Mulkay, Potter and Yearley (1983) which, as we read it, was an attempt to deconstruct our earlier work on parapsychology. [16] This is clearly a tactic they have learnt from SSK itself where it is common to deny that the SSK deconstruction of natural science carries any critical weight.

That is a nice twist to the argument, so it seems you actually did learn something at those workshops. You are right, normally proponents of reflexivity and so on argue that the SSKers' self-denial of any critical irony stemming from their work on science is unconvincing (e.g. Woolgar, 1983) – now you are saying it is equally unconvincing when it is claimed that no criticism of SSK is intended.

Exactly, why let the devil have all the good tunes? This also neatly explains much of the hostility generated by, for instance, Discourse Analysis. [17] Such work, just in examining the methodological basis of SSK threatened to deconstruct the findings of SSK. That is certainly why Collins and I, [18] and also MacKenzie (1981, 1984) felt it was necessary to reply to the Discourse Analysts.

I can sense you are building up to being really serious now so why not just go ahead and make a big point uninterrupted by me?

You certainly are getting sensitive to my style, but we had better watch it or people may suspect us of collusion. I have a suggestion. I will conclude this section on the 'move towards reflexivity' as it seems to have been going on for quite some time and then I will let you open the last section of the paper on New Literary Forms.

Agreed – with, of course, the usual proviso that in fact the last section started some time ago.

In summary, in order for any claims to be made some areas of discourse must be privileged. As we have seen, Bloor in effect privileges his own discourse, Collins privileges social science discourse and Mulkay, Woolgar and Ashmore claim to privilege nothing at all, and thereby as far as I can see claim nothing at all. But as I have argued, in deconstructing others' discourse these latter authors must privilege their own discourse and thereby they are caught in the very same trap.

Thus, the proponents of the strong version of reflexivity such as Ashmore, Mulkay and Woolgar, appear to want to have their cake and eat it. They critique the sort of argumentative moves made in which they themselves inevitably must engage. By deconstructing SSK they undermine their own premises. They are at best caught in the same self-referential circle as SSK and at worst, since their whole programme is parasitic upon SSK (a host which they inevitably undermine), it cannot expect to gain any credibility within SSK.

It is rather as if the fleas on a dog's back killed the dog. SSK is the dog and those that advocate reflexivity are the fleas. No doubt the proponents of reflexivity would say, 'Agh! What about the fleas on the fleas' backs?' – I for one am quite happy to ignore them!

Bravo! No need for me to deconstruct that passage – I shall let others more versed in the argument do that – after all we want to raise a few hackles, be provocative, and try to inspire a controversy. Also I liked your use of humour at the end, just to give the impression that you were not being too precious in your critique.

One serious point, though. Since this text is itself a dialogue this presumably means you too have taken the option of 'contradictions all round'?

I'm pleased to see that you too can be serious on occasions. You are quite right, the time has come for the contradictions to be resolved. So why don't you type your sub-heading in and let's get down to the real business.

It seems a bit misleading to put in a concluding sub-heading since like most papers the conclusion of this one was formulated long before we reached this point. If it is all right with you I shall just make one last remark and let you, as senior author, conclude the paper.

Surely you first want to summarize the points you have been making? I may be senior author but fair is fair, and I am quite happy, as we agreed earlier, to let you start off this section.

No, it seems counter-productive for me to conclude in that way; I would merely be falling into the trap of doing a normal concluding summary as happens in most conventional texts (Ashmore, 1985: ch. 6). What I would rather do is make one point which addresses the section you are about to write.

New Literary Forms: a Means to an End or Just a Means to Many Ends?

I put in the sub-heading anyway as your next point will specifically relate to my concluding section.

Great sub-heading! The point I wish to make concerns the fact that you as senior author will always have the last word in this text. If I have done my job well then the freedom you have given me to interrupt you should have raised a question mark in the readers' minds. I hope at the very least to have provided something of an antidote to the realist rhetoric of your critique by drawing the readers' attention to the textual devices, argumentative ploys and other 'tricks' embedded within your text. But now I am to be silenced.

It is your own choice.

However, I hope that my absence will not go unnoticed. The readers need not necessarily have got to like me, but hopefully they will miss me.

I wouldn't count on it.

My absence means that in the final part of the text you will have gone back to the conventional way of writing. And no doubt you, having had some experience of realist texts, will do a good job on the conclusion and without me here, you will thoroughly demolish New Literary Forms.

How very perceptive of you.

However, that is exactly my point. The more convincing you become in writing conventionally the more that part of the text will contrast with the earlier sections and hopefully this will in itself draw attention to the issue of textuality and how it is used in argument. Some readers used to these unconventional texts may even be able to reconstruct what I might have said in response to your points.

Well reasoned, if I might say so. You have indeed laid quite a clever trap for me. If I go on at length in the conventional manner and I seem more convincing than I did earlier then, as you say, it might draw undue attention to the conventional nature of the form I am using. On the other hand, if I stop now, I will not have done my job properly and demolished these New Literary Forms. I will not be able to put down all those strong concluding arguments about New Literary Forms which I have up my sleeve. I must admit that when I let you talk me into producing an unconventional text I had assumed you would be making comments throughout the text.

You are senior author so it's up to you to come up with a solution.

Well I think I have the answer; I hope it will allow me to have my cake and eat it too. In true John Fowles *French Lieutenant's Woman*-style I shall have two conclusions.

Nice idea.

I shall first have a proper serious ending in which I attack NLFs in the way which I know the editor of this volume is expecting. Then I shall finish with a short New Literary Forms-style ending (which probably no one will bother to read anyway after my devastating criticisms). Overall this will help to reduce the contrast with the earlier stages of the text. My conclusion will just be a long speech within a two-voiced text.

That is fine by me. One thing, though, are you sure you want your long conclusion to go before the short one? Surely it would be appropriate for you to have the last word?

I have given some thought to that and I think my plan works better because these are not alternative conclusions but are to be read serially. All my best points will have been made in the first conclusion and if you are right about them appearing as convincing because of

the textual form adopted, then no one will pay much attention to the last section anyway. Also, to make this text really convincing as a criticism of New Literary Forms we have got to have a silly non-serious final dialogic flourish.

But it may be serious in its non-seriousness.

Conclusion

It is time for you to go. I am senior author. Indeed, there has only ever been one author behind the text. So, dear junior author, I have just killed you off. And I will not even allow you to come back and say 'I left voluntarily' which I know you would have wanted to say. From now on it's just me.

He really has gone. And I must apologize to you, dear readers, as I have led you a little astray. No doubt you have been assuming that the 'typewritten' sections represented an independent voice. Well I've got news for you, it was me all along! That point made by my co-author, I mean me, when he went on about the possible difficulties I faced in concluding this text, was really just a little ploy on my part to give me the final say. It is like playing chess with yourself by playing both colours at the same time. You can set a trap, and sometimes you may even find you can't get out of it, but it is not the same thing as playing chess against a real opponent. However, I must say I was getting quite fond of his voice and maybe *I* shall bring him back for one final airing after all.

Anyway, all that is left for me to do is to clear up a few misunderstandings about New Literary Forms, or unconventional texts as I prefer to call them.

The first point I would like to make is that such unconventional texts, by their unconventionality, will inevitably irritate readers. Whether we like it or not, just as there are good manners, there are also conventions about the appropriate form sociology texts should take. Sociology texts are not novels. To break the conventions is to run the risk of irritating the reader, and thus there is a responsibility upon the authors of such unconventional texts to address the potential irritation they may produce. In other words, there is a special burden upon the breaker of conventions to show why breaking the conventions is warranted. It is not enough simply to be playful or to present such texts as a fait accompli. Just as if we break some rule of good manners, say by greeting a representative of a funding agency visiting our department with a kiss rather than with a handshake, the obligation is on the rule-breaker to give some account for such strange actions. Of course, if unconventional texts become more common then this burden will be removed.

Some of the irritation can be ameliorated by taking account of where the conventional reader is coming from. However, at the moment conventional texts will dominate the sociological reading of even the leading aficionados of New Literary Forms, and textual ploys such as those adopted in the present text inevitably will appear initially as distractions or at least will be noticeable as textual devices. This cannot make for good reading – the most enjoyable texts (including unconventional ones) are those where the text does not get in the way of the reading. Of course the most convincing way of overcoming the initial irritation is to make the text-as-a-whole *work*. In other words, the aim should be to make the argument more compelling in the unconventional form than a conventional text would have permitted. For example, Lakatos's (1963–4) brilliant 'Proofs and Refutations', although written unconventionally, works as a text and it is difficult to imagine how it might have been improved if he had used a conventional form.

With such caveats in mind I do not find anything especially worrisome about unconventional texts – indeed, it is not clear to me that unconventional texts per se raise particularly important issues for sociology. Such texts are a matter of the author's choice of style to suit the particular purposes at hand. However, I think it is important to draw a distinction between the use of unconventional texts in general and their explicit use in connection with the display of so-called 'constitutive reflexivity' within the sociology of science. It goes without saying that unconventional texts are often used in many other fields of discourse for a variety of purposes (even science – or rather Natural Philosophy – in the seventeenth century used a range of textual forms [19]). Moreover, they even have a history of use within SSK, but not explicitly for reflexive purposes.

If I may just cite a few examples with which I am familiar. It is not generally known that Harry Collins has employed such forms when the occasion merits. For instance, he has played with the notion of authorship. His less serious texts are published under the name 'Harry Collins' [20] (or in one case anonymously) [21] rather than the more austere and serious 'H. M. Collins'. Also he has written several spoof articles in the *New Scientist* magazine under the name 'Irwin Friml'. [22] In these articles outlandish physical devices are described, such as a Victorian 'fade out theatre' which produces a fading away of music by evacuating air from the theatre. Friml soon found he was engaged in a debate with a 'real' American historian about the technicalities of these sorts of devices!

Collins and I (Collins and Pinch, 1982) also originally had a chapter in our book *Frames of Meaning* which was written as science fiction. It had excerpts of dialogue among leading members of the sociology of science community engaged in a snooker match in the senior common room of a provincial university. In such games the use of the occasional pyschokinetic swerve or screw was quite normal. Sociology of science issues were readily discussed by participants between shots. The names of the SSKers were reversed – 'Nice shot, Senrab'! This chapter was taken out by the publishers because it was considered to be an outrageous detraction from the rest of the book. I even published an article (Pinch, 1979) which was a spoof on how a rationalist philosopher might treat the 'fraud hypothesis' as an explanation of parapsychology. Ashmore (1985: ch. 6) has this listed as an example of the use of 'fictioning' devices in SSK (and thus as a spoof precursor to his own work), although the paper had nothing to do with reflexivity.

I have cited only the texts with which I am personally familiar, but it is clear that there is not much 'new' about NLFs and more importantly that they can be used for other purposes in SSK than for displaying constitutive reflexivity. Indeed, Mulkay (1985) has used a variety of forms for a variety of purposes. Thus it is only the use of unconventional texts for the particular purpose of making a reflexive argument where, for instance, authors or voices try continually to deconstruct each other, that is of special concern to me here. Unconventional texts per se are a good thing, especially when they are well done. They are usually fun and surely we need more fun in sociology. It would be absurd to bar unconventional texts from sociology or from SSK. And here I hope the conservatism of some colleagues in sociology and the residual objections of publishers to anything new is not mistaken by those who advocate a heady mixture of SSK, reflexivity and New Literary Forms as confirmation that they are the latest 'true radicals' in SSK.

My reservations in this paper have concerned only the use of such texts for the particular purposes of deconstruction within SSK. [23] In other words, I think there are special difficulties when a particular voice becomes the subject of what Woolgar (1983) calls a 'critical irony'. When used for the purposes of deconstruction within our own field a crucial problem of such texts is the imputation of the *authenticity* of the voices espoused within the text.

In multi-voiced texts each voice is presented as being a genuine representative of those for whom they are supposed to speak. In this text, for example, I have used the voice of 'junior author' to present the position of those who advocate NLFs. How do we know that the voice of the junior author which I have constructed does mirror what an advocate of NLFs might authentically say in these circumstances? [24] 24

Citing or quoting direct from conventional texts in order to authenticate the voices produced in the unconventional text (as, for instance, favoured by Mulkay [1984] in a recent play) does not necessarily help either. It is quite likely that in the *new textual context* different things might have been said by the author of the quote anyway. Such forms produce many more ways in which to quote 'out of context'.

The problem of imputing authenticity is compounded because the purposes of unconventional texts are usually playful. It is often not clear in such unconventional texts whether the voices are meant as caricatures, or are meant to be taken ironically, or as reductio ad absurdums or whatever fantasy you can build into your reading of the voice. The author is usually encouraging the reader to think of new interpretations.

Conventional criticism becomes much harder to do and challenging the portrayal of a particular position in an unconventional text could become frustrating. For instance, if it is claimed by advocates of New Literary Forms that junior author has at various points in this text not quite got it right what is to stop me from replying: 'But, of course, didn't you realize he was being ironic there?'

This is not to say that realist texts are unambiguous or that there are no devices within conventional writing for displaying subtle shifts in what is being said and for distancing authors from voices. However, if the text is intended as criticism or deconstruction – the use to which NLFs have been put within SSK – it is surely more important and conducive to a good debate to avoid the extra layer of potential in-authenticity, which an unconventional text could produce. In other words, since most debates are liable to involve misunderstandings anyway, why start off by adopting a textual form which is likely to compound misunderstandings?

If the authors of these New Literary Forms were prepared to grant that they really had tried authentically to represent how the voice would speak in the new textual context, then the above criticism would not apply. We would simply have genuine criticism and debate occurring within one text rather than between several texts. However, it would seem that the authors of these texts are risking taking an absurd burden on their shoulders if they are claiming to represent multiple voices in an authentic manner. Why not just wait for a genuine debate to happen and use that as the basis for an unconventional text? This is in effect what Lakatos did in his 'Proofs and Refutations' paper.

Finally, we must not forget that lurking behind multi-voiced texts is the 'real' single author, as is the case with this text. Although the textual form chosen undoubtedly does place a constraint on what can be said (Mulkay, 1985) are we really to believe that an author has no axe to grind, and will represent all positions with equal sympathy and so on? Do you believe that Pinch is value neutral in this text and is giving New Literary Forms and reflexivity a fair hearing? Junior author did, by his textual existence, take on a life of his own and raise some problems for 'senior author', but has stopped interrupting for the moment – power ultimately lies with the one 'real' author. To repeat an analogy used above – it is like trying to play chess with yourself (i.e. playing both white and black): you can have a few good moments and set a few short-term problems but ultimately the game as a whole is pointless because you cannot be two players at once and truly play chess. That is the problem of authenticity raised by multi-voiced texts.

My contention is that in multi-voiced texts the voice behind the text is kept hidden. The reason for this is that if the author's own voice was allowed to come through in an obvious way, we as readers would immediately be suspicious of such texts. For instance, if it is apparent that a particular outcome of the debate staged in the text is that one voice loses and that the voice which wins happens to square with the position which we know the 'real' author advocates then we say 'surprise, surprise' and take the text to be a parody. Thus, in order to make these sorts of text work the 'real' or meta-author must in effect disguise his or her own voice – as indeed I have tried to do in the present text. In other words, there is a kind of bogus democracy permeating the text with all voices allowed equal rights. [25] Again to use the chess analogy, writing a credible dialogic text is like contriving a draw with yourself, but again such a draw, like an even-handed dialogic text, is bogus.

In summary, such multi-voiced texts are fine for many playful purposes, but for the purposes of making a serious contribution to SSK, especially when part of that contribution is to deconstruct positions within SSK, they have their limitations. As I have argued it is harder to establish the authenticity of the views portrayed and if multi-voiced texts are constructed with equal rights for all voices they are impotent. [26] Indeed, if I am correct, such texts when used as vehicles for criticism will produce even more misunderstandings or, more likely, reviewers and commentators will not take such texts seriously or will be at loss as to what to write in their commentaries apart from making arguments about form per se. [27] In this latter case sociology would become indistinguishable from literary criticism.

Some authors (e.g. Mulkay) seem to advocate unconventional writing, not as a means to deconstruct work in SSK, but just in the general sense of providing writers with greater freedom to make points in different ways. This is how such unconventional texts have traditionally been used. For instance, I have a lot of sympathy with the claim that technical and esoteric topics can be better clarified by the use of unconventional textual forms. Indeed, that is part of the reason I have used such an unconventional text for this critique – reflexivity and New Literary Forms are not in themselves exactly easy topics. Also novelists' techniques seem ideally suited for many purposes in interpretative sociology where the aim is to convey participants' understandings and to immerse the reader in the world of some group of actors. For example, William Faulkner's *The Sound and the Fury* is a powerful example of how different voices accounting for particular events can be put together to produce insights which it is difficult to imagine could have been produced by a conventional textual format.

When detached from their particular use as part of the reflexive wing of SSK such textual forms become really just a matter of preference – they are better suited to some tasks than to others. I only hope, dear readers, that you have found my present purposes suitable for this unconventional text. I would like to thank you for staying until the end, and please forgive me for breaking so many conventions.

Conclusion

Well I see some possible contradictions in your argument, but I suppose my voice is inauthentic because I am deconstructing your very serious position within SSK?

Exactly. Indeed, that is the first authentic thing you have said.

And all those 'conventional' uses of New Literary Forms by yourself never deconstructed anybody else's position?

Well perhaps just a few philosophers, but they are fair game anyway. However, there you go again making the deconstructive move.

And, of course, you are never the type of author to 'damn with faint praise'?

Well I did say that there were also tricks in conventional writing.

Yes you put such tricks to good use; as always you were at your most convincing with your more imaginative writing. I liked the chess analogy. It is a pity, however, that you didn't compare multi-voiced texts with a chess master giving a simultaneous display, but that I suppose would be stretching the analogy too far?

Quite.

Finally, just to show I am truly inauthentic and am really your puppet let me end by saying how right you are and that your critique is completely valid.[28]

Notes

1. For elaboration of 'quoting out of context' in conventional texts and how contexts are constructed to be the 'same' or 'different', see Ashmore (1985: ch. 4).

2. Pinch, personal communication, September 1986.

3. For a similar bad joke on my name see Hardin's (1981: 250) comment: 'Is what seems to be a formidable fortress of fraud to be taken with a Pinch assault?'

4. **An anthropologist attending Discourse Analyst Workshops and reading some of Ashmore's texts (e.g. Ashmore, 1985) could conclude that Woolgar, when mentioned as an advocate of New Literary Forms, is always referred to as 'Steve'.**

5. If Woolgar (1982) isn't a programme what is?

6. Notice the conventional textual trick of not mentioning at the same time as mentioning.

7. I am grateful to Malcolm Ashmore for the Light Bulb Theory of Knowledge.

8. Unpublished paper, T. J. Pinch, written sometime in 1978.

8. **Imaginary paper, cited in Pinch and Pinch (this volume).**

9. Ashmore (1985: 57) quotes Pinch as saying: 'I actually thought I'd write a paper about reflexivity arguing against Harry and I haven't – I've got it somewhere half-written and some day I'll probably come back to that again.'

9. **The above quote is clearly ambiguous and in any case since Ashmore claims he deliberately tries to misrepresent his sources of data (Ashmore, personal communication, September 1986) we cannot rely on his work as a serious documentary source.**

10. Ashmore (1985: 451, n. 51).

10. **See note 9.**

11. This account is actually wrong. I only went into print on reflexivity (Pinch, 1983) five years later and that was in response to a pro-reflexive critique of my work.

12. It seems from Latour (1984) and Woolgar (1986) that genuine discourse analysis can only be done in France!

13. On the distinction between serious and humorous modes of discourse, see Mulkay (1986b).

14. For philosophical work which mentions SSK see Brown (1984) and Hacking (1983). For historical work informed by SSK, see Rudwick (1985) and Shapin and Schaffer (1985).

15. My co-author is again bending the truth – this whole text was actually produced on a word-processor. However, because of certain technical problems the superscripts were added by Letraset!

16. Jonathan Potter and Steve Yearley have both made this point to me in conversation.

17. For some of the debate over discourse analysis see Mulkay et al. (1983), Collins (1983a), Gilbert and Mulkay (1984a, 1984b) and Shapin (1984b).

18. See our response as an appendix to Collins (1983a).

19. For examples of some of the unconventional textual forms used by Boyle and Hobbes, see Shapin and Schaffer (1985).

20. See, for instance, Harry Collins (1983b).

21. Anon (1984).

22. See, for instance, Friml (1974, 1976).

23. My comments in this section apply mainly to multi-voiced texts. These form only a sub-set of unconventional textual forms. See Ashmore (1985) for a complete listing.

24. That I have indeed misrepresented the NLF position is confirmed by comments I have received from Mike Mulkay and Malcolm Ashmore. Mulkay writes: 'Maybe the voice responsible for those concluding remarks should in some way acknowledge that those said to be involved in NLFs have themselves tried to deal with the kind of assertion proposed.' And here Mulkay refers me to his dialogue with Spencer in Mulkay (1985) where he tried to show how conventional forms actually misrepresent the highly interpretative process involved in making sense of the world.

24. The above note does in fact 'in some way acknowledge' Mulkay's point.

24. cont. And Ashmore has written in response to junior author's supposed exposure of senior author's conventional textual tricks: 'I'm not convinced, anyway that Pinch 2 [junior author] has done *all* that much in that line, at least not in any manner vastly different to Pinch 1 on occasions.'

25. Again, Ashmore's response to this text neatly illustrates this point. He writes 'And generally, isn't Pinch 2 a bit too subservient to Pinch 1. Why not have them *contest* who is the dominant author/voice?'

26. Thus the present text in that it strives to be a genuine dialogic text is impotent as a criticism of New Literary Forms. For instance, Mulkay in response to it has written: 'Does this mean I should abandon NLFs – or pursue them more enthusiastically?' Interestingly enough, any potency this text possesses comes from its *failure* to be a genuine dialogue. Thus the long speech by 'senior author' at the end reverts to a conventional form and thus produces a more potent criticism of NLFs. Indeed, the potency of this conventional speech is indicated by over two-thirds of Mulkay's comments on this text referring to it alone. Similarly, nearly half of Ashmore's fourteen-page commentary on this text concerns the same speech by 'senior author'.

27. It can be argued that new textual forms for reviewing and commentary will also be needed. For instance, Mulkay and Janet Heaton in response to this text have produced very interesting dialogic commentaries. Of course, all the comments made above about unconventional texts apply equally to new textual reviews and commentaries, especially if the aim of such reviews is to further criticism.

28. The jokiness of parts of this text is deliberate and is meant to reflect the type of discourse found at the Discourse Analysis Workshops. We are grateful to Malcolm Ashmore, Mike Mulkay, Janet Heaton and Harry Collins for many helpful conversations. We would also like to thank Malcolm, Mike, Steve and Jan for providing comments on an earlier draft of this text and thereby providing more data. We would also like to acknowledge the invaluable input which the Discourse Analysis Workshops have provided.

Reflexion on the Pinches

The chapter by the Pinches exemplifies some important and intriguing issues opened up by explorations in reflexivity of the kind undertaken throughout this volume. One reading of this chapter, a reading which empathizes most clearly with the senior author (s/he of the bold, masterful typeface), takes it as a sustained attack on the notion of reflexivity as explored through 'new literary forms'. But the alternative reading, which finds more sympathy with the junior author (nondescript, ordinary typeface), rejoices in the failure of this 'attack'. This alternative reading is perhaps less obvious, precisely because the junior author is made out to be junior, and his/her arguments are presented as inferior. Indeed, junior author is denied a voice for long sections towards the end of the 'debate'.

Staying with the more obvious reading for the moment, the question arises as to whether or not the sustained attack succeeds and, if so, how and with what consequences. The curious paradox is that the success of the attack depends on the use of (one of) the forms which is being attacked for being of (little or) no value. The successful use of a new literary form is necessary to argue for its failure, and the failure of the two voices technique is one of the reasons for the chapter's success. Clearly, the strength of the chapter is that it sets off and sustains the ambivalences which stem from this paradox. As a result of reading this piece, should readers abandon new literary forms, or pursue them more enthusiastically? The point is not that the reader has to make a choice, but that the choice is continually available. The openness of choice is exhibited and remains lively throughout the chapter. (For a discussion of this and other reactions to the chapter, see Pinch et al., 1987.)

But was this 'ambivalence effect' intended by (either) author? (And to what extent does it matter what was intended?) One referee's comment included the observation that the piece by the Pinches was 'one of the best defences of realism seen in a long time'. The irony of this remark resonates at several levels. Was it intended ironically by the referee? Was a defence of realism intended (or even anticipated as a reading) by the author(s), given that the discussion appears to presume a commonality of relativism between all participants? We could, of course, try to 'settle' this kind of question – by adducing evidence about the motives of the authors, drawing on readings of their past work and so on. However, this (relatively straightforward) option would amount to closure on just those issues which so enliven the discussion by opening the text to further questions.

The Pinches' chapter thus succeeds, perhaps despite itself, because it keeps alive the paradox upon which it is based: the critique of form through the use of that form. The liveliness is evident in that attempts to read or comment upon the chapter themselves generate paradox. But the chapter also fails because its author(s) seem(s) to assume that the adoption of a particular form guarantees a particular effect. The presumption is that the use of a New Literary Form – in this case 'the second voice device' – means that ipso facto reflexivity is being done. However, this volume has demonstrated that reflexivity is far more intricate and elusive than that.

I OBJECT TO THAT DENIGRATION OF THE SECOND VOICE DEVICE.

Why did you have to spoil everything by reappearing right at the end. . .?

Bibliography

Anon (1984) 'On Behalf of the Personae', *Social Studies of Science*, 14: 283.

Ashmore, M. (1983) 'The Six Stages', paper presented to the Discourse Analysis Workshop, University of York, April.

Ashmore, M. (1985) 'A Question of Reflexivity: Wrighting Sociology of Scientific Knowledge.' DPhil thesis, University of York.

Atkinson, J. M. and Drew, P. (1979) *Order in Court: the Organisation of Verbal Interaction in Judicial Settings*. London: Macmillan.

Atkinson, J. M. and Heritage, J. C. (eds) (1985) *Structures of Social Action: Studies of Conversational Analysis*. Cambridge: Cambridge University Press.

Austin, J. L. (1962, 1982) *How to Do Things with Words*. Oxford: Oxford University Press.

Barnes, B. (1974) *Scientific Knowledge and Sociological Theory*. London: Routledge and Kegan Paul.

Barnes, B. (1977) *Interests and the Growth of Knowledge*. London: Routledge and Kegan Paul.

Barnes, B. (1982) *T. S. Kuhn and Social Science*. London: Macmillan.

Barnes, B. and Bloor, D. (1982) 'Relativism, Rationality and the Sociology of Knowledge', pp. 21–47 in Hollis and Lukes (1982).

Barnes, B. and Shapin, S. (eds) (1979) *Natural Order: Historical Studies of Scientific Culture*. Beverly Hills and London: Sage.

Barth, J. (1972) 'Life Story' pp. 120–32 in *Lost in the Funhouse*. Harmondsworth, Middx: Penguin Books.

Barthes, R. (1975) *S/Z*. London: Jonathan Cape.

Barthes, R. (1977) *A Lover's Discourse* (trans. R. Howard, 1978). London: Jonathan Cape.

Barton, A. (1974) *Three Worlds of Therapy*. Palo Alto, CA: National Press Books.

Bastide, F. (1985) 'Introduction to Semiotics', unpublished paper, Centre de Sociologie de l'Innovation, Ecole des Mines, Paris.

Bell, C. (1974) 'Replication and Reality or the Future of Sociology', *Futures* (June): 253–60.

Belsey, C. (1980) *Critical Practice*. London: Methuen.

Berger, J. (1985) 'Postscript', pp. 93–7 in Brody and Ignatieff (1985).

Berne, E. (1961) *Transactional Analysis in Psychotherapy*. New York: Grove Press.

Bloor, D. (1976) *Knowledge and Social Imagery*. London: Routledge and Kegan Paul.

Bloor, D. (1981) 'The Strengths of the Strong Programme', *Philosophy of the Social Sciences*, 11: 173–98.

Bloor, D. (1982) 'Sociology of (Scientific) Knowledge', pp. 391–3 in Bynum and Porter (1982).

Blum, A. (1971) 'Theorizing', pp. 320–35 in Douglas (1971).

Blum, A. (1974) *Theorizing*. London: Heinemann.

Blum, A. and McHugh, P. (1984) *Self-Reflection in the Arts and Sciences*. Atlantic Highlands, NJ: Humanities Press.

Boas, F. (1888) *The Central Eskimo*. Washington: 6th Annual Report of the Bureau of Ethnology.

Bocock, R. (1976) *Freud and Modern Society*. Sunbury-on-Thames, Middx: Thomas Nelson.

Boltanski, L. (1984) 'La Dénonciation', *Actes de la Recherche en Sciences Sociales*, 51: 3–40.

Borges, J. L. (1970) 'Pierre Menard, Author of the *Quixote*', pp. 62–71 in *Labyrinths*. Harmondsworth, Middx: Penguin Books.

Braudel, F. (1985) *The Perspective of the World: 15th to 18th Century*. New York: Harper and Row.

Brody, H. and Ignatieff, M. (1985) *Nineteen Nineteen*. London: Faber.

Brown, J. (ed.) (1984) *Scientific Rationality: the Sociological Turn*. Dordrecht: Reidel.

Brunel–ARMS Research Unit (1983) 'Discovering the Diagnosis of Multiple Sclerosis', *General Report No 2*.

Bynum, W. and Porter, R. (eds) (1982) *Dictionary of the History of Science*. London: Macmillan.

Callon, M. (1986) 'Some Elements of a Sociology of Translation: Domestication of the Scallops and the Fishermen of St Brieuc's Bay', pp. 196–229 in Law (1986).

Callon, M. and Latour, B. (1981) 'Unscrewing the Big Leviathan: How Actors Macrostructure Reality and How Sociologists Help Them', pp. 277–303 in Knorr-Cetina, K. D. and Cicourel, A. (eds) (1981) *Advances in Social Theory and Methodology: Toward an Integration of Micro-and Macro-Sociologies*. London: Routledge and Kegan Paul.

Callon, M., Law, J. and Rip. A. (eds) (1986) *Mapping the Dynamics of Science*. London: Macmillan.

Calvino, I. (1982) *If On a Winter's Night a Traveller*. London: Picador.

Carroll, L. (1939) 'What the Tortoise Said to Achilles' in *Complete Works*. London: Nonesuch Press. Cited in Winch (1958).

Caute, D. (1971) *The Illusion*. London: André Deutsch.

Charcot, J. M. (1868) 'Leçons sur les Maladies Chroniques du Système Nerveux: 1. Des Scléroses de la Moelle Epinière', *Gaz d. hôp*, 41: 405–6 and 409.

Charcot, J. M. (1872) *Leçons sur les Maladies du Système Nerveux*. Paris: Delahaye.

Charcot, J. M. (1877) *Lectures on the Diseases of the Nervous System* (trans. George Sigerson). London: New Sydenham Society.

Chaudry et al. (1986) TRICK reference.

Clifford, J. (1981) 'On Ethnographic Surrealism', *Comparative Studies in Society and History*, 23: 539–64.

Clifford, J. (1983a) 'Power and Dialogue in Ethnography: Marcel Griaule's Initiation' pp. 121–56 in Stocking (1983a).

Clifford, J. (1983b) 'On Ethnographic Authority', *Representations*, 1 (2): 118–46.

Clifford, J. (1986) 'Introduction: Partial Truths', pp. 1–26 in Clifford and Marcus (1986).

Clifford, J. and Marcus, G. E. (eds) (1986) *Writing Culture: the Poetics and Politics of Ethnography*. Berkeley and Los Angeles, CA: University of California Press.

Cohen, S. and Taylor, L. (1976) *Escape Attempts: the Theory and Practice of Resistance to Everyday Life*. London: Allen Lane.

Cole, D. (1983) ''The Value of a Person Lies in His Herzensbildung': Franz Boas' Baffin Island Letter Diary', pp. 13–52 in Stocking (1983a).

Collins, H. M. (1975) 'The Seven Sexes: a Study in the Sociology of a Phenomenon, or the Replication of Experiments in Physics', *Sociology*, 9: 205–24.

Collins, H. M. (1976) 'Upon the Replication of Scientific Findings: a Discussion Illuminated by the Experiences of Researchers into Parapsychology', *Proceedings of 4S/ISA Conference*, Cornell University, November.

Collins, H. M. (1978a) 'Replication of Experiments: a Sociological Comment', *The Behavioural and Brain Sciences*, 3: 391–2.

Collins, H. M. (1978b) 'Science and the Rule of Replicability: a Sociological Study of Scientific Method', unpublished paper, presented to 144th National Meeting of the AAAS, Washington, DC.

Collins, H. M. (1981a) 'What is TRASP? The Radical Programme as a Methodological Imperative', *Philosophy of the Social Sciences*, 11: 215–24.

Collins, H. M. (1981b) 'Knowledge and Controversy: Studies in Modern Natural Science', special issue of *Social Studies of Science*, 11 (1).

Collins, H. M. (1981c) 'Stages in the Empirical Programme of Relativism', *Social Studies of Science*, 11: 3–10.

Collins, H. M. (1981d) 'Son of Seven Sexes: the Social Destruction of a Physical Phenomenon', *Social Studies of Science*, 11: 33–62.

Collins, H. M. (1981e) 'The Place of the "Core-Set" in Modern Science: Social Contingency with Methodological Propriety in Science', *History of Science*, 19: 6–19.

Collins, H. M. (1982a) 'Special Relativism – the Natural Attitude', *Social Studies of Science*, 12: 139–43.

Collins, H. M. (1982b) 'Knowledge, Norms and Rules in the Sociology of Science', *Social Studies of Science*, 12: 299–309.

Collins, H. M. (1982c) 'Scientific Replication', p. 372 in Bynum and Porter (1982).

Collins, H. M. (1983a) 'An Empirical Relativist Programme in the Sociology of Scientific Knowledge', pp. 85–113 in Knorr-Cetina and Mulkay (1983).

Collins, Harry (1983b) 'Magicians in the Laboratory: a New Role to Play?', *New Scientist*, 98: 929–31.

Collins, H. M. (1984) 'When Do Scientists Prefer to Vary Their Experiments?', *Studies in History and Philosophy of Science*, 15: 169–74.

Collins, H. M. (1985) *Changing Order: Replication and Induction in Scientific Practice*. London and Beverly Hills, CA: Sage.

Collins, H. M. (1987) 'Misunderstanding Replication?', *Social Science Information*, 26: 451–59.

Collins, H. M. and Cox, G. (1976) 'Recovering Relativity: Did Prophecy Fail?', *Social Studies of Science*, 6: 423–44.

Collins, H. M. and Cox, G. (1977) 'Relativity Revisited: Mrs Keech, a Suitable Case for Special Treatment?', *Social Studies of Science*, 7: 372–80.

Collins, H. M. and Pinch, T. J. (1982) *Frames of Meaning: The Social Construction of Extraordinary Science*. London: Routledge and Kegan Paul.

Collins, H. M., Pinch, T. J. and Shapin, S. (1984) 'Authors' Preface', *Social Studies of Science*, 14 (4): ii.

Coulter, J. (1979) *The Social Construction of Mind*. London: Macmillan.

Coulter, J. (1983) *Rethinking Cognitive Theory*. London: Macmillan.

Coulter, J. (1984) 'Untitled' paper presented to the Sociology of Language Conference. Plymouth, Devon.

Coulter, J. (1985) 'Two Concepts of the Mental' pp. 129–44 in K. Gergen and K. Davis (eds) *The Social Construction of the Person*. New York: Springer.

Crosman, R. (1980) 'Do Readers Make Meaning?' pp. 149–64 in S. Suleiman and I. Crosman (eds) *The Reader in the Text*. Princeton, NJ: Princeton University Press.

Crowcroft, A. (1967) *The Psychotic: Understanding Madness*. Harmondsworth, Middx: Penguin Books.

Culler, J. (1981) *The Pursuit of Signs: Semiotics, Literature, Deconstruction*. London: Routledge and Kegan Paul.

Dawe, A. (1978) 'Theories of Social Action' pp. 362–417 in T. Bottomore and R. Nisbet (eds) *A History of Sociological Analysis*. London: Heinemann Educational.

de Man, P. (1979) *Allegories of Reading: Figural Language in Rousseau, Nietzsche, Rilke and Proust*. New Haven: Yale University Press.

de Man, P. (1983) *Blindness and Insight: Essays in the Rhetoric of Contemporary Criticism*. London: Methuen.

Derrida, J. (1976) *Of Grammatology* (trans. G. Spivak). Baltimore: Johns Hopkins University.

Derrida, J. (1977) 'Limited Inc abc', *Glyph*, 2: 162–254.

Derrida, J. (1978) *Writing and Difference* (trans. A. Bass). London: Routledge and Kegan Paul.

Douglas, J. (ed.) (1971) *Understanding Everyday Life*. London: Routledge and Kegan Paul.

Durkheim, E. (1912) *The Elementary Forms of the Religious Life* (trans. J. W. Swain, 1954). New York: Free Press.

Erikson, E. (1958) *Young Man Luther*. New York: Norton.

Erikson, E. (1964) *Insight and Responsibility*. New York: Norton.

Firth, D. (1945) 'The Case of Augustus d'Este', *Cambridge University Medical Society Magazine*, 23 (1): 13–22.

Foreman, A. (1977) *Femininity as Alienation: Women and the Family in Marxism and Psychoanalysis*. London: Pluto Press.

Foucault, M. (1972) *The Archeology of Knowledge* (trans. A. Sheridan Smith). London: Tavistock.

Foucault, M. (1974) *The Order of Things* (trans. A. Sheridan Smith). London: Tavistock.

Fowles, J. (1977) *The French Lieutenant's Woman*. St Albans: Triad/Panther.

Fowles, J. (1982) *Mantissa*. New York: Little, Brown and Company.

Freud, S. (1898) *Sexuality in the Aetiology of the Neuroses*, Standard Edition 13 of *The Standard Edition of the Complete Psychological Works of Sigmund Freud* (trans. and general ed. James Strachey). London: Hogarth Press and The Institute of Psychoanalysis.

Freud, S. (1901) *The Psychopathology of Everyday Life*. St. Ed. 6.

Freud, S. (1905) *Three Essays on the Theory of Sexuality*. St. Ed. 7.

Freud, S. (1909) *Five Lectures on Psychoanalysis*. St. Ed. 11.

Freud, S. (1912) *Totem and Taboo*. St. Ed. 13.

Freud, S. (1926) *The Question of Lay Analysis*. St. Ed. 20.

Freud, S. (1927) *Future of an Illusion*. St. Ed. 21.

Freud, S. (1930) *Civilisation and its Discontents*. St. Ed. 21.

Freud, S. (1939) *Moses and Monotheism*. St. Ed. 23.

Friml, I. (1974) 'The Fade Out Theatre', *New Scientist*, 61: 23.

Friml, I. (1976) 'Bosenquet and his Spasmograph', *New Scientist*, December: 748–50.

Fromm, E. (1957) *The Art of Loving*. London: George Allen and Unwin.

Fromm, E. (1980) *The Greatness and Limitations of Freud's Thought*. New York: Harper and Row.

Fuller, S. (1986) 'Making Reflexivity Safe for Relativism', paper presented to Society for Social Studies of Science, session on Reflexivity, Pittsburgh, PA, October.

Furhman, E. R. and Oehler, K. (1986) 'Discourse Analysis and Reflexivity', *Social Studies of Science*, 16: 293–307.

Garfinkel, H. (1967) *Studies in Ethnomethodology*. Englewood-Cliffs, NJ: Prentice-Hall.

Geertz, C. (1973) *The Interpretation of Cultures*, New York: Basic Books.

Geertz, C. (1975) 'From the Native's Point of View: On the Nature of Anthropological Understanding', *American Scientist*, 63: 47–53.

Gieryn, T. F. (1982) 'Relativist/Constructivist Programmes in the Sociology of Science: Redundance and Retreat', *Social Studies of Science*, 12: 279–97.

Gilbert, G. N. and Mulkay, M. J. (1983) 'In Search of the Action', pp. 8–34 in G. N. Gilbert and P. Abell (eds) *Accounts and Action*. Aldershot, Hampshire: Gower.

Gilbert, G. N. and Mulkay, M. J. (1984a) *Opening Pandora's Box: A Sociological Analysis of Scientists' Discourse*. Cambridge: Cambridge University Press.

Gilbert, G. N. and Mulkay, M. J. (1984b) 'Experiments are the Key: Participants' Histories and Historians' Histories of Science', *Isis* 75: 105–25.

Gilbert, J. J. and Sadler, M. (1983) 'Unsuspected Multiple Sclerosis', *Archives of Neurology*, 40: 533–6.

Girard, R. (1978) *Des Choses Cachées Depuis La Fondation Du Monde*. Paris: Grasset.

Greimas, A. J. and Courtes, J. (1983) *Semiotics and Language. Analytical Dictionary* (trans. L. Cris et al.). Bloomington, IN: Indiana University Press.

Grice, H. P. (1975) 'Logic and Conversation', pp. 41–58 in P. Cole and J. L. Morgan (eds) *Syntax and Semantics 3: Speech Acts*. New York: Academic Press.

Gruenberg, B. (1978) 'The Problem of Reflexivity in the Sociology of Science', *Philosophy of the Social Sciences*, 8: 321–43.

Habermas, J. (1984) *The Theory of Communicative Action Vol. 1: Reason and the Rationalisation of Society* (trans. T. McCarthy). London: Heinemann.

Hacking, I. (1983) *Representing and Intervening*. Cambridge: Cambridge University Press.

Hammersley, M. and Atkinson, P. (1983) *Ethnography: Principles in Practice*. London and New York: Tavistock.

Hardin, C. L. (1981) 'Table Turning, Parapsychology and Fraud', *Social Studies of Science*, 11: 149–50.

Harvey, B. (1981) 'Plausibility and the Evaluation of Knowledge: a Case Study of Experimental Quantum Mechanics', *Social Studies of Science*, 11: 95–130.

Heidegger, M. (1967) *Being and Time* (trans. J. Macquarrie and E. Robinson). Oxford: Basil Blackwell.

Heritage, J. C. (1984) *Garfinkel and Ethnomethodology*. Cambridge: Polity Press.

Herndon, R. M. and Rudick. R. A. (1983) 'Multiple Sclerosis: the Spectrum of Severity', *Archives Neurology*, 40: 531–2.

Hirsch, E. D. (1976) *The Aims of Interpretation*. Chicago, IL: Chicago University Press.

Hofstadter, D. R. (1980) *Gödel, Escher, Bach: an Eternal Golden Braid. A Metaphorical Fugue on Minds and Machines in the Spirit of Lewis Carroll*. Harmondsworth, Middx. Penguin Books.

Hofstadter, D. R. (1985) *Metamagical Themas: Questing for the Essence of Mind and Pattern*. New York: Basic Books.

Hollis, M. and Lukes, S. (eds) (1982) *Rationality and Relativism*. Oxford: Basil Blackwell.

Hughes, T. P. (1983) *Networks of Power: Electric Supply Systems in the US, England and Germany, 1880–1930*. Baltimore: Johns Hopkins University.

Husserl, E. (1931) *Ideas: General Introduction to Pure Phenomenology*. London: George Allen and Unwin.

ICA (1986a) *In Conversation*. Seminar Series. London.

ICA (1986b) *Talking Psychoanalysis*. Lecture Series. London.

Jung, C. (1954) *The Practice of Psychotherapy*. New York: Pantheon Books.

Kidder, T. (1981) *The Soul of a New Machine*. London: Allen Lane.

Klein, M. (1948) *Contribution to Psychoanalysis*. London: Hogarth Press.

Knorr, K. D. (1979) 'Tinkering Towards Success: Prelude to a Theory of Practice', *Theory and Society*, 8: 347–76.

Knorr, K. D., Krohn, R. and Whitley, R. (eds) (1980) *The Social Process of Scientific Investigation. Sociology of the Sciences Yearbook, Vol. 4*. Dordrecht: Reidel.

Knorr-Cetina, K. D. (1979) 'Tinkering Towards Success: Prelude to a Theory of Scientific Practice', *Theory and Society*, 8: 347–76.

Knorr-Cetina, K. D. (1981) *The Manufacture of Knowledge: an Essay on the Constructivist and Contextual Nature of Science*. Oxford: Pergamon.

Knorr-Cetina, K. D. (1983) 'The Ethnographic Study of Scientific Work: Towards a Constructivist Interpretation of Science', pp. 115–40 in Knorr-Cetina and Mulkay (1983).

Knorr-Cetina, K. D. and Mulkay, M. J. (eds) (1983) *Science Observed: Perspectives on the Social Study of Science*. London: Sage.

Kurtzke, J. F. (1979) 'Epidemiology of Multiple Sclerosis in US Veterans: 1. Race, Sex, and Geographical Distribution', *Neurology*, 29: 1228–35.

Kurtzke, J. F. (1980) 'Multiple Sclerosis: an Overview', pp. 170–95 in F. C. Rose (ed.) *Clinical Neuroepidemiology*. London: Pitman Medical.

Lakatos, I. (1963–4) 'Proofs and Refutations', *British Journal for the Philosophy of Science*, 14: 1–25, 129–39, 221–43, 296–342.

Latour, B. (1975) 'Les Raisons Profondes du Style Répétitif de Péguy', pp. 75–94 in *Péguy Ecrivain, Colloque de Centenaire*. Paris: Klinsieck.

Latour, B. (1980) 'Is it Possible to Reconstruct the Research Process? Sociology of a Brain Peptide', pp. 53–73 in Knorr et al. (1980).

Latour, B. (1982) 'Review of Karin Knorr-Cetina's The Manufacture of Knowledge', *Society for Social Studies of Science Newsletter*, 7 (4): 30–4.

Latour, B. (1983) 'Give Me a Laboratory and I Will Raise the World', pp. 141–70 in Knorr-Cetina and Mulkay (1983).

Latour, B. (1984) 'Where Did You Put The Black-Box Opener?' *EASST Newsletter*, 3 (3): 17–21.

Latour, B. (1986) 'Visualisation and Cognition' pp. 1–40 in H. Kuklick (ed.) *Knowledge and Society. Studies in the Sociology of Culture Past and Present*. Greenwich, CT: Jai Press.

Latour, B. (1987) *Science in Action*. Milton Keynes: Open University Press.

Latour, B. (1988) *The Pasteurisation of France* followed by *Irreductions: a Politico-Scientific Essay*. Cambridge, MA: Harvard University Press.

Latour, B. and Bastide, F. (1982) 'Essai de Science-Fabrication', *Etudes Francaises*, 19 (2): 111–26.

Latour, B. and de Noblet, J. (eds) (1985) *Les Vues de L'Esprit: Visualisation et Connaissance Scientifique*. *Culture Technique*, 14.

Latour, B. and Woolgar, S. (1979) *Laboratory Life: the Construction of Scientific Facts*. (2nd ed, 1986) Princeton, NJ: Princeton University Press.

Laudan, L. (1981) 'The Pseudo-Science of Science?', *Philosophy of the Social Sciences*, 11: 173–98.

Laudan, L. (1982) 'A Note on Collins' Blend of Relativism and Empiricism', *Social Studies of Science*, 12: 131–2.

Law, J. (ed.) (1986) *Power, Action and Belief. A New Sociology of Knowledge?* Keele: Sociological Review Monograph no. 32 (University of Keele). London: Routledge and Kegan Paul.

Lawson, H. (1985) *Reflexivity: the Post-Modern Predicament*. London: Hutchinson.

Levinson, S. (1983) *Pragmatics*. Cambridge: Cambridge University Press.

Livingston, E. (1986) *The Ethnomethodological Foundation of Mathematics*. London: Routledge and Kegan Paul.

Lynch, M. (1985) *Art and Artifact in Laboratory Science: A Study of Shop Work and Shop Talk in a Research Laboratory*. London: Routledge and Kegan Paul.

Lynch, M. and Woolgar, S. (eds) (1988) *Representation in Scientific Practice*, Special issue of *Human Studies*.

McAlpine, D. (1972) 'Some Aspects of the Natural History of Multiple Sclerosis (continued)', pp. 99–131 in McAlpine et al. (1972).

McAlpine, D., Lumsden, C. E. and Acheson, E.D. (eds) (1972) *Multiple Sclerosis: a Reappraisal*. London and Edinburgh: Churchill Livingstone.

McCloskey, D. N. (1985) *The Rhetoric of Economics*. Madison, WI: Wisconsin University Press.

McHugh, P. Raffel, S. Foss, D. and Blum, A. (1974) *On the Beginning of Social Inquiry*. London: Routledge and Kegan Paul.

MacKenzie, D. (1981) 'Interests, Positivism and History', *Social Studies of Science*, 11: 498–504.

MacKenzie, D. (1984) 'Reply to Steven Yearley', *Studies in the History and Philosophy of Science*, 15: 251–9.

Malinowski, B. (1926) 'Myth in Primitive Psychology', pp. 93–148 in *Magic, Science and Religion*. Garden City, New York: Doubleday Anchor.

Malinowski, B. (1961) *Argonauts of the Western Pacific*. London: Routledge and Kegan Paul.

Marcus, G. E. (1980) 'Rhetoric and the Ethnographic Genre in Anthropological Research', *Current Anthropology*, 21 (4): 509.

Marcus, G. E. and Cushman, D. (1982) 'Ethnographies as Texts', *Annual Review of Anthropology*, 11: 25–69.

Marcus, S. (1984) *Freud and the Culture of Psychoanalysis*. Winchester, MA: George Allen and Unwin.

Marcuse, H. (1955) *Eros and Civilization*. Boston, MA: Beacon Press.

Marwick, A. (1970) *The Nature of History*. Harmondsworth, Middx: Penguin Books.

Masson, Mousaieff J. (1984) *Freud: The Assault on Truth*. London: Faber.

Matthews, B., Acheson, E. D., Batchelor, J. D. and Weller, R. C. (eds) (1985) *McAlpine's Multiple Sclerosis*. London and Edinburgh: Churchill Livingstone.

Merton, R. K. (1973) *The Sociology of Science*. Chicago IL: University of Chicago Press.

Mulkay, M. J. (1979) *Science and the Sociology of Knowledge*. London: George Allen and Unwin.

Mulkay, M. J. (1980) 'Sociology of Science in the West' (Trend Report, part 1), *Current Sociology*, 28 (3): 1–184.

Mulkay, M. J. (1981) 'Action, Belief, or Scientific Discourse? A Possible Way of Ending Intellectual Vassalage in Social Studies of Science', *Philosophy of the Social Sciences*, 11: 163–71.

Mulkay, M. J. (1984) 'The Scientist Talks Back: a One-Act Play, with a Moral, About Replication in Science and Reflexivity in Sociology', *Social Studies of Science*, 14: 265–82. Also pp. 156–70 in Mulkay (1985).

Mulkay, M. J. (1985) *The Word and the World: Explorations in the Form of Sociological Analysis*. London: George Allen and Unwin.

Mulkay, M. J. (1986) 'A Black Day for the 4S: Bernal Prize Acceptance Speech', *Science and Technology Studies*, 4 (3/4): 41–3.

Mulkay, M. J. (1988) *A Sociology of Humour*. Oxford: Polity Press.

Mulkay, M. J. and Gilbert, G. N. (1982a) 'What is the Ultimate Question? Some Remarks in Defence of the Analysis of Scientists' Discourse', *Social Studies of Science*, 12: 309–20.

Mulkay, M. J. and Gilbert, G. N. (1982b) 'Accounting for Error: How Scientists Construct their Social World When they Account for Correct and Incorrect Belief', *Sociology*, 16: 165–83.

Mulkay, M. J. and Gilbert, G. N. (1984) 'Replication and Mere Replication', unpublished paper, Universities of York and Surrey.

Mulkay, M. J., Potter, J. and Yearley, S. (1983) 'Why an Analysis of Scientific Discourse Is Needed', pp. 171–203 in Knorr-Cetina and Mulkay (1983).

Naess, A. (1972) *The Pluralist and Possibilist Aspect of the Scientific Enterprise*. London: George Allen and Unwin.

Nickles, T. (1984) 'A Revolution that Failed: Collins and Pinch on the Paranormal', *Social Studies of Science*, 14: 297–308.

Nietzsche, F. (1909) *Thus Spoke Zarathustra* (trans. R. J. Hollingdale, 1969). Harmondsworth, Middx: Penguin Books.

Oehler, K. (1983) 'Two Interpretations of Reflexivity in Sociology of Science: an Examination of H. M. Collins' Radical Programme', unpublished paper, Virginia Polytechnic Institute and State University.

Péguy, C. (1914) *CLIO: Dialogues de l'Ame Paienne et de l'Ame Charnelle*. Paris: Gallimard.

Pickering, A. (1981) 'Constraints on Controversy: the Case of the Magnetic Monopole', *Social Studies of Science*, 11: 63–94.

Pickering, A. (1984) *Constructing Quarks: a Sociological History of Particle Physics*. Edinburgh: Edinburgh University Press.

Pinch, T. J. (1977) 'What Does a Proof Do if it Does Not Prove?, pp. 171–215 in E. Mendelsohn, P. Weingart and R. Whitley (eds) *The Social Production of Scientific Knowledge. Sociology of the Sciences Yearbook*, Vol. 1. Dordrecht: Reidel.

Pinch, T. J. (1979) 'Normal Explanations of the Paranormal: the Demarcation Problem and Fraud in Parapsychology', *Social Studies of Science*, 9: 329–48.

Pinch, T. J. (1981) 'The Sun-Set: the Presentation of Certainty in Scientific Life', *Social Studies of Science*, 11: 131–58.

Pinch, T. J. (1983) 'Reflecting on Reflexivity: Comment on Verhoog', *EASST Newsletter*, 2 (2): 5–7.

Pinch, T. J. (1986) *Confronting Nature*. Dordrecht: Reidel.

Pinch, T. J. and Collins, H. M. (1984) 'Private Science and Public Knowledge: the Committee for the Scientific Investigation of the Claims of the Paranormal and its Use of the Literature', *Social Studies of Science*, 14: 521–46.

Pinch, T. J., Pinch, T. J. and Friends (1987) 'On Reading Pinch and Pinch', paper presented to Bradford Discourse Analysis Workshop, April.

Poser, C. M., Paty, D., McDonald, W. I., Scheinberg, L. and Ebers, G. G. (eds) (1984) *The Diagnosis of Multiple Sclerosis*. New York: Thieme-Stratton.

Potter, J. (1983) 'Speaking and Writing Science: Issues in the Analysis of Psychologists' Discourse'. DPhil thesis, University of York.

Potter, J. (forthcoming) 'Reading Repertoires: a Preliminary Study of Some Procedures Scientists Use to Construct Readings', *Science and Technology Studies*.

Potter, J. and Mulkay, M. J. (1985) 'Scientists' Interview Talk: Interviews as a Technique for Revealing Participants' Interpretive Practices', pp. 247–71 in M. Brenner, J. Brown and D. Canter (eds) *The Research Interview: Uses and Approaches*. London: Academic Press.

Potter, J. and Wetherell, M. (1987) *Discourse and Social Psychology: Beyond Attitudes and Behaviour*. London: Sage.

Potter, J. and Wetherell, M. (forthcoming) 'Discourse Analysis and the Identification of Interpretive Repertoires', in C. Antaki (ed.) *Analysing Lay Explanation: a Casebook of Methods*. London: Sage.

Potter, J., Stringer, P. and Wetherell, M. (1984) *Social Texts and Contexts: Literature and Social Psychology*. London: Routledge and Kegan Paul.

Prigogine, I. and Stengers, I. (1979) *La Nouvelle Alliance: Métamorphose De La Science*. Paris: Gallimard.

Ricoeur, P. (1970) *Freud and Philosophy* (trans. Denis Savage). New Haven and London: Yale University Press.

Ricoeur, P. (1981) *Hermeneutics and the Human Sciences* (trans. and ed. J. B. Thompson). Cambridge: Cambridge University Press.

Ricoeur, P. (1984) *Time and Narrative Vol 1*. Chicago, IL: University of Chicago Press.

Rogers, C. R. (1942) *Counselling and Psychotherapy: Newer Concepts in Practice*. Cambridge, MA: Houghton Mifflin.

Rorty, R. (1978) 'Philosophy as a Kind of Writing', *New Literary History*, 10: 146–60.

Rudwick, M. (1985) *The Great Devonian Controversy: the Shaping of Scientific Knowledge amongst Gentlemenly Specialists*. Chicago, IL: University of Chicago Press.

Russell, S. (1986) 'The Social Construction Of Artifacts', *Social Studies of Science*, 16: 331–46.

Sacks, H. (1972) 'On the Analysability of Stories by Children', pp. 329–45 in J. Gumperz and D. Hymes (eds) *Directions in Sociolinguistics. The Ethnography of Communication.* New York: Holt, Rinehart and Winston. Also pp. 216–32 in Turner (1974).

Sandywell, B., Silverman, D., Roche, M., Filmer, P. and Phillipson, M. (1975) *Problems of Reflexivity and Dialectics in Sociological Inquiry: Language Theorising Difference.* London: Routledge and Kegan Paul.

Schegloff, E. (1968) 'Sequencing in Conversational Openings', *American Anthropologist* 70: 1075–95.

Serres, M. (1983) *Hermes. Literature Science Philosophy* (Trans. J. Harari and D. E. Bell). Baltimore: Johns Hopkins University Press.

Shapin, S. (1982) 'History of Science and its Sociological Reconstructions', *History of Science*, 20: 157–211.

Shapin, S. (1984a) 'Pump and Circumstance: Robert Boyle's Literary Technology', *Social Studies of Science*, 14: 481–520.

Shapin, S. (1984b) 'Talking History: Reflections on Discourse Analysis', *Isis*, 75: 125–8.

Shapin, S. and Schaffer, S. (1985) *Leviathan and the Air Pump: Hobbes, Boyle and the Experimental Life.* Princeton, NJ: Princeton University Press.

Sharratt, B. (1982) *Reading Relations. Structures of Literary Production: a Dialectical Text/Book.* Brighton, Sussex: Harvester Press.

Sharrock, W. W. (1974) 'On Owning Knowledge', pp. 45–53 in Turner (1974).

Sharrock, W. W. and Anderson, R. J. (1982) 'On the Demise of the Native: Some Observations on and a Proposal for Ethnography', *Human Studies*, 5: 119–36.

Silverman, D. (1986) *Communication in the Clinic.* London: Sage.

Silverman, D. and Torode, B. (1980) *The Material Word: Some Theories of Language and its Limits.* London: Routledge and Kegan Paul.

Simmel, G. (1950) *The Sociology of Georg Simmel* (trans. and ed. K. H. Woolf). New York: Free Press.

Smith, D. (1978) 'K is Mentally Ill', *Sociology*, 12: 23–53.

Sorrentino, G. (1979) *Mulligan Stew.* London: Picador.

Stocking, G. W. Jr (ed.) (1983a) *Observers Observed: Essays on Ethnographic Fieldwork. History of Anthropology, Volume 1.* Madison, WI: University of Wisconsin Press.

Stocking, G. W. Jr (1983b) 'The Ethnographer's Magic: Fieldwork in British Anthropology from Tylor to Malinowski', pp. 70–120 in Stocking (1983a).

Stringer, P. (1985) 'You Decide What Your Title is to be and (Read) Write to that Title', pp. 210–31 in D. Bannister (ed.) *Issues and Approaches in Personal Construct Theory.* London: Academic Press.

Travis, D. (1981) 'Replicating Replication? Aspects of the Social Construction of Learning in Planarian Worms', *Social Studies of Science*, 11: 11–32.

Traweek, S. (forthcoming) *Particle Physics Culture.* Cambridge, MA: Harvard University Press.

Turner, R. (ed.) (1974) *Ethnomethodology.* Harmondsworth, Middx: Penguin Books.

Walker, T. (1982) 'The Cultivation of Dependence', BSc dissertation, Brunel University.

Walker, T. (1984) 'On Beginning an Enquiry', paper presented to the Discourse Analysis and Reflexivity Workshop, Brunel University, March.

Walker, T. (1986) 'The Re-enactment of Social Order.' PhD thesis, Brunel University.

Walker, T. (1987) 'Reflexivity: the Appliance of Science', working paper presented to the Discourse Analysis Workshop, University of Bradford, April.

Watson, G. (1987) 'Make Me Reflexive, But Not Yet: strategies for managing essential reflexivity in ethnographic discourse', *Journal of Anthropological Research*, 43: 29–41.

Weber, M. (1947) *The Theory of Social and Economic Organisation.* Glencoe, IL: Free Press.

Wilson, B. R. (ed.) (1970) *Rationality*. Oxford: Basil Blackwell.

Winch, P. (1958) *The Idea of a Social Science and its Relation to Philosophy*. New York: Humanities Press.

Wittgenstein, L. (1953) *Philosophical Investigations*. Oxford: Basil Blackwell and Mott.

Woolgar, S. (1980) 'Discovery: Logic and Sequence in a Scientific Text', pp. 239–68 in Knorr et al. (1980).

Woolgar, S. (1981) 'Science and Ethnomethodology: a Prefatory Statement', pp. 10–15 in S. Restivo (ed.) *New Directions in the Sociology of Science, International Society for the Sociology of Knowledge Newsletter*, Vol. 7.

Woolgar, S. (1982) 'Laboratory Studies: a Comment on the State of the Art', *Social Studies of Science*, 12: 481–98.

Woolgar, S. (1983) 'Irony in the Social Study of Science', pp. 239–66 in Knorr-Cetina and Mulkay (1983).

Woolgar, S. (1984) 'A Kind of Reflexivity', paper presented to the Discourse Analysis Workshop, University of Surrey, September.

Woolgar, S. (1986) 'Discourse and Praxis', *Social Studies of Science*, 16: 309–18.

Woolgar, S. (1988) *Science: The Very Idea*. London: Ellis Horwood/Tavistock.

Woolgar, S. (forthcoming) 'The Ideology of Representation and the Role of the Agent', in H. Lawson and L. Appignanesi (eds) *Dismantling Truth: Science in Post-Modern Times*. London: Weidenfeld and Nicolson.

Wynne, A. (1983) 'Accounting for Accounts of the Diagnosis of Multiple Sclerosis', paper presented to the Discourse Analysis and Reflexivity Workshop, Oxford Polytechnic, September.

Wynne, A. (1986) 'Reading and Writing: Sociology', paper presented to the Discourse Analysis and Reflexivity Workshop, University of York, April.

Wynne, A. (1987) 'Talk: Transcript: Text', unpublished paper, Brunel University.

Wynne, A. (forthcoming) PhD thesis in preparation, Brunel University.

Yearley, S. (1982) 'The Relationship Between Epistemological and Sociological Interests. Some Ambiguities Underlying the Use of Interests Theory in the Study of Scientific Knowledge', *Studies in the History and Philosophy of Science*, 13: 353–88.

Zimmerman, D. and Pollner, M. (1971) 'The Everyday World as a Phenomenon', pp. 80–103 in Douglas (1971).

Zuckerman, H. (1977) 'Deviant Behavior and Social Control in Science' pp. 87–138 in E. Sagarin (ed.) *Deviance and Social Change*. Beverly Hills and London: Sage.

Index